the remains of war

POLITICS, HISTORY, AND CULTURE

A series from the International Institute at the University of Michigan

SERIES EDITORS:

George Steinmetz and Julia Adams

SERIES EDITORIAL ADVISORY BOARD: Fernando Coronil, Mamadou Diouf, Michael Dutton, Geoff Eley, Fatma Müge Göcek, Nancy Rose Hunt, Andreas Kalyvas, Webb Keane, David Laitin, Lydia Liu, Julie Skurski, Margaret Somers, Ann Laura Stoler, Katherine Verdery, Elizabeth Wingrove

Sponsored by the International Institute at the University of Michigan and published by Duke University Press, this series is centered around cultural and historical studies of power, politics, and the state—a field that cuts across the disciplines of history, sociology, anthropology, political science, and cultural studies. The focus on the relationship between state and culture refers both to a methodological approach—the study of politics and the state using culturalist methods—and to a substantive approach that treats signifying practices as an essential dimension of politics. The dialectic of politics, culture, and history figures prominently in all the books selected for the series.

the remains of war

Bodies, Politics, and the Search

for American Soldiers Unaccounted For in Southeast Asia

THOMAS M. HAWLEY

DUKE UNIVERSITY PRESS DURHAM & LONDON 2005

© 2005 Duke University Press
All rights reserved

Designed by Katy Clove
Typeset in Cycles by
Tseng Information Systems, Inc.
Library of Congress Cataloging-
in-Publication Data appear on the
last printed page of this book.

For Tim Kaufman-Osborn, teacher, colleague, and friend without peer.

contents

Acknowledgments ix

1 Body Trouble 1

2 From Unrecoverable to Unaccounted For 39

3 The Body of the Accounted-For Soldier 81

4 "Our Stateside MIAS":
The Body of the Vietnam Veteran 115

5 Practices of Memorialization: The Vietnam Veterans Memorial, the Tomb of the Vietnam War Unknown Soldier, and the POW/MIA Flag 158

6 The Ethics of Accounting 211

Epilogue. Same as It Ever Was 242

Notes 253

Bibliography 261

Index 277

acknowledgments

This book is the material result of years of research and writing, a process that began on March 5, 1995, with the discovery of an article in the *Honolulu Advertiser* about the efforts being made by the United States to account for soldiers still missing in Southeast Asia. Along the way, I have had the exceedingly good (and, I gather, somewhat rare) fortune of greatly enjoying the research, the writing, and the editorial process that necessarily accompanies such a project. Apart from personal deficiencies that lend themselves to taking satisfaction in this sort of work, the rewarding aspects of this enterprise have resulted in substantial degree from the assistance I've received from many people, most of whom were too generous to know better and each of whom will not here receive the full measure of the gratitude they are truly due from me. Nonetheless, I hope the following individuals will take my word for it when I say that the positive elements of this book are a result of their contributions, and will understand my desire for an equally generous group of people onto whom I might slough off the numerous shortcomings that are ultimately my own.

The staff at the Joint Task Force-Full Accounting (JTF-FA) at Camp H. M. Smith in Honolulu, Hawai'i, was gracious with both their time and their insights during my research visits there in the spring of 2000. My thanks in particular to Raymond Spock, then-Director of Intelligence and to Lt. Col. Franklin Childress, the always-accommodating Public Affairs Officer at that time. I am also indebted to Paul Mather, Senior Analyst at the Department of Defense Prisoner of War/Missing Personnel Office (DPMO), who agreed to be interviewed in Honolulu on very short notice. My thanks as well to Jefferson Willard, former Linguist/Analyst with Detachment Two of the JTF-FA in Hanoi for his time and conversation during an impromptu meeting there in December 1997. I regard it as one of the more pleasurable ironies of this project that Jeff turned up four years later as a student in two of my political science classes at the University of Hawai'i at Manoa in Honolulu.

The staff at the Central Identification Laboratory, Hawai'i (CILHI) was very helpful as well. I am particularly indebted to Staff Sergeant Earl Bushong, Jr., External Liaison, U.S. Army CILHI, for facilitating my visit there, also made in spring 2000. Others gave generously of their time during the visit, including Major Andrew Irwin, Executive Officer, U.S. Army CILHI, Dr. John E. Byrd, Physical Anthropologist, and Bradley J. Adams, Forensic Anthropologist.

Many thanks are also due to Dee Spock and Sara Collins, whose assistance contributed greatly to my understanding of the effort to account for American soldiers missing in Southeast Asia. Katherine Maria Schlatter also generously shared her primary materials with me.

I have benefited greatly from strong personal and intellectual support throughout the duration of this project. I am particularly indebted to Sanford Schram, now at Bryn Mawr College Graduate School of Social Work and Social Research, for unfailing support during his stay in Honolulu and subsequently. Geoffrey White was generous with his time and thoughtful commentary, while Craig Howes provided both indefatigable enthusiasm and a breadth of knowledge without which this project would never have advanced beyond the planning stages. Kathie Kane and Carolyn di Palma gave the sort of encouragement that comes from people gifted enough to see diamonds in the analytical rough that accompanies any research project. The Department of Political Science at the University of Hawai'i at Manoa provided a warm and thoroughly supportive environment for this project, through both financial support and an intellectual setting whose equal I have yet to encounter. My thanks in particular to Kathy Ferguson, Michael Shapiro, Jon Goldberg-Hiller, Sankaran Krishna, and Phyllis Turnbull, each of whom guided this project through its many phases with a combination of moral, intellectual, and personal support. Every researcher should be so lucky to benefit from such support. My thanks as well to Nevzat Soguk, Neal Milner, Manfred Henningsen, Noenoe Silva, John Wilson, and Deane Neubauer. Other friends and colleagues have sustained me in ways they likely never fully realized, including Marie Thorsten, Allison Yap, Brian Richardson, Eric Ishiwata, Fred Klemmer, Gina Pusateri, Kamuela Young, Kennan Ferguson, Kerry Burch, Jill Keesbury,

Spike Bradford, John Pincince, Debbie Halbert, Jorge Fernandes, Karen Sprague, Christopher Bondy, Lisa Pasko, and Alison Zecha. Dr. Laura Heffernan (*née* Boeschen) provided invaluable assistance in my effort to understand the readjustment experiences of Vietnam veterans. Vicky Lebbin of Hamilton Library at the University of Hawai'i at Manoa was a constant source of research assistance.

The editors of the Politics, History, and Culture series provided provocative commentary and enthusiastic support throughout this project, particularly during a visit to Ann Arbor, Michigan, in December 2001. My thanks in particular to the series coeditors, Julia Adams and George Steinmetz, for their amiable and exceptionally intelligent critique of this work at the manuscript stage as well as support along the way. My thanks as well to the other members of the editorial board, including Fernando Coronil, Mamadou Diouf, Geoff Eley, Müge Göcek, Nancy Hunt, Webb Keane, David Laitin, Julie Skurski, Margaret Somers, Katherine Verdery, and Elizabeth Wingrove. It has also been a great pleasure working with Duke University Press, in particular with my editor, Raphael Allen, who has been unfailing in his assistance to me. My thanks also to Imani Owens, Courtney Berger, Mark Mastromarino, and Cherie Westmoreland, as well as to three anonymous reviewers whose insightful commentary contributed greatly to this project.

An earlier version of chapter 6 appeared as "The Ethics of Accounting: The Search for American Soldiers Missing in Vietnam" in *Millennium: Journal of International Studies* 31, no. 2. The revised version is reprinted with permission.

To my family, Malvern, Nancy, and Charlie Hawley, goes an expression of appreciation that simply defies adequate articulation. In particular, I want it known that each of them *voluntarily* read this book in manuscript form and offered editorial suggestions throughout. We all should be so lucky to enjoy such support. To my parents, an extra thanks for providing the space for three months of uninterrupted writing in the summer of 2003, and for the presence of mind to wait a full three weeks before asking what I was *doing* all those hours in the basement. To the gang in Twickenham, my thanks for helping stave off the lunacy that would surely have been my lot without you.

Finally, a word of immeasurable gratitude to Tim Kaufman-Osborn, to whom this book is dedicated. I know I speak for many when I say that life itself would be substantially more solitary, poor, nasty, brutish, and short were it not for the innumerable ways in which he supports the efforts of his students at Whitman College and beyond. If "throw-away comments too oblique to be intelligible" have here been kept to a minimum, it is because of Tim's long-standing and selfless attention to my personal, intellectual, and professional endeavors over the course of many years.

chapter one

Body Trouble

> Prospects for successful recovery and identification of remains of U.S. personnel in Southeast Asia diminish significantly with the passage of time.
> —U.S. Congress, House, 1976: 204

> We have an absolute, sacred obligation to do whatever we can to look for our missing in action. We will do that and not fail in that effort. We place the return of our missing in action as the very highest of our priorities.
> —U.S. Secretary of Defense William S. Cohen, in Kozaryn, 2000

On May 14, 1998, at Arlington National Cemetery just outside Washington, D.C., the Tomb of the Unknown Soldier from the Vietnam War was opened and the remains removed for purposes of forensic examination. With the assent of the Department of Defense and the support of organizations dedicated to advancing the cause of families with relatives still unaccounted for in Southeast Asia, that examination was performed at the request of the family who had come to believe the remains in the tomb might be those of its loved one. Ever since its interment in 1984, speculation had grown that the identity of the body in the tomb, though for the moment unknown, might not necessarily be unknowable. Improvements in forensic identification procedures, for example, had made even the most minute and highly fragmentary quantities of human remains potentially identifiable, while the increasingly refined technique of DNA analysis enabled scientists to determine the identity of such remains in the absence of the unique morphological or dental characteristics normally used for such purposes. Indeed, in June 1998, the Department of Defense announced that the unknown soldier from the Vietnam War was in fact U.S. Air Force First Lieutenant Michael J. Blassie of St. Louis. The identification thus ended a lengthy period of uncertainty in the Blassie family as to Michael's fate and whereabouts after his plane was shot down in 1972 near An Loc in South Vietnam.

While the identification of Michael Blassie's remains may have put an end to the episode for his family, it marked both a chronological and a conceptual continuation of efforts by the United States to account for soldiers still missing in Southeast Asia as a result of the Vietnam War. Chronologically, that effort began well before the war was over with attempts in the late 1960s to ensure the humane treatment and eventual release of American prisoners of war and the repatriation of the remains of those killed in action. Now in its fourth decade, the search is primarily concerned with recovering and positively identifying the remains of just over eighteen hundred American servicemen killed during the Vietnam War whose bodies were not recovered at the time of their deaths. As in previous American wars, however, a certain number of those killed in Southeast Asia were not identifiable, and so an unknown soldier from the Vietnam War eventually found a place beside his compatriots amid the symbols of the nation at Arlington National Cemetery. Such commemoration has been a long-standing tradition in Western nations, a means of symbolizing and honoring the sacrifice of one for the good of the democratic whole (Mosse, 1990; Inglis, 1993). It was thus remarkable that the nameless body of the Vietnam War unknown soldier later became a problem to be solved, one so serious that it ultimately trumped the symbolic value that had for so long attached to precisely that anonymity. At the same time, the problem was unique in that the concern shown for the identity of the Vietnam unknown soldier was not extended to the anonymous soldiers with whom he had shared sacred space for the previous fourteen years. Indeed, no one has seriously proposed that the representational innards of the other tombs dedicated to unknown warriors be eviscerated in the manner that eventually became the only possible course of action for the Vietnam War unknown. That Michael Blassie managed to make it out of the Tomb of the Unknowns and into a marked grave at Jefferson Barracks National Cemetery in Missouri thus represented the apotheosis of the peculiar logic that animates efforts by the United States to account for missing

Vietnam War soldiers, an effort unlike any undertaken by any nation in history.

Put briefly, that logic is one in which the body is invested with the sole power of adjudicating the many questions comprised in the contentious legacy of the Vietnam War. Not simply a moment of relief and closure for his family, positive determination of Blassie's identity answered a series of questions that have become an integral part of the post–Vietnam War era in the United States and that, until the moment of his identification, could not be laid to rest. In particular, the question of precisely what had happened to Lieutenant Blassie (he was killed in action) was now resolved, thus definitively refuting the possibility that the Vietnamese had held him back as a prisoner of war. Further, Blassie's identified body indicated the veracity of the U.S. government's attempts to account for missing Vietnam War soldiers, attempts whose sincerity has long been called into question by family organizations, members of Congress, various intelligence services, and the public. Still more, identification of the Vietnam unknown soldier was a victory of sorts and not an unsubstantial one given the sense that the defeat in Vietnam has lingered with the United States in all sorts of unpleasant ways in the years since the withdrawal of American forces in 1973. Broadly, Blassie's body generated *certainty*, for his family in the form of a body that could be properly interred and mourned and for the nation as confirmation of its ability to resolve, if only incrementally, one of the major ambiguities of the Vietnam War.

Yet the quest for certainty in the form of the identified body itself marks a dramatic change from previous wars, in which circumstantial evidence often sufficed to account for missing soldiers. The prior sufficiency of such evidence marked the acceptance of an unavoidable, if unwelcome, side effect of mechanized warfare, namely, the permanent obliteration of the bodies of some combatants. The uniqueness of the current accounting standard that requires the identified body is further dramatized by the United States government's own admission that those soldiers who failed to return from Southeast Asia in any form are in fact deceased and that no credible evidence exists to suggest otherwise. Thus, rather than expressing uncertainty concerning a given soldier's fate, *unaccounted for* in this context refers strictly to the absence of the body, meaning in turn that to account for missing Vietnam War soldiers requires the repatriation and positive identification of their remains. These circumstances are still more significant when the numbers of those missing from other American wars—roughly eight thousand from the Korean War and approximately seventy-eight thousand from World War II—are borne in mind. Were it a question of overall quantity, one might expect that the bulk of American personnel recovery efforts would be directed toward those missing from these two wars. Yet such an expectation would fail to account for the vast political, cultural, and ontological significance assumed by the body of the absent Vietnam War soldier. Among other things, that body has come to stand for deceit on the part of both the Vietnamese and U.S. governments, who have allegedly prolonged its absence in ways large and small. Further, it indicates the failure of the United States to truly end the war in Vietnam: some of its warriors, after all, have failed to return home. Perhaps still more compelling, the absent body stands as the most material indication of the defeat that occurred in Southeast Asia, an ever-present reminder of the catastrophe that continues to afflict the American body politic. Its recovery, therefore, functions materially in the resolution of these many ambiguities and ontologically through what it indicates about the United States. As President George H. W. Bush once claimed, "The POW/MIA [Prisoner of War/Missing in Action] issue is a question of honor, of oath-sworn commitment kept. It's a Nation's test of its own worth, measured in the life of one lone individual" (U.S. President, 1993: 1933). That the body of the Vietnam War unknown could not rest in peace until its identity as Michael Blassie had been positively determined speaks to the intensity of the interpretive battles that have been waged over the meaning of missing and unidentified military bodies in the years since the end of the Vietnam War.

Such battles are an initial confirmation of this book's central premise, namely, that the contentious legacy of the Vietnam War is first and foremost one of bodies and that this circumstance can be most clearly observed in U.S. attempts to account for soldiers still missing from that war. And while the body of the unaccounted-for soldier obviously figures prominently in that effort, the search for the missing implicates other bodies as well, in particular the identified body that occasionally results from forensic examination of remains, the body of the Vietnam veteran, and the American body politic. The significance of these bodies, however, is not simply given in the nature of postwar things; neither is it an expression of antecedent truth about them. These bodies are not to be understood as substantives to which "we," in some equally substantive sense, enjoy unambiguous recourse in our effort to make sense of what happened to those who never came home. Rather, the bodies at issue in the search for missing soldiers are better understood as effects of the various practices that enable them to assume intelligible meaning. They are the result of particular ways of representing the post-Vietnam War era and one of the ways in which the intelligibility of that era—and, by extension, the Vietnam War itself—is made possible.

KNOWING THE ABSENT BODY

In view of these considerations, this book adopts a genealogical perspective as a means of exploring more thoroughly how the body has come to assume such significance within the accounting for American soldiers missing as a result of the Vietnam War. In the context of this study, genealogy forestalls the quest to arrive at the truth of the missing, some unambiguous claim as to what "really happened" to those who never returned from the war in Vietnam. The reasons for this forbearance include the absence of any single explanation concerning the fate and whereabouts of those soldiers still unaccounted for in Vietnam or why these particular soldiers became so important while those missing from other wars did not. Indeed, one of the greatest difficulties in analyzing the accounting effort is the sheer quantity of theories, explanations, accusations, and counteraccusations concerning the fate of the missing. Moreover, evidence in support of these theories, while in some cases plausible, often must be believed in order to be seen. As a result, the quest for truth has not infrequently been complicit in the very problem its pursuit is allegedly intended to solve. About the only conclusion that can be reached with any degree of certainty is that the absent bodies of Vietnam War service personnel have beguiled the United States like no other absent bodies in the history of the republic.

In lieu of a quest for truth, genealogy begins with the present and works backward. This does two things. First, it encourages a view of the present as peculiar and therefore in need of explanation rather than as the realization of an immanent essence whose determining features lie outside the realm of human cognition. Second, working backward from a distinctive present requires inquiry into the (often obscure) conditions that enabled the emergence of a given thing in the first place. Accordingly, genealogy is uninterested in the sort of boilerplate historiography that seeks to trace the evolutionary arc of history. Instead, it looks for moments of discontinuity, focuses on the production rather than the discovery of knowledge, and inquires into the interpretive categories upon which the very possibility of the present rests (Foucault, 1977). In light of the complicated twists and turns taken by the search for missing soldiers in Southeast Asia, a genealogical perspective helps to situate the political, cultural, and historical events that contributed to the production of this entirely peculiar present.

In virtue of these analytical commitments, genealogy's relationship to the body is especially clear; it is "situated within the articulation of the body and history. Its task is to expose a body totally imprinted by history and the process of history's destruction of the body" (Foucault, 1977: 148). Accordingly, the genealogical insight perhaps most central to this analysis is the admonition that, short of a suspect process of abstraction, there is no such thing as "the body" per se. In virtue of this, all claims about the body must be rendered provisionally. Such caution stems from the observation that, when treated as given or beyond the purview of critical reflection, invocations of the body all too often deny gendered or racialized elements of embodiment, the importance of materiality to an understanding of bodies, or the epistemic conditions required to speak of the body at all. Genealogy thus explicitly foregrounds these circumstances in the act of directing attention to the conditions of possibility under which bodies come to be and the various practices through which corporeal intelligibility is secured.

If, in light of this epistemological discretion, there is no such thing as the body apart from the interpretive conditions that enable its emergence as such, then an analysis of the bodies at issue in U.S. efforts to account for missing Vietnam War soldiers must explain how those bodies have been represented in the years since the end of the war. A genealogical perspective is helpful once again because it emphasizes discourse as a way of assessing how the body has assumed meaning and value within that effort. Discourse can be thought of here as the rules and procedures that condition the meaningfulness of the things to which any given language refers (Shapiro, 1992). For this reason discourse is often said to be productive. Absent some means by which the things of this world can be intelligibly represented, those things remain, quite literally, nonexistent. The study of discourse in the context of the search for missing soldiers can therefore be understood as something of a first-order analysis, an effort to determine what has to happen *before* the objects, categories, and identities comprised in the search can even be talked about, much less understood.

On this basis, analyzing the bodies at issue in the search for absent soldiers in terms of their discursive antecedents entails the acceptance of two closely interrelated and by now quite familiar claims. First, language is not a transparent tool to be used in representing a pre-given reality but is instead opaque. Hence, the process of ascribing words to things is never neutral. It must be scrutinized with a view toward the power relations and authority structures that not only permit the appearance of meaningful statements but also secure their meaning. J. L. Austin's (1975) well-known example of the phrase "I now pronounce you man and wife" illustrates the point. The very possibility of this phrase depends at one level on the authority of (in this case) the priest to back it up. Not just anyone can utter it and have it *mean* the union of one man and one woman in matrimony. On another level, our ability as listeners to draw this particular meaning from the phrase depends on our understanding of the individual words that compose it, understanding that is by no means automatic but always dependent on some process of acquisition. Both elements here (that is, the authority of the priest and the meaning of the individual words) are thus never given in the nature of things. Instead, they are produced—the authority of the priest via the investiture, the meaning of words via the agreement of some group of speakers. This underscores the importance of focusing on discourse rather than on language, since the genealogical concern is with the production of meaning and value rather than with the relationship between words and things (Shapiro, 1989: 14).

The issue of value is especially relevant here. How did the absent Vietnam War body become so meaningful and so valuable? and how have that meaning and that worth been sustained to such an extraordinary degree? This question directs attention toward the second claim concerning the discursive antecedents of the body. If language is a human artifact and if statements are therefore best viewed as productions of meaning rather than reflections of reality, then statements can never be simply descriptive. Instead, they must be thought of as strategies by which the meaning of any given thing is inclined this way rather than that. Put somewhat differently, if the conditions of any statement's coherence are political and therefore contingent, the existence of one way of characterizing the world must be seen as a victory achieved at the expense of alternative representations. This entails the consequent recognition that reality itself is a production dependent upon some mode of representation and, further, that the alleged facticity of reality can no longer be treated as either self-evident or "uncaused" (Shapiro, 1989: 13–14). By way of example, take one especially frequent means of representing absent Vietnam War soldiers—that their absence is due to deceit on the part of the Vietnamese, which therefore makes it their responsibility to account for them—and compare it with one possible alternative, that such absences resulted from more than a decade of American military intervention in Southeast Asia that, as in prior wars, could not help but produce a certain number of absent bodies. Clearly, both of these representations take unaccounted-for soldiers as their point of departure. However, the absence of bodies does not have to be represented as the fault of the Vietnamese, that is, that particular meaning is not given in the nature of absence. Rather, it is produced. Further, if we recall the strategic dimension of discourse, representing unaccounted-for American soldiers as the fault of the Vietnamese is an instance of producing them as one sort of thing rather than another. To point out the obvious political and perhaps psychological superiority of one interpretation over the other does not dilute the overall argument. Indeed, it shows that even the interpretation of events whose character has come to seem especially self-evident nevertheless requires that choices be made, a circumstance that returns us to the importance of attending to the strategic considerations that always accompany such a choice. The analytical value of genealogy lies in its concern for the productive role of discourse and the correlative recognition that meaning is not a discovery but an imposition that results from particular interpretive practices (Shapiro, 1989: 11).

This argument in no way suggests that everything is discourse and that therefore the events associated with the search for missing American soldiers somehow lack a material dimension. To illustrate the point, take the two interpretations of absent servicemen offered in the preceding paragraph. Each points the U.S. response in a different direction, the former toward some way of securing greater cooperation from the Vietnamese, the latter toward the recognition that one of the unavoidable effects of mechanized warfare is absent bodies. Either way, both are indisputably material in that their consequences with respect to those bodies are vastly different. It now becomes possible to see with greater clarity why and how the body has assumed such importance within the process of accounting for missing soldiers, since the materiality of the body is so often represented as an expression of antecedent truth about it. It is quite obviously materially absent, nothing could be more true than that, and therefore something must be done about it. Yet if we bear in mind the productive dimension of discourse, even the materiality of the body cannot be separated from the interpretive practices that enable it to acquire meaning. This is the argument advanced by Judith Butler in her book *Bodies That Matter: On the Discursive Limits of "Sex"* (1993). In particular, Butler argues that the materiality of the body must be seen not as an unambiguous indication of its extradiscursive reality but instead as a dissimulated effect of power—an effect we fail to discern because of its appearance of facticity and naturalness. By interrogating the matter of the body and its production within discourse as a certain kind of body, Butler offers insights into the means by which bodies secure meaning and value.

The immediate relevance of Butler's project to an analysis of the bodies of missing American soldiers lies in her apparently counterintuitive inquiry into the discursive antecedents of materiality. Counterintuitive, of course, because it's not immediately clear how anything so obviously material as the body could possibly be constructed in language. We may readily admit that our understandings of the body are constituted discursively, but to suggest in the process that the body itself is a creature of discursive convention is a whole other matter indeed. Nevertheless, Butler's argument forces us to wonder how it could be otherwise—how it is possible, in other words, to have culturally constructed understandings of the body on the one hand, and, on the other, a body that supports those understandings but is not itself a construction. As indicated, the immediate rejoinder cites the body's materiality and the claim that it is too palpable, evident, and factual to be a construction. Yet to suggest on this basis that the body serves as the uncaused cause of its sundry cultural understandings is to place that body beyond the purview of critical reflection. This placing in turn marks our tacit acceptance of an all-too-deterministic status quo in which the material "facts" of the body unproblematically stand for antecedent truths about it.[1]

The discursive antecedents of materiality thus suggest that the significance of the body is not to be derived either through recourse to an immanent essence or from a principle external to discourse. Such recognition also implies that our knowledge of the body is not given in the nature of the material things that distinguish one body from another.

Accordingly, the materiality of the absent Vietnam War body does not automatically or necessarily distinguish that body from those missing as a result of other American wars. Such distinction is produced and continually mediated in the discourse of the absent Vietnam War soldier. Furthermore, that mediation is always a moment of producing the absent body as such, an instance of inclining the meaning of absence in a particular way. It is for this reason that the absence of the body does not result in the absence of intelligibility and still less in the absence of meaning. Indeed, the unaccounted for Vietnam War body is by far the most meaningful of its kind in U.S. history. Meaning is always effected, a process whose particulars are obscured when materiality is cited as an expression of indisputable truth about the thing in question. Genealogical analysis of the unaccounted-for body in terms of the discursive antecedents of its materiality is thus an active attempt to *avoid* linking the significance of the missing to unequivocal truths about them. Instead, my inquiry is concerned with how the various truths that animate the accounting for missing soldiers became possible at all.

Certainly one of the engines driving the production of truth in the context of American soldiers missing in Southeast Asia has been previous studies of the issue. Accordingly, along with theoretical, historical, and sociological literature, this book enters into conversation with a dozen or so previous works on the subject of the search, all of which take the body of the missing soldier for granted and therefore fail to explore how it has achieved significance within the accounting effort specifically and the post–Vietnam War era more generally. Aside from works which present either firsthand experiences or an informational overview of the search (the work of Mather [1994], Lesinski [1998], Smith [1992], Stern [1995], and Bell [2004] belongs here), previous analyses of the search for the missing are noteworthy for their commitment to one of two interpretive possibilities concerning the absent Vietnam War soldier. The first argues that the United States either knowingly or inadvertently left American soldiers behind in Southeast Asia at the conclusion of the Vietnam War and/or that the Vietnamese withheld American prisoners for later negotiating purposes. Examples here include Frank Anton (1997), Scott Barnes (1987), Monika Jensen Stevenson and William Stevenson (1990), Malcolm McConnell and Ted Schweitzer (1995), Larry O'Daniel (1979), Chimp Robertson (1995), and George Veith (1998). That not a single living, unaccounted-for American has returned from Southeast Asia since the withdrawal of forces in 1973 does not pose a problem for arguments of this kind since it merely confirms that "there exists in the government a policy of deceit and coverup concerning the fate of MIAS" (O'Daniel, 1979: 168). The return of Marine Pfc. Robert Garwood in 1979 is illustrative of the claims making here. Before his return, the U.S. government had consistently argued that Garwood was never technically unaccounted for; rather, he was suspected of collaborating with the enemy following his capture near Da Nang on September 28, 1965, an offense for which he was court-martialed and convicted in 1980 (Mather, 1994: 43; Franklin, 1993a: 115). Yet this event only proved the point. Activists in the POW/MIA movement—many of whom are authors of works in this category—cited Garwood's return as proof the United States left prisoners behind in Southeast Asia and accused the government of plotting to conceal this fact. Right on cue, Garwood began talking of having seen such prisoners himself despite extensive debriefings upon his return in which he consistently claimed that no such Americans were left in Southeast Asia (Howes, 2000).

The second interpretive possibility argues that belief in the existence of living American prisoners of war either today or at any other point following the cessation of hostilities is, in the words of H. Bruce Franklin (1993a: 168), a myth symptomatic "of a profound psychological sickness in American culture." That myth, composed of "self-deception, amateur research anecdotes, half-truths, phony evidence, slick political and media manipulation, downright lies, and near-religious fervor," has, according to this view, infected the American body politic throughout the past three decades and thus prevented the United States from truly ending the Vietnam War (Franklin, 1993a: xvi). Franklin is the most vocal and best-known exponent of this position, and his work constitutes the only other academic treatment of the search for the missing. Other authors in this second category include Douglas Clarke (1979) and Susan Katz Keating (1994). Finally, in the midst of these hostilities there are the innumerable studies, commissions, delegations, and special reports commissioned by the government in the years since 1973, the most important of which for my purposes include the House Select Committee on Missing Persons in Southeast Asia (U.S. Congress, House, 1976), the Woodcock Commission (U.S. Department of State, 1977), and the Senate Select Committee on POW/MIA Affairs formed in 1991 (U.S. Congress, Senate, 1993). As might be imagined, these investigations are constrained by the rhetorical and representational milieus in which they are produced, meaning that they cannot help but reproduce and contribute to the interpretive battles outlined above. The quest for the truth about the missing, in other words, has not exactly been assisted by the substantial resources of the government or by the epistemological neutrality that allegedly characterizes such inquiries.

If these books, studies, and broadsides about American soldiers unaccounted for in Southeast Asia have done anything well, they have underscored Foucault's (1977: 154) point that "knowledge is not made for understanding; it is made for cutting." Indeed, within the contentious legacy of the Vietnam War, the endeavor to determine the fate and whereabouts of missing soldiers has strayed far from the otherwise laudable goal of providing closure for the families of the missing; further, it has radically exceeded the customary postwar effort to recover the bodies of soldiers that has been part of American military regulations since the Civil War. Instead, that effort has become a forum for the production of knowledge that almost without exception not only fails to redress the hostilities and ambiguities handed down by the Vietnam War but actively contributes to their continuation. Knowledge is therefore not a step toward the truth, and the truth shall not set us free. As indicated, my study adopts a methodological posture designed to engage with this state of affairs rather than redress it, since "the genealogical thinker too swims in the culture that establishes these settings and because one does not expect to locate a space wholly outside them. The goal is to problematize the present by recourse to the past without promising a perfect time in the past to return to" (Connolly, 1991: 182). This aim is abetted by a final feature of the genealogical perspective, namely, its treatment of context not as support for the emergence of the "real story" but as constitutive of that story in the first place. A review of various contextual elements is thus provided as a means of further suggesting how and why the absent Vietnam War body has come to matter like none other in American history.

A LONG NATIONAL NIGHTMARE: UNACCOUNTED-FOR BODIES AND THE VIETNAM WAR

With the signing of the Paris Peace Accords in January 1973, the Vietnam War finally came to an end for the millions of American service personnel who had served in Southeast Asia and for the American people as a whole, who had either opposed the war or who had silently provided their support. Operation Homecoming in the spring of that year resulted in the repatriation of 591 prisoners of war, thereby resolving questions about the fate and whereabouts of at least these American soldiers. As had been the case following every one of its previous wars, however, the United States was left with a certain number of soldiers whose fate was unknown (those listed as missing in action, or MIA) or whose fate was known but whose whereabouts were not (those listed as killed in action/body not recovered, or KIA/BNR). In 1973, the combined total of the two categories stood at 2,583, the smallest number ever for an American war of such magnitude (DPMO Website, 2004). As a result, in the months and years immediately following the war, little about the absent body was noteworthy save for the very small number of missing as compared to those of previous wars.

As indicated, however, a distinguishing feature of the Vietnam War missing was the degree to which the absence of the body was seen as a problem to be solved rather than as an unavoidable result of modern warfare. This circumstance was in turn related to another distinctive feature of the Vietnam War: its status as a defeat. The implications of that fact far outstripped those of the stalemate that had occurred in Korea two decades earlier. Indeed, the Vietnam War marked a crisis of the warring body with which extant interpretive structures were decidedly ill-equipped to cope. As Tom Engelhardt observes in *The End of Victory Culture: Cold War America and the Disillusioning of a Generation* (1995), in Vietnam "the war story finally lost its ability to mobilize young people under 'freedom's banner' except in opposition to itself, a loss experienced by a generation as both a confusing 'liberation' and a wrenching betrayal. There, the war story's codes were jumbled, its roles redistributed, its certitudes dismantled, and new kinds of potential space opened up that proved, finally, less liberating than frightening" (15). This was an especially powerful blow given that throughout the Cold War the United States had represented itself both to itself and to the outside world as the defender of freedom against the external menace posed by Communism generally and the Soviet Union in particular. In the act of staking a claim to this identity in Vietnam, the United States had replaced a geostrategic imaginary with an ontological one in which the capturing of the "hearts and minds" of the Vietnamese people and, later, of the Americans themselves was the mission. The defeat in Vietnam was therefore substantially more damning and disorienting than anything that had occurred in Korea because the American project in Indochina had been explicitly linked to virtually every value for which the United States believed it stood.

The eventual relationship of this defeat to the bodies who went off to war in Vietnam was an intimate one, a circumstance due in large measure to the almost exclusive reliance upon the body as a means of assessing progress (or the lack thereof) during the Vietnam War. In particular, the body count meant that the significance of the soldier's body would be largely restricted to what it indicated about the overall success of the war effort—success which never materialized. Defeat in Vietnam was thus explicitly a problem of bodies, if for no other reason than that the United States was ultimately unable to sacrifice as many bodies for as long a period of time as the enemy. Further, "because the (enemy) body had meaning only in death, its signification was fragmented—pieces of bodies 'counted'; some American soldiers collected and strung Vietnamese ears into ornamental necklaces, severed limbs were bagged and burned at military hospitals. The body became the site for multiple display, *as each part became meaningful in itself*, not as synecdoche for larger and more coherent forms, but as unintegrated bits of information that did not reassemble themselves into classic narrative" (Jeffords, 1989: 8; emphasis added). In combination with the defeat in Vietnam, the body count had a powerful effect on how the soldier's body would come to be known. In particular, the body of the soldier became an instrumentality of warfare in a manner unlike those of previous conflicts, in which additional metrics (territory, for example) were at least as crucial to an overall assessment of the war effort. For better or worse, the materiality of the body would be the most salient expression of the American military adventure in Southeast Asia. Second, fragmentation became a principle of the warring body's intelligibility. Randomly disassociated parts of the body not only assumed meaning as material, verifiable evidence of the death of the whole but because of the body count were ascribed special significance. In combination with the substantial unrest that afflicted the American body politic during the war years, it was hard to escape the impression that the loss in Vietnam was due to an explicitly corporeal failure. That the United States had suffered its first outright military defeat was bad enough, but this was something else altogether. Defeat in Southeast Asia called attention to a unique sort of breakdown, namely, "the failure of the Vietnam War to produce a valorization of warring male bodies as well as a failure to unify the national body with coherent and unambivalent support for warring violence" (Shapiro, 1997: 154).

Of the many bodies at issue in this failure, one that was counted unusually enthusiastically was that of POW. Given the emphasis on body counts, this preoccupation fit altogether comfortably within an interpretive framework that invested bodies both living and dead with extraordinary levels of significance. Much of this preoccupation was owing to relentless efforts by the Nixon administration and its Go Public campaign, which, by dramatizing the experiences of POWs, was designed to publicize American prisoners of war as a rationale aimed at shoring up the American body politic's flagging zeal for the war in Vietnam. I will take up the specifics in chapter 2, but here I want to note that the similarity of the Go Public campaign to pre–Revolutionary War captivity narratives opens a window on America's sense of itself in the world. Drawing on widespread fear of threats from without, such narratives customarily featured white women being taken captive by Native Americans and subjected to unimaginable savagery and depredation. In addition to their contributions to American identity, the historical inversions effected by these tales are especially key. In particular, "history in North America begins with the capture of white women and the idea of white victimization. Without necessarily straying far from the often horrific facts of any given experience . . . captivity narratives instantly turned the invader into the invaded and created the foundation for any act of retribution that might follow" (Engelhardt, 1995: 23). Imprisonment, rescue, and retribution thus emerge as themes written into the very earliest years of the American sense of self.

The political usefulness of such representational strategies made it easy for Americans to see themselves as victims, even under circumstances marked by substantial American aggression. Characterizations of the Vietnam War as a quagmire suggest the point. In particular, "the initial benefit of the word *quagmire* was that it ruled out the possibility of planned aggression. The image turned Vietnam into the aggressor, not only transferring agency for all negative action to the land, but also instantly devaluing it. It undoubtedly called to mind as well movie scenes in which heroic white adventurers misstepped in some misbegotten place and found themselves swallowed to the waist, with every effort at extrication leading toward further disaster" (Engelhardt, 1995: 199). American violence in Vietnam was being officially obliterated long before it could be taken as a point of reference in a larger discussion about the merits of belligerence as a policy option. A sanitizing discourse soon followed, one in which the U.S. experience in Vietnam was represented as a trauma. Representing the war as a quagmire was all the more effective when linked to American POWs because it contained "the first glimmerings of a postwar sense that victimhood was the essence of national identity. In the idea of the land as aggressor lay the future obliteration of the memory of the Vietnamese victors; in an acceptance that all efforts at extrication only embedded Americans deeper in the muck of war lay proof that, had they been in control of events, all they would have wanted was to depart" (Engelhardt, 1995: 199–200).

On these bases, captive American soldiers were diligently represented during the late 1960s and early 1970s as victims of the depraved and treacherous North Vietnamese. During a televised ceremony in June 1970, an exhibit featuring two American soldiers confined to bamboo cages was dedicated at the nation's capitol: "One sits in the corner of a bare cell, staring bleakly at an empty bowl and chopsticks on which a huge cockroach is perched. On the floor are other cockroaches and a large rat. The other figure lies in a bamboo cage, ankles shackled" (in Franklin, 1993a: 54). POW/MIA bracelets began appearing on the wrists of Americans across the United States, bracelets which the wearer vowed never to remove until the person whose name was inscribed upon it was returned. The result was the creation of a group of Americans on whose behalf the latter years of the Vietnam War would be waged and for whom the Vietnamese would be expected to account long after the American defeat. Again, the relationship between the war and the body was profound. The unaccounted-for soldier became the most material indication of loss, a lingering absence whose debts to American violence were denied and whose presence in the years following the war was rendered still more acute because the United States had no access to the battlefields and thus could not unilaterally resolve the many questions surrounding the fate of the missing. No one could really say what had happened to those who never returned, and still less whether they might be captives of the Vietnamese.

Not surprisingly, numerous governmental analyses in the postwar years took the body of the absent soldier as their point of departure. At the same time, given the small number of unaccounted-for soldiers compared to those of previous American wars, the very existence of such studies was indicative of just how deeply a sense of victimhood had permeated the American response to the Vietnam War. The House of Representatives Select Committee on Missing Persons in Southeast Asia in 1976 and President Jimmy Carter's Woodcock Commission in 1977, for example, were explicitly conceived to assess rumors of captive American soldiers and the prospects of securing the repatriation of the remains of those killed in action (U.S. Congress, House, 1976; U.S. Department of State, 1977). Both of the inquiries concluded there was no credible evidence to suggest that live prisoners were being held against their will in Southeast Asia. Further, both recommended normalized relations between the United States and Vietnam as offering the greatest likelihood for a full accounting of the missing. For a brief moment, it appeared that the end to America's "long national nightmare" might simply be declared rather than staked to the painstaking and often frustrating effort to resolve individual unaccounted-for cases. Put differently, it seemed as though the balance sheet of the Vietnam War might resemble those of prior American wars, in which the unaccounted-for body was regarded as a more or less unavoidable consequence of mechanized warfare.

Yet the desire of some officials to move on did not prove strong enough to overcome the significance with which the body of the Vietnam War soldier had been invested during the war years. On the contrary, the United States began leveraging various international organizations to force Vietnam to account for missing American soldiers. It went so far as to block Vietnam's admission to the United Nations in September 1976 with the argument that Vietnam "had failed to meet the charter's standard as a 'peace-loving state' by not satisfactorily accounting for the MIAs of the Vietnam War" (Zasloff and Brown, 1978: 9). Later, the United States also blocked Vietnam's efforts to pay its debts to the International Monetary Fund and the World Bank (Stern, 1995: 80). Instead of subsiding, then, the discourse of the absent body was pushed well beyond whatever boundaries were recognized following wars in which the permanent absence of some soldiers was accepted. In particular, the captivity narrative that had determined to such a large degree how that body came to be known during the war retained its force and enabled the body to become indicative of continued American suffering at the hands of the duplicitous Vietnamese. Moreover, as to the question of missing Americans, it mattered little whether the captive body was dead or alive. Its significance would be restricted to the fact of its absence, and that absence would be self-evident confirmation that all was not right with the American world. The result was a pervasive tendency "to see the United States as the nation in need of reparations. If even in flight from Vietnam, the United States hardly fit the image of a defeated nation, the postwar project of its leaders nonetheless became a new kind of domestic reconstruction" (Engelhardt, 1995: 258).

As will be seen, that reconstruction has been staged on the body of the unaccounted-for soldier to a degree unprecedented in the history of warfare. Yet the attempt to account for missing American soldiers is not the only instance in which dead bodies have been hitched to a project of national significance, a point which suggests that because they implicate "matters of accountability, justice, personal grief, victimization, and suffering, dead bodies as vehicles of historical revision are freighted with strong emotion." Dead bodies thus have a distinctly political utility because of "the associations they evoke for people whose feelings of disorientation make them receptive to arguments, stories, and symbols that seem to give them a compass" (Verdery, 1999: 115). Given the absence of an interpretive structure that could account for the loss in Vietnam, the disorientation of the postwar years was indeed palpable. After dominating virtually all the battlefields in Indochina yet still managing to lose the war, the United States was left with much doubt not only about the utility of its military power but also about its national identity as the world's foremost executor of containment. The post–Vietnam War era has accordingly been characterized by uncertainty among Americans as to whether the dead and unaccounted for could be redeemed by the political aims of the conflict. That aims of a different sort—accountability, national honor, certainty for the families—are so frequently and explicitly appended to unaccounted-for Vietnam War bodies attests to the felt need among Americans for a new kind of "compass."[2]

It is especially with respect to questions of accountability that dead bodies suggest their value to projects of national reconstruction like that undertaken in the aftermath of the Vietnam War. In this context, accountability "serve[s] to draw up a moral balance sheet, to settle accounts, as a condition of making the post[war] order a moral one" (Verdery, 1999: 38). Such an effort became all the more vital in the late 1970s as organizations like the National League of Families of Prisoners and Missing in Southeast Asia began agitating for increased cooperation from the Vietnamese and greater fervor on the part of the U.S. government in the search for missing soldiers. However, the results of such agitation all too often seemed to reprise the absence of accountability that had characterized the Vietnam War. The government would deny the existence of evidence concerning live prisoners, only to see its assertion refuted by an enterprising family member who discovered precisely such evidence in a missing soldier's case file.[3] The aforementioned return of Robert Garwood in 1979 threw still more fuel onto the fire. Accountability even for the accounting effort appeared decidedly lacking.

Because of the perilous trajectory of accountability during and after the war, the discourse of the absent body began to undergo certain shifts. These shifts do much to explain the current place of identifiable remains at the center of attempts to determine the fate and whereabouts of missing service personnel. In particular, the materiality of the body was increasingly viewed as *the* standard for determining the fate and whereabouts of missing soldiers, the site at which justice, accountability, and the U.S. aggrieved sense of self came together. Materiality came to be seen as the sole route to the truth of the absent body, the means by which the wildly proliferating theories and allegations about the missing could be resolved in favor of certainty. Circumstantial evidence, in many cases substantial and convincing, was cast aside as a stand-alone means of accounting for the missing since it was still more evidence of either Vietnamese duplicity or conspiracy on the part of the U.S. government to conceal the existence of living American soldiers left behind in Southeast Asia. As a consequence, the United States now officially requires the repatriation and identification of a soldier's body in order to remove his name from the list of the missing, the only such means of accounting for absent soldiers ever embraced by any nation in the aftermath of war.

Unique though it may be, the emphasis on the materiality of the unaccounted-for body nonetheless intersects with forms of commemorating and burying the dead that long predate the search for Americans missing in Southeast Asia. What these practices suggest is that although the effort to repatriate and identify the bodies of soldiers who failed to return from the war in Vietnam is a distinctively American phenomenon, it derives a certain degree of conceptual coherence from broader cultural and historical influences. In this context, the early Christian concern "about how parts of the body related to the whole being—that is, how they would be reintegrated after death" is a good example (Hogle, 1999: 28). Such concerns were especially intense when the dead body was fragmented because it wasn't immediately clear how God could reassemble the various parts if they had been widely separated or, worse, consumed and digested. The doctrine of resurrection thus achieved much of its cultural salience from the response it offered to anxieties about corporeal integrity. In particular, "to rise with our bodies and its [sic] parts intact was a victory over digestion, dissemination, and assimilation into another form as much as a victory over death" (Hogle, 1999: 29). The Eucharist also played a pivotal role, particularly in the twelfth and thirteenth centuries as the relationship between the material body and emergent notions of the self became more intertwined. Of special note here was the Eucharist's basis in "the belief that the human body would be made whole and holy through Christ and would therefore be protected from decay" (Hogle, 1999: 29). Further complementing this relationship between the body and the self is the connection between the individual body and the collectivity, a connection which has in many countries generated the belief that "our 'sons' must be buried in 'our' soil, lest we be plagued by misfortune arising from the soul's continued distress" (Verdery, 1999: 47). While the relationship of the soul to burial practices may be less immediate in the comparatively secular age of the nation-state, a shift in emphasis from the ecclesiastical principality to Hobbes's (1968 [1651]) body politic as the unity of the many in the creation of the one suggests the importance to the collectivity retained by the individual body.

Still other beliefs about the dead body derive from the life lived prior to death, as illustrated by disparate burial rights accorded the poor and the wealthy. Beginning in seventeenth-century Europe, for example, upper-class dead retained their right to the connection between individual identity and bodily integrity that was a hallmark of bourgeois existence, while the poor were often disposed of in mass graves without a formal funeral ceremony (Hogle, 1999: 33). Proper burial thus became a marker of the place one occupied in the social order during life. This phenomenon would also later be true in the United States, where "death was regarded as the epitome of life. How one died, and how one's body was treated after death, fixed for eternity one's moral, aesthetic and social status" (Sappol, 2002: 31). On this basis, one can more clearly understand the importance of military bodies in a country like the United States where the social order has long drawn strength from the instantiation of specifically martial virtues in the bodies of its (male) citizens (Ferguson and Turnbull, 1999). Defilement of the military body by the failure to ensure its proper burial becomes a defilement of the body on which the defense and maintenance of the republic have allegedly come to depend. The meaning of the dead Vietnam War body—descended from its significance in life as a result of the body count—might thus be said to derive from this interpretive tradition in which the life of the deceased governs its subsequent treatment. Again the social order is implicated, in this case via the understandings of honor and duty that have long animated American understandings of the martial experience.

While forms of honoring and interring the dead in the United States can be traced in many ways to practices originating in Europe, certain uniquely American attitudes toward the dead body can also be cited in the context of the protocol used to account for missing Vietnam War soldiers. A comparison of cremation rates in Germany and the United States is especially helpful here. In Germany, 60 to 70 percent of bodies are cremated. Further, "when a body is buried, the plot is not permanent; rather, it is leased for about twenty years. Coffins are made of simple wood, and bodies are not embalmed. They are allowed to disintegrate and disseminate into the earth naturally—dust to dust" (Hogle, 1999: 26). In the United States during the 1970s, by contrast, 92 percent of burials were earth burials and 78 percent were preceded by funerals featuring a full viewing of the body. More than 90 percent of bodies not cremated are embalmed (Hogle, 1999: 27). The difference between these practices and those found in Germany suggests an American preoccupation not just with the body in death but with a particular sense of bodily integrity and the capacity to retain that integrity long after burial. Put somewhat differently, "American customs of handling the dead suggest a desire to make the individual's corporeal existence permanent . . . [and] reflect the belief that, even in death, property can be owned. Each individual has his own place for eternity; this is his memorial" (Hogle, 1999: 27). Simply allowing the body to disappear after death, regardless of circumstances, does not appear to have been an option in the United States to anywhere near the extent it was in Germany.

Further evidence for this conclusion comes from Michael Sappol (2002) in his captivating account of the history of anatomy and dissection in eighteenth- and nineteenth-century America. Sappol reveals that anatomical knowledge of the body became a marker of American bourgeois identity and an indispensable part of the scientific credibility of the physician. This, in turn, ramped up the demand for cadavers—demand that was not easily met given the aforementioned beliefs about the relationship between individual identity in life and bodily integrity in death. Not surprisingly, the bodies of the poor, the indigent, and racial minorities bore the brunt of this "traffic of dead bodies." Yet even though cadavers were being drawn from the lower classes, anatomy in its early days roused considerable popular opposition for reasons that will now sound familiar:

> Medical dismemberment and exhibition of the human body were seen as the inverse of a Christian burial that deposited the body whole into the ground and placed it safely out of view. The dissected human was demoted to the status of slaughtered meat, in the words of one commentary, "a raw head and bloody bones" taken up by a "Tribe of Dissectors." Even worse, the exhumation and dissection of bodies rendered them risible: a New Yorker of the 1790s complained that corpses were "being violently dragged" from the grave "to become a subject of mirth to a licentious set of men and the laughter of fools . . . who cut and mangle the body." And worse still, dissection was seen as having affinities to necrophilia, cannibalism, and satanic ritual. (Sappol, 2002: 104)

At times, such sentiments led to "anatomy riots"—a mêlée in New York City in April 1788 featured a horde of five thousand stick- and rock-wielding demonstrators—usually triggered by the discovery of the recently robbed grave of a white citizen or a laboratory in which dissections were quietly taking place. One observer at the time said the destruction of the body occasioned by anatomical dissection is "'an immense injury to the living,' to society as a whole: it 'breaks up the sympathies which unite us with the dead' and 'make life serious, rational, and religious.' Anatomy 'must produce a state of mind at war [with] feeling,' a callous indifference to the 'continued identity of being' that links the living and the dead" (Sappol, 2002: 133-34).

These examples suggest that the life of the deceased, corporeal integrity, and proper burial have long been critical components in Americans' understanding of death generally and how to care for the dead body. Accordingly, I present them in the context of the search for missing Vietnam War soldiers for two reasons. First, they furnish a backdrop and something of a conceptual chronology to the contemporary accounting protocol requiring the repatriation and identification of human remains. Such a requirement, though unique in the history of warfare, nonetheless shares certain affinities with beliefs about the "proper" relationship to and handling of the dead body. Second, such background is offered as a way of saying that my analysis of the search for missing soldiers and of the accounting protocol does not amount to blaming the families of the missing for seeking the return of the body of a loved one. Such desire is clearly written into both the Western and the American experience of death and the body to which that death pertains. As a result, the argument here does not deny either that the loss of a loved one is difficult or that the absence of the body might compound the grief that accompanies the loss of life. Repatriation, commemoration, and proper burial of the body ought not now become the stuff of which future hostilities are made. Instead, the overriding task is to engage the political, interpretive, and ethical consequences that follow from an accounting protocol committed to the repatriation of nameable, identifiable bodies.

As it happens, however, hostility has predominated among these consequences and in many ways continues to govern the endeavor to account for soldiers missing in Vietnam. While there can be little doubt that the manipulations and deceptions of the later years of the Vietnam War played a substantial role in generating and sustaining such tensions, the extraordinary emphasis placed on the body of the absent soldier has ensured their continuation. In particular, the requirement of an identified body to remove a name from the list of the missing has opened a discourse of certainty in which no claim about the absent body can be considered true in the absence of its identified materiality. Not surprisingly, this discourse has been embraced with alacrity by the families of the missing. As the wife of a Navy pilot missing since 1966 once remarked, "If [he] is still alive, I want him home; if he is dead, his remains need to be returned to this country. He has a right to come home—and I need to know" (in Steele, 1992: 37). Certainty, closure, the body—this is the holy trinity of the American effort to account for missing Vietnam War soldiers. Understandable though the quest for certainty may be given the extensive political manipulation of the issue in the late 1960s and early 1970s, it has also done its part to ensure that the striving to account for the body of the absent Vietnam War soldier would repeat the animosity, distrust, and bitterness of the war itself.

Still more, emphasis on the repatriation of remains revivifies the infamous body count that determined the interpretive parameters of Vietnam War bodies in the first place. During the war, of course, "this numerology of death was not just a set of passive measurements. The numbers were an active element in Vietnamese affairs. *They initiated death as they recorded it*, for it was on the basis of deaths recorded that future deaths were to be ordered up. The numbers would determine the next set of 'quotas' to be met" (Engelhardt, 1995: 209; emphasis added). In like manner, identification of one body requires the identification of still more since it implies that despite the circumstances of loss and the extreme fragmentation of remains, such identifications can be—and will be—made. Certainty in the form of the identified body, in other words, is presented as the only means of resolving the deep-rooted uncertainty generated by missing soldiers specifically and loss of the Vietnam War generally. While the United States pursues what it calls "the fullest possible accounting" of its soldiers in Southeast Asia as a means of hinting that not every single soldier will be accounted for, this cautionary note is almost entirely belied by the intensity of the repatriation effort and the emphasis placed on the identified body. Because of this situation, the refusal to find fault with the impulse behind retrieving the dead body must be accompanied by the recognition that mechanized warfare results in a uniquely violent form of death, that some bodies simply do not come back, and that profound political and ethical implications arise when the refusal to accept often overwhelming circumstantial evidence concerning the fate and whereabouts of a loved one comes to define government policy regarding the missing. While the history of death and the dead body no doubt partly informs the current accounting protocol, that same protocol—and the quest for certainty in the form of the identified body which it expresses—affects in numerous ways the interpretive practices that inform the American response to the Vietnam War and those unaccounted for.

To begin the process of demonstrating these consequences—and as a means of showing just how thoroughly the discourse of certainty has come to govern the American response to the ambiguity of the absent body—in chapter 3 I discuss the practices that support the accounting protocol. Consisting of archival research, archaeological excavation, and the forensic identification of recovered remains, these practices have developed not only as a result of the quest for certainty but also in response to one of the most noteworthy features of the unaccounted-for body, its extreme fragmentation. Such fragmentation is attributable to the violence of aircraft crashes, the effects of climate and soil on the decomposition of remains, and the passage of more than thirty years between the incident of loss and subsequent recovery efforts. Among other things, this means there is no body to repatriate to the United States, at least not in the complete sense implied by the name of a soldier on the list of the missing. Weeks of excavating a grave site or an aircraft crash site in accordance with the strictest archaeological standards very often result in little more than a few shards of bone or perhaps, under more providential conditions, some teeth.

Not surprisingly, such circumstances complicate the claim that "the body" of the absent soldier has been recovered in Southeast Asia and clearly impede the quest for certainty that animates the search in the first place. Furthermore, given the current accounting protocol, such a claim can be made only in the presence of identifiable remains or, more accurately, upon successful identification of those remains. We now begin to see why remains identification is of absolute centrality to the search for missing American soldiers. In view of the lingering belief that the Vietnamese held back a certain number of American prisoners as well as the more general "need to know" expressed most frequently by families of the missing, the only way to be sure the soldier in question has in fact returned to the United States is through positive identity of his remains. Identification effectively constitutes a complete body by enabling a definitive correspondence between the body named on the list of the missing and the fragmentary remains recovered in Southeast Asia. Conspicuous here is the materiality of identified remains and the degree to which that materiality underwrites the claim that the formerly absent soldier is now accounted for. Portrayed as an expression of antecedent truth, the materiality of identified remains provides the desired certainty in the form of a body that can be interred in a casket and buried in American soil.

Yet if we remain suspicious of materiality's standing as an expression of antecedent reality, we must explore how these fragmentary though identified remains are able to signify anything at all. Certainly part of their meaning is derived from the Vietnam War itself and the curious epistemology of the body count, in which parts of the body became meaningful in and of themselves. Put simply, body parts have always made a particular kind of sense in the context of the Vietnam War and its aftermath. More crucial, however, is the degree to which the significance of fragmented remains is an effect of the practices of modern forensic science and its ability to achieve the abovementioned correspondence between the name on the list and the remains recovered in Southeast Asia. What this underscores is that identification of remains is never a given, once again because of their extreme fragmentation. This, in turn, means there is always a risk that identification procedures will fail to attach a name to the remains in question, a situation that leaves said remains in the indeterminate status from which they were recovered and therefore fails to respond to the need to know. Though rare, such instances have occurred, sometimes as a result of problems at the government's Central Identification Laboratory (CIL), where identification of remains is performed, other times because families of the missing have refused to accept that such a small quantity of the body definitively indicates the death of their loved one. The need to know is thwarted on its own terms, an occurrence that brings one face to face with the political and ethical toll exacted by the discourse of certainty and its concomitant exclusion of circumstantial evidence as a stand-alone means of accounting for the missing. The quest for certainty becomes increasingly pernicious in that it enflames the hostilities that have characterized the post–Vietnam War era when the identified body fails to materialize.

In identifying the role of certainty in the continuation of Vietnam War hostilities some thirty years after the withdrawal of American forces, I refer to additional bodies implicated in the U.S. quest to account for its missing soldiers, a reference that reiterates this book's claim that the contentious legacy of the Vietnam War is one of bodies. To bolster this argument, in chapter 4 I discuss the body of the Vietnam veteran and its place within that legacy. As with the body of the absent soldier and the identified body recovered in Southeast Asia, the intersections of defeat in Vietnam, victimhood, and the certainty provided by the materiality of the body are again prominent, though in a manner starkly different from that seen in chapters 2 and 3. In particular, the body of the veteran is noteworthy for its inability to lay to rest the lingering uncertainties of the Vietnam War as the identification of the accounted for body does. Instead, the materiality of the veteran's body is the continual signification of the failure and loss in Vietnam, bearing as it does the immutable traces of the war's corporeal fragmentation and dismemberment. This circumstance in turn evokes Butler's claim that not all bodies can be affirmed within extant structures of normativity and intelligibility. As she argues, materialization (understood as the process by which bodies assume cultural intelligibility) always entails the production of opposites, "a domain of abject beings, those who are not yet 'subjects,' but who form the constitutive outside to the domain of the subject" (1993: 3). The abject thus designates "precisely those 'unlivable' and 'uninhabitable' domains of social life which . . . constitute the defining limit of the subject's domain; it will constitute that site of dreaded identification against which—and by virtue of which—the domain of the subject will circumscribe its own claim to autonomy and to life" (3). The "Vietnam vet" is no accident. Instead, he is an outcome of the insistence on identified bodies as a means of making sense of defeat in Vietnam.

In light of these considerations, understanding the Vietnam veteran in the context of the search for misssing Vietnam War soldiers requires analysis of the discourse of abjection as one of the primary means of knowing that veteran. Two paramount actualities frame this discussion: the comparatively low rates of psychiatric casualties suffered by Vietnam soldiers compared to soldiers in other American wars and the readjustment to civilian life, which, statistically speaking, at least, Vietnam veterans have accomplished with greater success than any other generation of warriors in American history. Next to these indicators, the persistence of the image of the Vietnam veteran as physically and psychically scarred, shunned upon his return to the United States, and likely to explode in a fit of violent rage at any moment is curious indeed. I argue that the abject body of the veteran serves needs, which means that rejection of the veteran from the realm of solicitude occupied by the unaccounted-for body is nonetheless a form of inclusion in the political work of making sense of the Vietnam War. Most important among those needs, the abjection of the veteran preserves the unaccounted-for body as something worth fighting for and holds it in a realm of postwar politics in which victory in the form of the identified body remains a possibility. Far from incidental to the accounting effort, the body of the abject veteran is one of the search's constitutive elements, the limit over and against which the body of the accounted for soldier comes to be defined.

As in the case of the body of the unaccounted-for soldier, a great deal of the interpretive impetus behind the image of the demented Vietnam veteran can be traced to the ways in which veterans were represented beginning in the later years of the Vietnam War. In some cases these were self-representations, as when returning veterans joined the antiwar movement and self-consciously implicated themselves, and by extension American policy, in the atrocities committed during the military project in Indochina. Such activism fit altogether too comfortably within the division then being created by the Nixon administration between good veterans (meaning primarily those from World War II) and the bad veterans of the Vietnam War, who, having laid their lives on the line in defense of American interests, were now returning home to protest the war in large numbers. In an environment literally unimaginable in the hyperpatriotic climate of the early twenty-first century, veterans of the late 1960s were vilified by such high-level American political figures as Vice President Spiro Agnew, who repeatedly accused antiwar veterans of aiding the enemy. Simultaneously, the Go Public campaign was doing its part to transform the war into something fought to secure the release of POWs and the repatriation of the remains of KIAs. On top of this, Hollywood began releasing films depicting the Vietnam veteran as a murderous, rampaging lunatic, a person not simply a danger to himself and society but also likely to be well beyond the purview of medical and psychiatric intervention. Perhaps the Vietnam veteran really was a little pale by comparison.

At the outset, then, the Vietnam veteran began the post–Vietnam War era as unaccounted for within traditional notions of valor, courage, and, above all, victory. Defeat spoke to the possibility that the men who went to fight in Vietnam lacked what it takes to win a war, that they hadn't been tough enough, indeed, that they weren't real men in the sense presupposed by prior American war narratives. For these reasons, "the representation of the soldier and combat in contemporary American culture is more than simply a resurgence of militarism or nationalistic fever, but is instead a forum for the reaffirmation and reconstitution of the masculine in the modern *polis*. Consequently, Vietnam narratives are to be read, not as a subgenre of popular fiction, but as an emblem of a cultural reformulation of masculinity" (Jeffords, 1989: 62). In the context of the search for the missing, however, that reformulation has only haltingly been extended to the Vietnam veteran because it is precisely the failure of masculinity that produced absent bodies in the first place. Failed masculinity thus becomes not only a principle that sustains the abjection of the Vietnam veteran but also a condition which must be reversed if the return of America's missing from Southeast Asia is to be achieved. The feminine, in other words, becomes that category of embodied existence which must be expelled if the Vietnam War and American masculinity are to be reclaimed. The need for such expulsion is reinforced by the tacit presumption that veterans have widespread psychiatric difficulties—difficulties which in the context of warfare have never quite shed the connotations of malingering and femininity they acquired with the advent of shell shock during World War I. Because the Vietnam veteran has demonstrated his failed manhood, the "cultural reformulation of masculinity" falls to the body unaccounted for in Southeast Asia and its repatriation. Not merely unsullied by defeat, missing bodies remain perhaps the only victim of the war whom the real men might still be able to save.

I argue in chapter 4 that the relationship between the body unaccounted for in Southeast Asia and the body of the Vietnam veteran both stands in for the impaired relationship between masculinity and femininity in the post–Vietnam War era and reprises the defeat in Vietnam and the American sense of victimhood which that defeat underscored. The absent body possibly imprisoned and certainly left behind in Vietnam is emblematic of our status as victims and the most material indication of defeat—problems not coincidentally produced and sustained by incursions of femininity into the masculine domain of warfare. Vietnam veterans share the interpretive wealth as the most immediate examples of what happens when femininity infects the body of the warrior. At the same time, both the unaccounted-for soldier and the Vietnam veteran can be victims, in this case

> of a government that not only failed to win the war but also failed in its responsibility to returning veterans. Chief among the characteristics of failure is the depiction of the government's negotiating posture toward the governments of both South Vietnam and the Republic of Vietnam. This posture is perceived as weak, passive, easily deceived (and yet capable of deceiving veterans), nonaggressive (read primarily as a failure to use aggression when appropriate rather than a decisive action itself), and, most important, ignoring or deliberately repressing the interests of the soldier/POW/veteran. (Jeffords, 1989: 150)

This almost dizzying array of interpretive possibilities indicates the breadth of cultural sources from which the effort to account for soldiers missing in Southeast Asia draws sustenance. As a receptacle of blame for loss in the Vietnam War, however, the abject veteran serves one predominant need in the context of the search: he is an indication of where we likely *won't* find a solution to the disorientation and fragmentation produced by the defeat in Vietnam.

While the encounter between the unaccounted-for body and the body of the Vietnam veteran lends much to the cultural salience of the search for American soldiers missing in Southeast Asia, the coherence of that endeavor is also derived from the body to which recovered remains are returned, that is, the American body politic. Return of absent bodies is sought, in other words, because of their meaningfulness as parts of a larger whole. In suggesting a connection between the individual body and its collective counterpart, I aim to highlight the degree to which nation-states constitute themselves as both ontological and corporeal entities. Often this is revealed through "the impulse or inward aim of the constitution of collective coherence, [and the] desire to represent the national body as unified and unambivalent" (Shapiro, 1997: 141). Such unification and coherence were patently called into question by the defeat in Vietnam and the lingering absence of a certain number of military bodies. The fragmentation of the individual body recovered in Southeast Asia might thus be said to extend to the American body politic, a circumstance that requires some process of repair (read: repatriation) like that undertaken by the effort to recover the bodies of soldiers missing from the Vietnam War. I take up these issues in chapter 5 through an analysis of three practices of memorializing the Vietnam War: the Vietnam Veterans Memorial in Washington, D.C., the Tomb of the Vietnam War Unknown at Arlington National Cemetery, and the POW/MIA flag. Memorials are chosen for this inquiry because such projects explicitly foreground the collectivity to which they refer. By linking the individual body to the collective body in the form of shared narratives about each, memorials contribute to the material and conceptual coherence of the body politic. Such contributions became especially important with the advent of the nation-state, which, as George Mosse (1990) argues, constantly requires practices capable of promoting a sense among individuals of their membership in the collectivity. Consecration of the death and sacrifice of individual soldiers to the nation has long been one especially salient means for the articulation of such themes.

One of the most vital links between the individual and the national body in the context of Vietnam War memorials is the sense that the American body politic remains wounded as a result of the fragmentation caused by the war and the absence of certain bodies. This extension of the sense of victimization means that much Vietnam War memorialization, the Vietnam Veterans Memorial above all, is largely guided by the discourse of healing, a discourse that derives much of its sense from the absence of individual soldiers. Vietnam War memorials therefore have their share of political work to do, work that is primarily oriented toward restoring the sense of corporeal integrity that allegedly marked the pre–Vietnam War years. At memorial sites, furthermore, this work is inextricably bound up with remembering and forgetting. Does healing occur when we remember the missing? or is it best achieved by a willed forgetting and a process of moving on? Still more to the point, does the naming of missing soldiers on the Vietnam Veterans Memorial rejoin them to the body politic? or does it effect a tacit forgetting of their most significant feature, namely, their continued absence? One answer is suggested by the extraordinary popularity of the Vietnam Veterans Memorial, a status that derives from the space of reconciliation it offers and its apparent refusal to take a position on the Vietnam War itself. A rejoinder comes from the Tomb of the Unknown Soldier and the problems occasioned by anonymous remains in the post–Vietnam War era as well as by the POW/MIA flag, conceived in 1971 by the wife of a soldier missing in Southeast Asia and then embraced by the National League of Families in response to the conviction that not enough was being done to ensure the return of American missing.

The answers to these questions are important, but it is not immediately clear that the body politic retains much conceptual coherence as a metaphor for political collectivities, especially given the democratic refiguration of the social that occurred "when the body of the king was destroyed, when the body politic was decapitated and when, at the same time, the corporeality of the social was dissolved" (Lefort, 1986: 303). That refiguration, according to Lefort, has left the social without anything at the center to give form and substance like that supplied by the body of the king during the age of the hereditary monarchy. Yet this transformation need not lead to the conclusion that the body has lost its relevance to democratically articulated collectivities. Rather, what can be seen is a move "from the 'body of the king' to the 'social body of citizens.' The *corpus politicum* became socialized; the *corpus* in question became society itself" (Neocleous, 2001: 33). On this basis, the repatriation of individual bodies, especially as a means of healing the body of the social, retains a certain logic in that the individual body is the very stuff of the body politic. Further, repatriation of the body connects with the uniquely modern and democratic memorial practice of listing the names of those either killed in war or whose bodies were never recovered (Laqueur, 1996). If the democratic revolution signals a new emphasis on the individual, then the individual's named existence becomes, as it were, all the collectivity has. While the tension between recovering the absent body and simply naming it, as occurs at the Vietnam Veterans Memorial, remains crucial, one can nevertheless see how the discourse of healing that animates both that memorial and the accounting for missing American soldiers draws from the continued vitality of the body even in the absence of the body of the monarch.

Although such examples suggest the continued relevance of the metaphor of the body politic to democratic republics, it is equally the case that the discourse of healing to which that metaphor gives rise brings with it substantial political and ethical implications, especially when healing is achieved through the repatriation and identification of the remains of missing soldiers. In particular, healing implies the possibility of getting beyond the injurious event in question, a political posture that ultimately fails to disable the representational practices that legitimate nation-state violence in the first place. Second, figuring the social in terms of a body implies that the social has a gender. On this basis, it is not surprising to see that the Vietnam War has been memorialized in a gendered idiom, given warfare's traditional figuration as an expression of the heroic masculinity of the national body and the defeat in Vietnam that so seriously called that masculinity into question. The addition to the memorial site of Frederick Hart's realist statue depicting three male Vietnam War soldiers, for example, confirms the suspicions of failed masculinity discussed in chapter 4, a failure that must be explicitly and unambiguously refuted in the presence of the nation's most important memorial to the Vietnam War. The addition of Glenna Goodacre's Vietnam Women's Memorial some years later performs a similar function, that is, to show women performing the allegedly natural women's task of caring for wounded soldiers. The message is unmistakable: the American body politic shall be healed, and the body of the absent soldier shall be subsumed into the larger project of returning to the status quo ante. Along the way, consideration of the institutionalized violence that contributed to absent bodies in the first place is forestalled, and the repatriation and identification of soldiers' bodies is naturalized as one among many normal postwar practices that contribute to the healing so fervently desired.

Perhaps not surprisingly, however, many families of missing Vietnam War soldiers take a dim view of this form of healing, seeing it as entirely premature if the body of the absent Vietnam War soldier remains absent. Naming like that which occurs at the Vietnam Veterans Memorial simply does not respond to the imperative of certainty in the manner achieved by the materiality of the identified body. Indeed, such naming is not only premature given the continued absence of so many bodies but further wounds the body politic insofar as the practice of memorialization constitutes a tacit forgetting of those still unaccounted for in Southeast Asia. The exhumation and identification of the Vietnam War unknown soldier suggests the point. Despite the previously vast symbolic significance attached to the anonymous body, that anonymity became a problem to which the discourses of certainty and healing called dramatic attention. Named, memorialized, remembered, forgotten—none of it really mattered in the absence of the certitudes that came with positive identity of Michael Blassie's remains. A still more palpable example in the context of Vietnam War memorialization is the POW/MIA flag, the third form of memorializing the Vietnam War taken up in chapter 5. Its stark message—"You Are Not Forgotten"—is, at one level, nourished by the value of the name to the democratic collectivity, value which in the post–Vietnam War era is measured solely by the identified body. At another level, however, the alleged risk of forgetting the individual missing soldier by naming him on the Vietnam Veterans Memorial yet failing to secure the return of his body is used by the flag for purposes of firing interpretive shots across the bow of the "fullest possible accounting." Its ammunition is the presentation of live American prisoners of war as fact despite the exceedingly dubious evidence marshaled in support of this claim. Further, the flag suggests that any failure to secure the return of the absent body means the missing have been forsaken, an offense for which responsible agents must consequently be located in the form of either the U.S government or the Vietnamese. Ethically speaking, then, the POW/MIA flag must itself be called to account for its contribution to the hostilities that motivate the desire to account for missing American soldiers.

Like the discourse of certainty, abjection, and healing, that of responsibility has played a major role in solidifying the interpretive parameters of the absent body and in shaping the political climate within which the drive to account for Americans missing in Southeast Asia assumes legitimacy. The attribution of unilateral responsibility to account for missing Americans has been especially forceful in this respect. since in placing before the Vietnamese an absent body represented not as the effect of mechanized warfare but as something for which they are required to account, the Vietnamese are remanded to the same position of inferiority they occupied during the war itself. Such positioning is all the more noteworthy given America's profound dependence on Vietnamese assistance at literally every moment in the accounting process. In addition to contributing to the contentiousness of the accounting effort, the relationship of superiority and inferiority it contains reflects just how lopsided the push to account for American soldiers has become. Even in 1973, the Vietnam War was the most accounted for war in U.S. history, yet the search for the missing continues. Some three hundred thousand Vietnamese soldiers remain unaccounted for and yet little effort is made to ensure the recovery and identification of their remains. Not unexpectedly, the absence of a similar accounting effort on behalf of Vietnamese missing has much to do with the economic embargo maintained by the United States against Vietnam for the first twenty years after the war, an embargo that helped drain Vietnam of the resources that might otherwise have been used to locate their unaccounted-for soldiers. Yet within the interpretive framework of the absent American body, not only are unaccounted-for Vietnamese ineligible for the sorts of solicitude extended to their American counterparts, the lion's share of the responsibility to account for those missing Americans is foisted onto the Vietnamese.

Like the POW/MIA flag, the assertion of the American self at the expense of the Vietnamese brings the ethical dimension of the search for missing soldiers to the forefront. In response, in chapter 6 I articulate an ethical relation that begins with the interpretive commitments that legitimize the search for the missing and then reframes them in a manner which disables the attributions of unitary responsibility that feature so strongly in American representations of the issue. One way to do this is to call attention to the dependence of responsibility on the belief that there must be an identifiable agent in the world who caused the suffering in question, what William Connolly (1991: 79) has characterized as "the demand for an equivalence between evil and responsibility." Because such categories require "that there be a responsible agent or purpose for suffering in the world, that human finitude and suffering be redeemed by an agency of responsibility" (79), contextual elements that might also have contributed to the suffering in question are obscured. Accordingly, the ethical relation foregrounds the recognition that American soldiers went missing not solely because of the Vietnamese but also as the result of the massive American military presence in Southeast Asia. This recognition then becomes a means of inhibiting the tendency to seek in the Vietnamese an unambiguous agent who might redeem the uncertainty of the absent body.

The ethical relation also seeks to forestall the production of the Vietnamese as the other within an accounting effort predicated entirely on the American self. Such rearticulation is achieved by engaging with the understandings of responsibility, humanitarianism, and the body that motivate the accounting effort — understandings which are frequently dissimulated through reliance on what Emmanuel Levinas (1981) characterizes as an ontological orientation that seeks to subsume the Other into the Same. Ontology, in other words, consists in the effort to establish a framework through reference to which events in the world can be judged true (because they correspond with the self) or false (as expressions of the other). The problem here is that, like the body, truth and falsity are themselves dependent and relational, deriving their force not from their status as pure existents but from the interpretive and representational practices that allow them to achieve meaning. Accordingly, the impetus behind the ethical relation is not *an* ethics against which the accounting effort might be judged. Rather, the goal is a more conciliatory and open relationship to the Vietnamese through diminished emphasis on the absent body, which has become the most insistent — and most insidious — expression of the American defeat in Southeast Asia. This in turn permits a confrontation with the sense of American exceptionalism that has underwritten the accounting effort from the beginning.

Staging this confrontation requires disavowal of the language of ontology and a turn toward the Saying, or a performative stating "in which our responsibility to the other is the basis for reflection" (Campbell and Shapiro, 1999: x). Foregrounded in this manner, the other is no longer comprehended in terms of the self, which is to say, no longer interpellated as the inferior term in a hierarchical dichotomization that equates the self with the true. Instead, the other is embraced as that which permits acknowledgment of the self's relational and contingent status. As a result, responsibility is no longer an attribution from one to another but responsibility for the other as both complementary to and necessary for the self in the first place. This is not simply a gesture toward reciprocity or an acknowledgment of shared interests. It is a political posture designed to short-circuit production of the glib verities and invidious categorical distinctions upon which the accounting effort depends. In the context of the search for missing soldiers, this posture compels attention to the racial and moral vocabulary employed by family organizations and the U.S. government when insisting on Vietnam's responsibility to provide the fullest possible accounting as well as to the long-standing claim by the United States that the accounting effort is a humanitarian mission to be pursued independently of other issues affecting the two countries. The problem here, once again, is not whether the search for the missing is truly humanitarian but that its invocation presumes a set of universal principles able to differentiate the humanitarian from its opposite, an impulse at odds with ethical relation's emphasis on a solicitation of the other.

A final value of the ethical relation lies in its ability to displace the body as the ultimate repository of the truth of the missing. As seen in the context of remains repatriation and identification, the body has become that irreducible thing whose materiality proves Vietnam's obligation to cooperate in the fullest possible accounting. Just like responsibility and humanitarianism, then, the body has assumed the character of a universal standard available for distinguishing truth from its opposite in a manner that both denies context and furthers the hostilities which the search for the missing was allegedly designed to placate. Given these circumstances, perhaps resolution of cases should be allowed to proceed in the absence of remains, a solution long proposed by the Vietnamese but consistently dismissed by the United States as a further example of their unwillingness to cooperate. Perhaps the families of the missing could commit themselves to the sometimes difficult work that accompanies the striving to move beyond the loss of a loved one in the absence of remains. Still more, perhaps the United States should be encouraged to see the search for missing soldiers as the all-too-American phenomenon it is and thereby unlink Vietnamese responsibility from the question of missing soldiers altogether.

Apart from any of these specific possibilities, the ultimate hope behind the ethical relation—and behind the larger critique of the effort to account for missing American soldiers contained in this book—is that the United States might somehow disable the still-active wartime representational economy in which the absent body signifies the continuation of so many Vietnam War hostilities. Only then does it seem possible to imagine an end to an accounting effort that has done so much to delay the closure and healing desired by so many. Only then can we begin to rethink the balance sheet of war in a manner that does not require recourse to the mathematical calculus of the list of the missing or to the truth allegedly provided by the materiality of the body but instead through a delegitimation of violence as a policy option in the first place. As will be seen in the epilogue, however, the prospects for such a refiguration are not promising, a state of affairs amply demonstrated by more recent events in which the legacy of Vietnam War missing and the representational strategies it has bequeathed are readily apparent. The most prominent example comes from the Persian Gulf War of 1991, a war that resulted in thirteen unaccounted-for American soldiers, among them Navy Lieutenant Commander (now Captain) Michael Scott Speicher, shot down over Iraq on January 17. Originally declared KIA/BNR, Speicher has been making a steady comeback in the years since, having been reclassified as MIA in 2001 and then missing-captured in October 2002, not coincidentally during the rhetorical and material buildup for the second war with Iraq. Virtually all of the usual suspects made appearances during this series of events, including Speicher's absent body, which preserved the possibility of life despite a CIL investigation in Iraq in 1995 that confirmed his initial status determination; family organizations that clamored for proof of Speicher's death and accused virtually everyone of deceit and conspiracy when no proof aside from the circumstantial variety was forthcoming; and live-sighting reports and other "intelligence" concerning Speicher's fate and whereabouts, which added fuel to the above two fires. Not surprisingly, great hopes were pinned on success in the second Gulf War, at which time unfettered American access to Iraq would finally lift the veil and find Captain Speicher moldering away in some obscure Iraqi prison. In light of the legacy of Vietnam War missing, however, the outcome was almost absurdly predictable. Speicher was not found, either alive or dead, and a renewed round of accusations, acrimony, and delusion was launched. First on the spot was the ever-reliable National Alliance of Families for the Return of America's Missing Servicemen, who claimed "Speicher has served his purpose. It is time to KOP [Kill on Paper] him, once again." Citing the always-handy unnamed source, they continued to charge deception, selective evidence, and cover-up when Speicher's body failed to materialize in Iraq (Bits n Pieces 2003).

As the most prominent example of the legacy of unaccounted-for Vietnam War soldiers, Speicher unwittingly confirmed the views of an American searcher working in Southeast Asia, who proclaimed, "The war won't really be over until they're all accounted for. We need to bring them all home" (in Dillow, 1995: A5). One suspects he's right, though not because the accounting effort might somehow fail but because the war in question continues to rage—just as it always has—in the very home to which the missing are being returned.

chapter two

From Unrecoverable to Unaccounted For

In every war America has ever fought, some fighting men and civilians disappeared. Many were never seen again. Significant numbers of these were never accounted for by their own government or by their enemy. It was common practice to close those cases within a short period after cessation of hostilities. Combat operations and losses in Indochina produced a different result, and the problems are still with us.
—U.S. Congress, House, 1976: 1

Given the committee's findings, the question arises as to whether it is fair to say that American POWs were knowingly abandoned in Southeast Asia after the war. The answer to that question is clearly no. But there remains the troubling question of whether the Americans who were expected to return but did not were, as a group, shunted aside and discounted by government and population alike. The answer to that question is essentially yes.
—U.S. Congress, Senate, 1993: 7

Having introduced some of the theoretical and contextual dimensions of the efforts made by the United States to account for servicemen missing in Southeast Asia, I can now devote specific attention to the unaccounted-for body and the significance it has assumed in the United States since the later years of the Vietnam War. As indicated in the preceding chapter, that importance is unique in part because substantially fewer Vietnam War soldiers remain unaccounted for as compared to those in earlier American wars. To this one might add a second important distinction: those missing from previous wars are categorized as unrecoverable, whereas those missing in Southeast Asia are listed as unaccounted for. Although the U.S. government readily acknowledges that some six hundred unaccounted-for Vietnam War soldiers are, in fact, unrecoverable (those lost over water, for example), this categorization has not generally been part of intelligible statements about personnel missing from the Vietnam War. Instead, unaccounted-for Vietnam War soldiers at first were understood to be something for which the Vietnamese should be held responsible and therefore a rationale for continuing the war in Southeast Asia. In addition to the attributions of Vietnamese responsibility, the unaccounted-for body in the immediate postwar years took on the role of ultimate arbiter of the sincerity of those in the United States charged with securing its repatriation. The intelligibility of the unaccounted-for body has thus long been tied both to American presumptions about the quantity and quality of knowledge the Vietnamese ought to have about it as well as to suppositions about what the U.S. government itself ought to do about absent soldiers. The upshot is a body granted exclusive power to adjudicate the many questions that have come to constitute the U.S. side of the balance sheet of the Vietnam War. Broadly speaking, the unaccounted-for body has become a litmus test for a host of issues that have never before been related either to unaccounted-for personnel specifically or to the aftermath of war generally.

Positioned thus, the unaccounted-for body might, one is tempted to hope, share our concern for the facts and therefore join in the effort to put to rest some of the many ambiguities resident within the contentious legacy of the Vietnam War. Yet, as we will see, the absent Vietnam War soldier is far from an ardent participant in such a project, in large part because there are no facts to which we might enjoy unproblematic recourse either in the determination of "what really happened" to those who never returned from Southeast Asia or for purposes of resolving the uncertainties occasioned by a lost war. Instead, what emerges with unrelenting clarity is factuality's status as contingent and ever fugitive, something which makes a consistent and sometimes cruel mockery of the "need to know." Because of this situation and because of my conviction that all bodies are mediated by discourse, genealogy immediately becomes a privileged instrument of analysis. As noted in chapter 1, genealogy refuses the impulse to seek truth in the materiality of the body and instead devotes attention to the historically constituted discourses that enable the emergence of any given thing. In this case, then, a genealogy of the unaccounted-for body does not aim to establish the facts of the matter, since the discourse of the absent body inaugurates what counts as a fact in the first place as well as the mode of comprehension upon which our understanding of the facts is predicated (White, 1978: 3).

The discourse of the absent Vietnam War soldier has typically cohered around two similarly situated yet ultimately quite different bodies. The first is the body of the POW, known at some point to have been in the custody of either North Vietnam, Laos, or Cambodia and who may or may not have been left behind after the withdrawal of American forces from Southeast Asia. The second is the body of the soldier killed in action, who, everyone agrees, is no longer living but whose remains have yet to be returned to the United States. Although, as noted, 591 prisoners of war were repatriated to the United States in the spring of 1973, many people believe the U.S. government either knowingly or inadvertently left some living prisoners behind in Southeast Asia after the Paris Peace Accords were signed in January of that year. Significantly, the controversy over whether live prisoners exist in fact or are figments of a twisted imagination rages between people who are often in similar situations but who nevertheless reach starkly divergent conclusions. They include family members of the missing, any number of current and former members of the Department of Defense, past and present employees of various intelligence services including the Defense Intelligence Agency (DIA), the Central Intelligence Agency (CIA), and the National Security Agency (NSA) as well as members of Congress and numerous journalists. Further, advocates of these two positions often cite exactly the same evidence in the act of reaching diametrically opposed conclusions. As a result, it has become virtually impossible to separate the truth of the missing from their many and disparate fictions.

Characterizing the issue of missing soldiers in this way might at first appear to emphasize the question of live prisoners in a manner that is at odds with this book's focus on the U.S. effort to repatriate the remains of soldiers known to be dead. However, because these two bodies are closely related it is important to situate the possibility that live American prisoners of war still exist in Southeast Asia within the overall effort to repatriate the remains of those killed in action. Although the U.S. government claims to lack credible evidence of the existence of living prisoners, it refuses officially to deny the possibility. Accordingly, given the impossibility of saying with absolute certainty what happened to those currently unaccounted for, the effort to account for missing soldiers is persistently (and officially) haunted by the possibility that some soldiers *were* left behind. As a result, the government's long-standing assertion that there is no compelling evidence of living prisoners has never quite managed to quell the claim that American POWs either were or continue to be held against their will in Vietnam.

This circumstance helps to explain why the matter of the (possibly) live body in Southeast Asia matters so much to the unaccounted-for body. As we will see in more detail in chapter 3, such significance is registered most prominently in an accounting protocol that requires the repatriation of identifiable remains before a name is removed from the list of the missing, a requirement which suggests that "unaccounted for" is really only a matter of getting the body back. Yet that protocol simultaneously gestures at the questions of fate that have long surrounded the issue of missing American soldiers. Indeed, the (possibly) live body and the body killed in action each become the condition of the other's possibility. Although no living, unaccounted-for serviceman has returned from Southeast Asia in the years since the war, the condition of some recovered remains implies the possibility that the soldier in question was alive in Vietnamese custody. Furthermore, evidence that the Vietnamese, despite repeated denials, have stored the remains of American soldiers fuels suspicion among some that Vietnam has something to hide—including living American prisoners—while the highly fragmentary nature of recovered remains leads others to conclude that the remainder of the body in question may have survived its incident of loss. Meanwhile, because the chance that there are living prisoners cannot be definitively discounted, the dead body becomes the only way of proving that Americans are no longer being held against their will in Southeast Asia. In other words, short of the possibility of live prisoners it seems unlikely, given the example of past American wars, that identifiable remains would be the sole means of accounting for the missing. Hence, although my analysis is primarily concerned with the effort to repatriate the remains of those killed in action, it must pay heed to the interconstitutive nature of the (possibly) live body and its dead counterpart because each functions to legitimate the corporeal terms in which the accounting effort is articulated.

What follows, then, is an analysis of selected events in the materialization of the unaccounted-for body, one that in many ways doubles as a history of the United States after the defeat in Vietnam. It begins with a discussion of the categories used during the Vietnam War to classify soldiers separated from their units, devoting specific attention to "missing in action" and the ambiguities to which that category gives rise both in wartime and afterward. Next, I consider efforts by President Richard Nixon and his administration to dramatize American prisoners and those missing as a means of restoring public support for the war. Along with increased activism by families of missing servicemen, the Go Public campaign would play a crucial role in how the unaccounted-for body came to be known. The discussion then turns to the immediate postwar years and the centrality of discrepancy cases, live-sighting reports, and private efforts to rescue American POWs allegedly still held against their will in Southeast Asia. Not unexpectedly, such events have done much to condition the intelligibility of the unaccounted-for body in the years following the war; as well, they have influenced the very possibility of renewed relations between the United States and Vietnam, relations which were delayed until 1995 exclusively over the issue of the missing. A genealogy of the unaccounted-for body is thus also a genealogy of both the American body politic and the bodies whose absence has come to matter like never before.

CATEGORIES

The faint outlines of the body of the unaccounted-for Vietnam War soldier began to take shape long before the end of the war, particularly during the massive U.S. troop buildup of the mid-1960s. The increased military presence in Vietnam, Laos, and Cambodia meant that mounting numbers of servicemen began to be separated from their units, the obvious precondition for any soldier to be listed eventually as unaccounted for. Such separations occurred for a variety of reasons, the most common including the shooting down of American aircraft, crashes of aircraft unrelated to hostile action, and ground losses in which American troops were captured, killed in action, or lost during hostile engagements. Other separations resulted when servicemen deserted or were absent without leave (AWOL), although because these losses are arguably not the direct result of hostile action the U.S. military does not list them among the separations discussed here.

Analysis of the issue of unaccounted-for soldiers from the Vietnam

War is complicated by the system of classification of missing soldiers used by the government during the war. At that time, the U.S. military employed three categories to specify both the circumstances of a soldier's loss and his subsequent status. POW referred to soldiers confirmed to be in enemy hands. Placement in this category was almost never left to speculation and thus required demonstrable evidence that the serviceman in question was both alive and being held captive. Normally, such evidence is provided by the governments of the respective combatants, as mandated by the Geneva Convention of 1949 governing the treatment of POWs. Among other things, the conventions require the release of lists of all captured enemy forces, the humane treatment of POWs, and certain privileges such as visits by international humanitarian agencies and regular mail service between prisoners and their families. During the Vietnam War, North Vietnam regularly disregarded these conventions, a dereliction that has profoundly affected the evolution of the issue of missing American soldiers. In particular, North Vietnam refused at any time during the war to furnish the United States with a list of prisoners, referring instead to American captives as war criminals whose treatment was not subject to the Geneva Convention. Much to the chagrin of the U.S. government, the few lists that were obtained during the war were often given to private American citizens affiliated with the antiwar movement, whose increasing influence the Vietnamese had learned to skillfully cultivate. Further, such lists were widely regarded by American officials as incomplete, partly because they failed to match admittedly imperfect American records and partly because North Vietnam continuously refused any form of independent verification.

The second category of servicemen separated from their units as a result of hostilities is composed of soldiers killed in action whose bodies were not recovered at the time of their death, abbreviated KIA/BNR. This designation bears one similarity to that of POW insofar as the evidence must conclusively demonstrate that the soldier in question perished during the incident of loss. As Air Force regulations stated at the time, the KIA/BNR categorization is to be made when "available information indicates beyond any reasonable doubt that a missing person could not have survived" (in Clarke, 1979: 14). The army employed equally strict criteria by stipulating that "conclusive evidence of death must be more than an indication of death. The facts must be such that death is the only plausible alternative under the circumstances" (in

Clarke, 1979: 14). On January 27, 1973, the date of the signing of the Paris Peace Accords ending the war in Southeast Asia, the U.S. Department of Defense listed 1,118 Americans in this category. Like POWs, KIA/BNRS have been a notable part of the issue of unaccounted-for soldiers in the post–Vietnam War era. Because the United States lost the war and thus did not have access to the battlefields, any postwar repatriation of the remains of dead soldiers required unilateral action by the Vietnamese. Although such action was mandated by Article 8(b) of the Paris Peace Accords, Vietnam's efforts to repatriate American remains have been viewed as insufficient by successive American presidential administrations, family members of the missing, and many others. This dissatisfaction has in turn fueled accusations of further Vietnamese duplicity in all other matters related to unaccounted-for soldiers.

The third wartime category is composed of soldiers missing in action (MIA). By design this category is the most nebulous of the three because it refers to personnel whose whereabouts and status are truly unknown. Evidence about their incidents of loss, if any, is either circumstantial, too inconclusive to allow listing in the other two categories or both. MIA does not rule out the possibility that soldiers so designated survived their incidents of loss. In the words of one observer, "Missing in action is an accounting limbo. It reflects a lack of knowledge concerning an individual rather than being truly descriptive of his condition" (Clarke, 1979: 1). In theory, then, the idea is to move soldiers out of this category and into one or the other of the alternatives as information permits, although this is difficult to do during wartime and often no less trying following the cessation of hostilities. Like POWs and KIAS, MIAS at the end of the Vietnam War are well represented in the controversy surrounding the fate of unaccounted-for soldiers. Indeed, such soldiers represent the greatest overlap between the possibility of prisoners left behind and the effort to repatriate the remains of those known to be dead. Precisely because of the ambiguity surrounding their fate, a virtually limitless number of scenarios can be proposed as to what happened to those who never returned from the war. Further, the acronym MIA has become a sort of cultural shorthand for the entire issue of unaccounted-for soldiers, a fact which, among other things, has effaced the evidentiary differences that formerly sought to distinguish the three categories with as much precision as possible. This, in turn, has contributed to confusion over just how many Americans remain unaccounted for in Southeast Asia and whether any might still be alive.

Such confusion is not necessarily the result of postwar factors only, but also of ambiguities built into the process of classifying military casualties. Although the system of classification strove for a high level of precision, many assignments were necessarily judgment calls because of lack of evidence. Captain Douglas L. Clarke (U.S. Navy) was a carrier-based aviator who served three tours of duty in Vietnam followed by eighteen months in the office of special assistant for prisoners of war matters to the chief of naval personnel. In *The Missing Man: Politics and the MIA* (1979), one of the first book-length treatments of the issue of missing Vietnam War service personnel, Clarke calls attention to the importance of the categorization process to the subsequent salience of the issue of missing soldiers. During the war, the responsibility for the initial classification of soldiers separated from their unit fell to the field commander. Clarke (1979: 13) points out that "no one should have more understanding of the circumstances surrounding a loss than the commander on the scene," but he notes that these commanders often had close personal ties to the men who served under them. That connection occasionally affected the commander's initial classification decision, especially when he was deciding between either KIA/BNR or MIA status. In the absence of remains, for example, the "conclusive evidence" of death required by the KIA/BNR category frequently became an unwelcome judgment call, thus tilting such decisions in favor of MIA status. MIA also meant that the service member's pay and benefits continued to go to his dependents, another factor that sometimes influenced the initial determination. As a result, Clarke argues it is not improbable that numerous servicemen initially classified as MIA were in fact killed in action.

An example helps illustrate the difficulties that plagued the initial status determination. Two American aircraft were on a mission over water during bad weather. The flight leader decided the conditions were too poor to continue and initiated a 180-degree turn. Emerging from a cloud bank upon completion of the turn, the lead pilot discovered he was alone. A subsequent search discovered a large oil slick in the area of the wingman's loss. Depending on the commander's inclinations, both KIA and MIA were defensible classifications in this case (this particular pilot was classified as MIA). The point is that "the system was driven toward a finding of MIA by the requirement for 'conclusive' evidence of death before an individual could be declared KIA" (Clarke, 1979: 17).

The significance of the original classification, particularly with respect to those listed as MIA during the Vietnam War becomes apparent upon consideration of the process through which a missing service member's status is changed from one category to another. There are two means by which that status can be changed, the first through receipt of information that indicates the soldier's current status is no longer warranted, and the second through the administrative procedures of the Missing Persons Act.[1] If upon cessation of hostilities a soldier listed as MIA fails to return as a POW, the U.S. military generally believes it reasonable to assume the soldier in question did not survive his incident of loss. Further, the financial interests of the government dictate that soldiers unaccounted for not be paid indefinitely. Accordingly, the Missing Persons Act contains provisions for a "presumptive finding of death" as a means of changing a soldier's status from MIA to KIA. To effect such a change, the secretary of the missing serviceman's branch of service must convene a review board within one year of the date of the soldier's incident of loss. Upon review of the case, the board can either maintain the soldier in the missing status, change the status if new information so warrants, or, if no new information has been obtained within one year of the soldier's date of loss, issue a presumptive finding of death (Clarke, 1979: 19-23). In other words, if no new information is received on a missing soldier, the earlier-noted "accounting limbo" of the MIA category is resolved through administrative fiat.[2] The importance of the initial classification of a soldier who is separated from his unit is clear. If the chances are comparatively slim that soldiers listed as MIA will return alive following the cessation of hostilities, then the odds of uncovering new information concerning their fate are slim as well. This is especially true following a war in which a nation is not allowed access to the battlefield, as was the case for the United States following the Vietnam War. The absence of additional information in turn presents the military branches with the onerous, though not especially unusual, task of issuing presumptive findings of death for the personnel still listed as MIA upon cessation of hostilities. Although such findings are mandated by the Missing Persons Act, they nevertheless create the appearance that large numbers of unaccounted-for soldiers are being administratively "killed off" even though many could in all probability have been originally classified as KIA/BNR. For reasons I explore below, this situation played a central role in the early stages of the controversy surrounding unaccounted-for soldiers following the Vietnam War. Families of the 1,392 men still classified as MIA were understandably distressed when the military began issuing presumptive findings of death, fearing such declarations would inhibit their effort to obtain an accounting of their loved ones. For the moment, the important point is that presumptive findings of death, in combination with the smaller than expected number of Americans who came home in spring 1973 during the official prisoner return known as Operation Homecoming, contributed much to the intelligibility of the absent Vietnam War soldier by creating the impression that some POWs had been left behind and that the government simply wanted to rid itself of the issue.

Two issues exposed by this element of the controversy speak directly to the salience of the issue of missing soldiers following the Vietnam War. The first concerns the chances that any soldier listed as MIA survived his incident of loss, chances which the United States military generally deems slim. Douglas Clarke (1979: 1), for example, cites the American experience in World War II and the Korean War as confirmation of his assertion that "virtually all MIAs are either dead or in enemy hands from the day they disappear—except this information is not available to their country." The second issue concerns the means by which such information can be made available to the country in question. Article 8(b) of the Paris Peace Agreement required both the United States and Vietnam "to help each other to get information about those military personnel and foreign civilians of the parties missing in action" (Clarke, 1979: 52). Because the United States had no access to the battlefields of Southeast Asia to conduct inquiries of its own, it had to rely on the cooperation of the Vietnamese in the resolution of MIA cases, cooperation which many on the American side believed to be wholly unsatisfactory. Administrative status changes thus did much to aggravate the already sensitive issue of unaccounted-for soldiers in Southeast Asia because they appeared to relieve Vietnam of its obligations under the peace treaty.

Here again the import of the original classifying of a soldier as MIA and the presumption of life built into that designation come into view. If additional information is required during war itself either to confirm or deny life, then a finding of death in the absence of such information following the war can legitimately be viewed by families as a betrayal of the soldier in question and by the military as simple acceptance of the odds. Rightly or wrongly, the perception of inadequate cooperation by the Vietnamese lent credence to the families' view of the situation, as did the U.S. government's extreme credibility problems as a result of the war itself. As a result, many Americans concluded that the United States was shunning its responsibility to account for the missing and/or that the Vietnamese had something to hide because of their refusal to abide by the stipulations of Article 8(b). These developments also marked the moment at which MIA began a gradual transformation from an "accounting limbo" to proof (for some) that living American soldiers had been left behind in Vietnam.

Still, the mere fact that some soldiers were still listed as MIA following the Vietnam War does not differentiate that war from those that preceded it. As noted, tens of thousands of Americans from World War II and the Korean War remain unaccounted for, and the government has acknowledged that "clearly hundreds" of American POWs from the Korean War were not returned following the end of hostilities (U.S. Congress, Senate, 1993: 51). What differentiates Vietnam War missing, of course, is the degree to which their fate became controversial in subsequent years. Much of the controversy can be linked to efforts—ranging from the entirely innocent to the overtly cynical—by both the government and organizations of family members of missing Americans. These organizations bear much responsibility for the contemporary salience of the issue of unaccounted-for soldiers, but actions by the government during and after the war also contributed. The examples presented below show how some families' belief that their loved one would return home following the cessation of hostilities is not entirely of their own making. The examples also reveal much about the early materialization of the body of the unaccounted-for soldier. Through them, it becomes possible to understand how and why the body of the unaccounted-for Vietnam War soldier became so much more important than that of previous wars

THE GO PUBLIC CAMPAIGN AND FAMILY ORGANIZATIONS

During the first few years of the Vietnam War, there was no such thing as a POW/MIA issue, as it has come to be known, a circumstance which reflected the strategic thinking of the time rather than callousness toward the families of the missing. One reason for the silence was the U.S. government's belief that "publicity in this matter would only be a hindrance to obtaining a prisoner release, which was to be brought about through bilateral diplomatic negotiations. It was felt that publicity might only harden the positions of the Southeast Asian Communist governments" (Clarke, 1979: 29-30). Beginning in the mid-1960s, however, this policy began to evolve in response to a desire by the Nixon administration to publicize the issue of prisoners and missing in Southeast Asia. While in some respects a legitimate effort both to improve the treatment of American POWs and to secure their prompt release, the 1969 Go Public campaign, as it came to be called, must also be seen in the context of rapidly deteriorating domestic support for the war in Vietnam. In addition to whatever other considerations motivated the decision to publicize Americans missing and held prisoner, it is also the case that President Nixon and his senior aides believed the issue of missing Americans to be one around which a majority of Americans could rally regardless of their stance on the war itself.

Along with the changes it brought to the American public's perception of the Vietnam War, the Go Public campaign inaugurated substantial changes in the nature of intelligible statements within the discourse of the unaccounted-for body and who was authorized to make them. As a strategy aimed at mobilizing public opinion in support of the release of American POWs, the campaign deliberately foregrounded the families of missing servicemen and their perspective on the issue. In September and October 1969, for example, a delegation of wives and parents of missing and imprisoned Americans flew to Paris amid much media attention to demand meetings with representatives of North Vietnam and the Viet Cong. Full-page advertisements placed by Ross Perot in various American newspapers featured a picture of two children praying, "Bring our Daddy home safe, sound, and soon" (Franklin, 1993a: 50). Such efforts contributed greatly to the evolving intelligibility of the unaccounted-for body. In particular, that body was no longer the effect of mechanized warfare and its capacity to render bodies totally and permanently absent. Rather, it became a link between a rapidly deteriorating military and political situation and the American family, an institution long signified as the bedrock of American culture and society. Accordingly, the interpretive possibilities of the absent body were increasingly restricted to those offered by families of the missing and their desire to have their loved one returned home as soon as possible. Understandable though this desire may be, failure to take Nixon's representation of the issue at face value meant tacitly opposing the family, an option that in the pantheon of late-1960s Cold War hatreds almost immediately indicated an affinity for the values of the enemy.

One would have to be cruel and coldhearted indeed not to want to see the missing soldiers returned home "safe, sound, and soon."

Additional publicity gambits the following year included the aforementioned display of American POWs in Washington and POW/MIA bracelets engraved with the name of an American POW or soldier MIA. Reports at the time estimated that between four and ten million Americans were wearing POW/MIA bracelets (Franklin, 1993a: 57). In addition to being the link between the unaccounted-for body and the family, the missing now concerned the nation as a whole. The presence of the bracelet on the wrists of so many members of the body politic became a metaphor for the absence of those bodies who had gone to fight for its interests. Perhaps more important, representational strategies like the display at the Capitol implied that each missing soldier was likely being held prisoner as well despite the evidentiary precautions built into the classification system. Construed in this way, continuing to fight for the prisoners and missing became not only a possibility but a principled requirement.

At the outset, then, the Go Public campaign is significant to the intelligibility of the unaccounted-for body because it altered the discourse of the absent soldier. In addition to no longer being one among many consequences of modern warfare, the absent body is proposed as an independent condition for which someone is to be held responsible. During the later war years, those responsible parties were the Vietnamese, an attribution that would in the years following the war be shared by the U.S. government. Further, the families of missing servicemen began assuming greater legitimacy as interlocutors on the subject of MIAS. Articulated as a domestic problem as well as a military one, their statements were a crucial interpretive link between the unaccounted-for soldier and the American body politic. Such circumstances deeply affected Americans' perception of the war in Southeast Asia. In particular, "America's vision of the war was being transformed. The actual photographs and TV footage of massacred villagers, napalmed children, Vietnamese prisoners being tortured and murdered, wounded GIs screaming in agony, and body bags being loaded by the dozen for shipment back home were being replaced by simulated images of American POWs in the savage hands of Asian Communists" (Franklin, 1993a: 54).

As intended, this perception generated wide domestic support for the prisoner issue during negotiations with Vietnam in the late 1960s and early 1970s. Determined to avoid the humiliation of an outright withdrawal of American forces, Nixon parlayed the POWs' newfound celebrity into "the most visible of all the current questions" concerning the end of the war (in Franklin, 1993a: 58). North Vietnam's refusal to release prisoners prior to a withdrawal of American forces became the occasion to vilify them still more, as when the U.S. government characterized this refusal as "unprecedented, inhuman, and barbaric" (in Franklin, 1993a: 58). The United States went even further on December 30, 1969, when it presented North Vietnam with a list of "military personnel missing in Southeast Asia includ[ing] personnel classified internally by the services as either missing or captured." The United States claimed it was "holding the Communist authorities in Southeast Asia responsible for every individual on this list whether or not he is internally classified by the services as captured or missing" (in Franklin, 1993a: 68). For the first time, the body of the unaccounted-for soldier materialized as both an effect of the Vietnam War and a justification for its continued prosecution. By contributing to a continuation of hostilities, the Go Public campaign was responsible for more service members being KIA, MIA, and taken prisoner. Further, the intense publicity surrounding American POWs was not lost on the Vietnamese, who "could only be expected to demand more for the men and information they held. In accordance with a diplomatic law of supply and demand, the value of the Vietnamese product was driven sharply up by the magnitude of the American demand" (Clarke, 1979: 36).

Roughly contemporaneous with the Go Public campaign were organizing efforts by family members of missing and imprisoned service personnel, efforts originally intended not so much as a political move as a means of offering moral support to each other. Only later did some of these organizations come to play a powerful role in the government's effort to publicize the prisoner issue. By far the most influential family organization has been the National League of Families of Prisoners and Missing in Southeast Asia. Organized in 1966 as an ad hoc group of families in and around San Diego, the organization grew as more families became aware of their shared status and realized how little direct effort was being made to secure the humane treatment and eventual release of American POWs. The league incorporated as a nonprofit organization in May 1970; its bylaws restricted membership to next of kin. In the short term, the work of the league was instrumental in enabling families to be treated not individually, as they had been under the government's more discreet approach to the issue of the missing, but as a group with shared needs that might be coordinated.

In particular need of coordination was regular mail communication between American POWs and their families, a provision of the Geneva Conventions which North Vietnam had routinely disregarded throughout the war. It was entirely unforeseeable at the time, but this innocuous effort was a further evolution in the materialization of the unaccounted-for body. That evolution again draws much from the categorization of missing soldiers, especially with respect to the presumption of life implied by the MIA category. Although "common sense and logic indicated that many of the MIAs—when they were viewed as a category—were dead, the possibility was very real that any one individual MIA would turn up alive." Consequently, "all the services recognized immediately that, for reasons of politics and public relations, POW and MIA families must be treated equally in all respects" (Clarke, 1979: 27-28). This meant establishing means by which the families of anyone listed as either POW or MIA could send mail to the soldier in question. The result as regarded the families of those listed as MIA, however, was to heighten their expectation that their loved one would return home following the war. Although it is true the MIA designation holds out the possibility of life, it is equally true that if that classification was made with sincerity, the possibility of life is at best a fifty-fifty proposition. As something of a middle point among the three categories, MIA means quite simply that the soldier in question may or may not be alive. As seen earlier, however, the original classification was not infrequently subject to pressures that inclined it toward MIA, which unavoidably preserved the possibility of life in a manner likely not justified by the circumstances of the incident of loss. By treating the families of MIAs and POWs the same, the government created among the families of MIAs the sense that the chances of their loved one returning home were much closer to 100 percent than they actually were.

As it was in virtually all facets of the U.S. prosecution of the war in Vietnam, the same absence of sincerity that sometimes plagued the classification system was featured in the attempts to facilitate communication between POWs and their families. Some of the details of the equal treatment policy suggest the point. Those with a family member missing in Laos, for example, were advised by the Navy's Bureau of Naval Personnel to forward a letter to the missing man via the head of the Pathet Lao Government, Prince Souphanouvong. The Prince could supposedly be reached in care of the Pathet Lao liaison officer in Vientiane, Laos, Mr. Sot Pethrase, and that official's exact address was supplied. The Navy's Casualty Branch further suggested "that such a letter might have a better chance of reaching the recipient if the date and general location where the service member was captured or became missing (if known) is listed in the forwarding letter. This is to assist forwarding personnel in determining where the captured/missing member is held." The families were warned that some letters had been returned to the sender, for the specified reasons of "erroneous sorting and misrouting by postal personnel. Capitalizing and underlining . . . is recommended as an aid to preclude such errors." It is now realized that there were no "forwarding personnel" in Laos and the letters were not usually returned because of sorting errors by postal employees, but for far more somber reasons. (Clarke, 1979: 28–29)

In the face of such extraordinary cynicism, it is hardly surprising that many families felt betrayed when their loved one failed to return home after the war. No longer another justification for belligerence, the matter of the absent body would now also serve as the fulcrum around which questions of U.S. government honesty on the issue of unaccounted-for soldiers would turn for the next three decades.

The combined effect of these developments was of extreme consequence to the materialization of the unaccounted-for body. Frequent, well-publicized demands that the Vietnamese account for all soldiers both taken prisoner *and* missing in action transformed the issue into one that implicated the entire American body politic. Further, by obfuscating the normally rigid distinction between POW and MIA, the U.S. government created the impression that the Vietnamese held far more prisoners than they ever did and that they knew much more about MIAs than they ever could. The result was a single, unaccounted-for body, one for which the United States had explicitly waged the final four years of the Vietnam War and which would single-handedly govern U.S.-Vietnamese relations in the post–Vietnam War era. As of the liberation of Saigon on April 30, 1975, 2,583 Americans were listed as MIA by the U.S. government (Command Briefing, JTF-FA, 2000).

THE UNACCOUNTED-FOR BODY, 1973-75

Events during the two-year period between the termination of hostilities in Southeast Asia in 1973 and the liberation of Saigon in 1975 saw the unaccounted-for body subjected to still more complicated political and epistemological construals. The Paris Peace Accords ending the war were signed on January 27, 1973, by the United States, the Democratic Republic of Vietnam (North Vietnam or DRV), the Provisional Revolutionary Government (the Viet Cong, or PRG), and the Republic of Vietnam (South Vietnam or RVN). The parties agreed to cease all military activities in Southeast Asia, and the United States and North Vietnam arranged a sixty-day timetable for the simultaneous withdrawal of American troops and the return of POWs. Concluded on March 29, 1973, Operation Homecoming resulted in the return to U.S. control of 591 Americans and the disengagement of all American forces from the region (U.S. Congress, Senate, 1993: 147). Further, Article 8(b) of the agreement required the signatories to assist each other in obtaining information on service personnel still listed as MIA and in repatriating the remains of those KIA, while Article 21 obliged the United States to "contribute to healing the wounds of war and to postwar reconstruction of the DRV and throughout Indochina" (in Stern, 1995: 19). Obscured by the abstemious prose of the peace agreement, however, were several factors that would prove crucial to later iterations of the issue of unaccounted-for soldiers.

Although a comprehensive peace agreement had been reached among the warring parties, the overall political and military situation in Southeast Asia remained extremely tenuous. Following the American withdrawal, both North Vietnam and the Viet Cong incrementally continued their assault on what was left of South Vietnam. Any U.S. efforts to account for missing soldiers were thus severely constrained by ongoing military activity. The determining of the fate of missing Americans was also hindered by the loss of many Americans in North Vietnam, Laos, and Cambodia—territory to which the United States was denied access by the governments in question. Still, time was of the essence concerning the resolution of MIA cases and the repatriation of remains. Access to battlefields and grave sites was still possible in South Vietnam, and people with information about missing Americans would never be more available and have clearer memories than in the early postwar period. Consequently, the United States created the Joint Casualty Resolution Center (JCRC) as a means of resolving as many unaccounted-for cases as it could. The JCRC compiled information on unaccounted-for Americans and conducted field searches, excavations, recoveries, and repatriations of the remains of Americans KIA (Mather, 1994; Bell, 2004). Their work was impeded, however, by the largely uncooperative attitude of the PRG and the DRV. Plenary sessions designed to coordinate the implementation of Article 8(b) were often used to further political aims not achieved earlier at the bargaining table, and numerous stalling tactics frustrated American search efforts (Mather, 1994: 7). Many requests to search crash and grave sites in areas under the control of the Viet Cong were rejected in spite of the provisions of Article 8(b). The situation worsened on December 15, 1973, when a recovery team was ambushed by the Viet Cong and suffered several wounded and the deaths of one American and one Vietnamese. Because it could no longer ensure its safety, the JCRC was forced to greatly restrict its recovery work in South Vietnam, and eventually it moved out of the country upon the liberation of Saigon in April 1975 (Mather, 1994: 20–29). In the process, many opportunities were lost during what was otherwise the most promising period for the resolution of MIA and KIA cases.

The complications on the ground in Vietnam were accompanied by serious doubts in the United States about the accuracy of the list of American POWs provided by North Vietnam on the day the Paris Peace Agreement was signed. These doubts have remained at the heart of the dispute over the fate of Americans unaccounted for in Southeast Asia and warrant detailed discussion. As indicated in chapter 1, North Vietnam had throughout the war viewed captured Americans as war criminals, not POWs. As a result, it refused to adhere to Geneva Conventions provisions requiring each side to supply the other with lists of personnel in its custody. U.S. intelligence on not only the identity but also the number of American prisoners in Southeast Asia was thus vague at best. Estimates in 1972, for example, placed the number of American POWs between 400 and 1,600. President Nixon, for his part, consistently made reference to the higher figure, while Congress passed a resolution demanding the release of 1,500 American POWs (U.S. Congress, Senate, 1993: 78). Worse still was the imprecision regarding Americans thought to be missing in Laos and Cambodia. Though heavy fighting had occurred in both countries, neither was party to the peace agreement that ended the Vietnam War. The United States thus found itself in the unenviable position of asking North Vietnam to account for soldiers about whom they likely knew little and who were missing in countries over whom the Vietnamese had little control. Not surprisingly, North Vietnam declined to assist. At the same time, American intelligence strongly indicated that both North Vietnam and the Pathet Lao should have been able to account for far more missing Americans than they seemed willing to. In particular, the Vietnamese claimed not to have had a military presence in Laos or Cambodia during the Vietnam War and further denied having any influence over the ruling government in Laos, the Pathet Lao, respecting their ability to account for missing Americans. While these assertions were clearly disingenuous, the United States had been party to similar deceptions throughout the "secret" wars in Laos and Cambodia and had even gone so far as to falsify the location of loss of all American personnel lost in those two countries, listing them instead as lost over South Vietnam. In addition to the problems this was later to cause with the families concerned, such falsification often meant even the United States could not always be sure a particular soldier had gone missing where claimed.

Such disputes came to a head in 1973 when, at the signing of the peace accords, North Vietnam provided the United States with a list of American prisoners in its custody. The immediate American response was one of disappointment over the relatively small number of prisoners included on the list when compared even to admittedly uncertain intelligence estimates. The American side protested that the Vietnamese omitted the names of American POWs who had previously appeared in photographs released by the Viet Cong or in other propaganda media. Additional skepticism came from other sources, including Air Force General Eugene F. Tighe Jr., who had been responsible for the preparation of the military's list of American prisoners and missing prior to Operation Homecoming in 1973. In testimony before the Senate Select Committee on POW/MIA Affairs in 1992, Tighe related that his response to the list provided by North Vietnam "was shock because I had a great deal of faith in the approximate numbers of those lists that we had compiled . . . and my reaction was that there was something radically wrong with the lists versus our information, that they should have contained many more names. That was my personal judgment and that was a collective judgment of all those that had worked compiling the lists" (U.S. Congress, Senate, 1993: 147).

Still more uneasiness centered on the absence in the list of any Americans known to have been taken prisoner in Laos. Indeed, not until February 1, 1973, five days after the peace treaty, did North Vietnam finally supply a list of American prisoners in Laos. Like the list of those missing in North Vietnam, this one fell well short of intelligence agency estimates, which suggested that perhaps as many as 352 Americans were MIA in Laos in addition to 41 POWs (U.S. Congress, Senate, 1993: 82). Yet the list given to the United States on February 1 included the names of but ten servicemen, each of whom had been captured by North Vietnam during American incursions into Laos, meaning it omitted any mention of Americans captured by the Pathet Lao themselves. Worse still, as noted, Laos was not a signatory to the peace agreement, and Vietnam had ultimately agreed only to a largely unenforceable verbal commitment to try to account for Americans missing in neighboring countries.

The United States responded with a cable from President Nixon to the prime minister of North Vietnam, Pham Van Dong. The president made clear his dissatisfaction with the Laos list and threatened to cancel an upcoming trip to Hanoi by Secretary of State Henry Kissinger during which economic aid was to be discussed. Oddly, the threat appears neither to have generated a response from North Vietnam nor to have been made especially seriously by the administration (U.S. Congress, Senate, 1993: 84). Still, in late March 1973, Chairman of the Joints Chiefs of Staff Admiral Thomas Moorer (USN) reported that "it was 'highly likely' that the Pathet Lao was holding live U.S. POWs in addition to" those on the February 1 list (U.S. Congress, Senate, 1993: 89). The likelihood of this possibility had been bolstered by the Lao themselves, who on several occasions acknowledged holding American prisoners in addition to those captured by Vietnamese forces and who insisted that any release of such prisoners would require direct negotiations with the Lao government. This led Admiral Moorer to propose a suspension of the American troop withdrawal then in progress until a more adequate list of Americans being held in Laos was produced. Complicating this proposal, however, was the lack of provisions for the release of the ten Americans listed on the February 1 list. Reluctance to lose ten accounted-for American prisoners over others whose existence could not be verified forced the United States to abandon plans to halt the troop withdrawal. As a result, the return of American POWs during Operation Homecoming came to a conclusion as scheduled.

At one level, the significance of these lists to the materialization of the body unaccounted for in Southeast Asia lies in the absence of any similar listing of North Vietnamese missing by the United States. The importance of this unidirectionality rests partially in what it indicates about U.S. anxieties over its ability to account for North Vietnamese prisoners. Turned over to South Vietnam as a matter of policy, such prisoners were not kept track of to nearly the extent required of North Vietnam vis-á-vis American prisoners and were widely believed to have been subjected to treatment at least as barbaric as any endured by American prisoners in the north. Had the United States been held accountable for the fate of these prisoners and their eventual return to their families, its effort to account for missing Americans could have been impugned. At another, arguably more important level, however, investing the list of missing Americans with the sole power to adjudicate all claims about the adequacy of the accounting effort created conditions to which the *accounted*-for body would later have to respond. In particular, the list created a calculus that defined absence in terms of nameable bodies whose repatriation in the form of identifiable remains would be the only means to account for missing Americans and for which the Vietnamese would be held largely responsible. The intelligibility of all future statements concerning the body missing in Southeast Asia would now be contingent upon their correspondence with the truth imposed by the list.

With the completion of Operation Homecoming and the withdrawal of American forces from the region in the spring of 1973, the optimum time for meaningful action on American POWs possibly left behind in Southeast Asia had expired. Although some in Congress attempted to preserve the possibility of a military response to the prisoner issue, such initiatives were overwhelmingly blocked by intense domestic pressure for a complete American withdrawal from Vietnam and by the growing Watergate scandal, which occupied more and more government attention. At the same time, since the return of 591 American prisoners was the only issue the United States could celebrate, the Nixon administration was eager to dramatize their return, which it did by throwing a massive party for the POWs at the White House. President Nixon stated on various occasions following the completion of Operation Homecoming that "1973 . . . saw . . . the return of all our prisoners of war" and "for the first time in eight years, all of our prisoners of war are home here in America" (U.S. Congress, Senate, 1993: 94). Shortly thereafter, Dr. Roger Shields, head of the Defense Department's POW/MIA Task Force, announced during a news conference, "We have no indications at this time that there are any Americans alive in Indochina" (U.S. Congress, Senate, 1993: 97). Finally, given the continuing absence of cooperation by the Lao government and the U.S. lack of leverage, the DIA was forced to admit at the end of 1973 that "one can only speculate about the current fate of the Americans who were known to have been held captive by the Pathet Lao in previous years" (U.S. Congress, Senate, 1993: 115).

Although the United States had strong indications that Americans may have been alive in Laos at the end of Operation Homecoming, high-level disappointment over the comprehensiveness of the prisoner return does not constitute conclusive proof that prisoners were in fact left behind, a point which many equally high-level sources have been quick to point out. Shields emphasized before the Senate Select Committee in 1993 that "most of the intelligence about suspected prison camps or U.S. prisoners in Laos, received while I was in the Pentagon, was very vague and impossible to verify. And the fact remains that we knew, and I believe know today, very little specifically about our men missing in Laos" (U.S. Congress, Senate, 1993: 126). Still, the groundwork had been laid for a controversy in which everyone was bound to be dissatisfied. The Go Public campaign had created a series of expectations which not only went unfulfilled but also were obscured by overly positive administration statements about the success of Operation Homecoming. In the meantime, status changes in accordance with the Missing Persons Act had begun, thereby contributing to the impression that the government was attempting to brush the issue aside. In the balance flourished the conditions of possibility for the further formation of the unaccounted-for body. Perhaps paradoxically, it was not knowledge about that body so much as the absence of knowledge that enabled its materialization as either proof of government duplicity or evidence of a successful prisoner return. The materialization of the unaccounted-for body continued in the space opened up between the strong indications of Americans still alive in Indochina and the absence of definitive proof thereof.

POST-1975:
DISCREPANCY CASES AND LIVE-SIGHTING REPORTS

Virtually everything that came to characterize the matter of the unaccounted-for body from 1975 onward can be traced to how that body came to be known during the later stages of the Vietnam War and the signing of the Paris Peace Accords in 1973. In the years following North Vietnam's victory in 1975, the production of knowledge about the absent body would continue to draw from the vast archive of events, classifications, and statements that had enabled its intelligible materialization in the first place. Of enduring salience were the lists of American prisoners and missing compiled at the time of the peace agreement. As noted, the completeness of the lists provided by the Vietnamese was viewed with suspicion at the highest levels of the U.S. government, especially concerning Americans missing in Laos. Despite the absence of conclusive proof that Americans had been left behind, there were a number of cases in which the possibility that Americans had been left behind in Southeast Asia could not be summarily dispatched as a figment of the conspiratorial imagination. These have come to be known as discrepancy cases and have long formed the basis for claims that either the U.S. government has done too little to secure an adequate accounting of missing personnel or the Vietnamese withheld American prisoners as bargaining chips for use in future negotiations. Again, the importance of the (possibly) live body to the materialization of the unaccounted-for body must be underscored, as during this period it helped to form the ground for what later came to count as a fact within the troubled process of accounting for Americans missing in Southeast Asia.

During the negotiations leading up to the Paris Peace Accords, Kissinger presented North Vietnam with file folders containing the names and details of eighty discrepancy cases. In many cases, the files named Americans whom the Vietnamese had acknowledged taking prisoner but whose names did not appear on any list and who did not return during Operation Homecoming. In other instances, a discrepancy case simply referred to a missing American about whom the United States believed Vietnam should be able to supply more information. Either way, the United States was eager to do as much as possible as soon as possible to account for these soldiers. Unfortunately, the initial list of discrepancy cases was more or less rebuffed by the Vietnamese, who claimed, perhaps disingenuously in some instances, that they had no further information on missing Americans and that they had returned all American prisoners during Operation Homecoming. In addition, the United States had virtually no leverage with which it might have forced greater cooperation on this issue, and the Vietnamese knew it. Congress had passed numerous resolutions prohibiting any form of military response, and domestic sentiment was firmly against any form of military intervention in Southeast Asia regardless of the reason. Nevertheless, the United States continued to press Vietnam in subsequent years to provide information on discrepancy cases and for a time continued to add names to the list of discrepancy cases as additional intelligence analysis warranted. As a result, the list eventually grew to include the names of 305 Americans (U.S. Congress, Senate, 1993: 161).

The importance of discrepancy cases to the materialization of the unaccounted-for body can be understood through a brief review of the nature of the evidence in question—evidence which, in a few cases at least, is quite compelling. On May 18, 1965, for example, Air Force Captain David Hrdlicka was shot down over Laos and captured by forces of the Pathet Lao. Over the next few years, Hrdlicka was used for propaganda purposes. A photograph of him in captivity appeared in the Soviet magazine *Pravda* and a Radio Peking broadcast quoted Lao sources as confirming his status as a prisoner. Nevertheless, Hrdlicka's name was not on the list of ten prisoners held in Laos given to the United States on February 1, 1973, and he did not return during Operation Homecoming (O'Daniel, 1979: 46–48). Although there can be no question Hrdlicka survived after being shot down and lived for a period of time in Lao captivity, both the Lao and the Vietnamese have consistently denied any knowledge of his fate, and neither he nor his remains have ever been returned to the United States. A presumptive finding of death was eventually issued but because *unaccounted for* is defined as the absence of the body rather than the absence of knowledge as to a given soldier's fate, Hrdlicka was, and still is, listed as unaccounted for by the U.S. government (DPMO Website, 2004).

Another discrepancy case concerns Navy Lieutenant Ronald Dodge, shot down over Vietnam on May 17, 1967. Dodge managed to eject safely from his aircraft, and he reached the ground alive, albeit in enemy territory. Upon completion of his descent, Dodge radioed a message to his wingman, "Here they come. I'm destroying my radio." Later that same day, a Vietnamese radio broadcast publicized the capture of a "U.S. bandit pilot" (in O'Daniel, 1979: 46). Over the ensuing years, Dodge was also used for propaganda purposes. A photograph of him being led by his captors through an undisclosed area of North Vietnam appeared in *Paris Match* a few months after his capture, and he was featured in an East German propaganda movie entitled *Pilots in Pajamas* (O'Daniel,

1979: 45). Like Hrdlicka's, Dodge's name was not on the list of prisoners to be returned upon the signing of the peace agreement, and he too failed to return at Operation Homecoming. In 1981, his remains were repatriated to the United States without explanation by the Vietnamese (DPMO Website, 2004).

A third example concerns Army Sergeant Donald Sparks, who was cut off from his unit when it was ambushed in South Vietnam on June 17, 1969. Sparks was observed lying wounded on the ground, but no one could reach him because of the fierce fighting. When soldiers returned to the area several days later, Sparks's body was gone, and he was classified as MIA. On April 11, 1970, however, a letter from Sparks to his parents was found on the body of a dead Viet Cong soldier; in it he reported that he was in good health and that he had not seen another American during his ten months in captivity (O'Daniel, 1979: 49). His status was then changed to POW, but the Vietnamese claimed to have no knowledge of Sparks at the time of the Paris Peace Accords, and no remains have ever been repatriated to the United States. A presumptive finding of death was eventually issued, and he too remains on the list of those unaccounted for (DPMO Website, 2004).

Just as official suspicion of the lists of the missing substantiates nothing, so discrepancy cases such as these do not constitute definitive proof that Americans were left behind after the Vietnam War. Some observers have gone so far as to argue that "if these are the cases that argue most strongly for the existence of live American prisoners in Indochina today, widespread devout belief in such beings needs to be explored as myth" (Franklin, 1993a: 34). There is a point to be made here insofar as such assessments are based on the admittedly poor odds that a POW could have survived in captivity for so long, especially in Laos, where conditions are often harsh. By the same token, at least some of the discrepancy cases make it impossible to say with certainty that every American unaccounted for at the end of the Vietnam War was necessarily deceased. This actuality has been seized upon by those who believe the United States either concocted an elaborate conspiracy to obscure its knowledge of surviving Americans or was simply deceived by the Vietnamese after they held back American prisoners. Referring to precisely the same discrepancy cases, another observer argues that "the United States government has destroyed evidence, has probably behaved in an illegal manner, and has attempted to deceive the American people" (O'Daniel, 1979: 40).

For present purposes, the truth of the matter as respects discrepancy cases is less imperative than their contribution to the epistemic conditions under which the body of the unaccounted-for soldier has come to be known. In particular, the salience of discrepancy cases means that statements about the possibility of there being live American prisoners are increasingly possible while statements suggesting that no living Americans were left behind in Southeast Asia are increasingly marginalized. The intelligible materialization of the unaccounted-for body comes to depend on the interplay between the absence of the body of the POW and the presence of indications that the serviceman in question survived his incident of loss. Discrepancy cases matter, therefore, not only because they sometimes present compelling evidence that a given soldier may have survived in captivity beyond the end of the war, but also because they underscore the indispensability of the body to the accounting calculus instituted by the list of the missing.

Another body was to play a role: that designated by what have come to be known as live-sighting reports. These are reports that a living American prisoner has allegedly been seen in Southeast Asia. Sometimes firsthand, other times merely hearsay, and all too often simply fabricated, live-sighting reports have assumed a crucial position in the issue of unaccounted-for Vietnam War soldiers. Moreover, despite the extremely thin evidentiary basis that undergirds the vast majority of live-sighting reports, the U.S. government, given its inability to say with absolute certainty that all servicemen who failed to return from the Vietnam War are in fact dead, has little choice but to take each of them seriously. Indeed, the House select committee convened in mid-1975 to study the issue of missing Vietnam War servicemen was formed in part because of the steady flow of such reports in the years following the war, and live-sighting reports have been the subject of numerous other congressional and executive branch investigations (Franklin, 1993a: 117). As in discrepancy cases, the body named in the live-sighting report is not a fact external or prior to the effort to account for the missing, but an effect of the ways in which that effort has been constructed over time. By suggesting the continued existence of the (possibly) live body, live-sighting reports invigorate its dead counterpart as the only means of definitively determining the fate of missing servicemen within an accounting calculus based on nameable, identifiable bodies. First, such reports appear to confirm extant suspicions concerning the adequacy of the list of the missing, and, second, they articulate those suspicions in precisely the same terms which locate the truth of the missing in the materiality of the body. Thus, live-sighting reports assume prominence within the attempts to account for missing Americans as much by their confirmation of the epistemic terms of the accounting process as by what they reveal about the possibility of living American prisoners.

The number of live-sighting reports increased exponentially with the massive exodus of Vietnamese refugees following the official end of the war in 1975. In some cases, refugees mistakenly believed they would be granted automatic entry into the United States if they could provide information about missing American servicemen, a belief that has almost certainly contributed to an artificial inflation of such reports. As of April 2004, the U.S. government had received a total of 22,442 reports pertaining to possibly live Americans in Southeast Asia, of which 1,953 were firsthand live sightings. Of the firsthand sightings, all but 50, or 2.56 percent, have been resolved, meaning they either correlated with already accounted-for personnel, were fabrications, or were pre-1975 sightings of Americans in Southeast Asia. Of the 50 unresolved live sightings, 44 pertain to Americans reported in a captive environment and 6 pertain to Americans in a noncaptive environment (DPMO Website, 2004). Like discrepancy cases, live-sighting reports have made clear the impossibility of making unproblematic truth claims about the status of unaccounted-for soldiers.

Such absence has been nowhere more observable than on the domestic front, where live-sighting reports are interpreted along lines that will now look familiar. On one side are those who see in the failure of even a single live-sighting report to correlate with a living unaccounted-for American definitive proof that there never were such Americans in the first place. On the other side are those who believe the U.S. government has a "mindset to debunk" any and all reports of living Americans in Southeast Asia. The skeptical position was audaciously dramatized by the chief of the Pentagon's Special Office for POW/MIA Affairs, Millard Peck, who upon leaving his post in 1991 went so far as to tack his resignation letter—which included precisely this phrase—to his office door. The Senate Select Committee in 1993 commented that, although it discovered no mindset to debunk, "until recently, these reports were not treated as important, and accorded a high priority by DIA" (U.S. Congress, Senate, 1993: 177–78). Change eventually came in the wake of the Senate's investigation, and the military now emphasizes that "resolution of these live sightings is JTF-FA's first priority" ("Joint Task Force-

Full Accounting: Fiscal Year 1999"). Others, however, argue that the "drop everything" priority accorded to each and every live-sighting report diverts attention from more promising leads because "investigators are required to work on cases that are obvious fabrications, just to make sure no one can say that the information wasn't checked out" (Smith, 1992: 162). Because each live-sighting report is treated as genuine, investigators often spend time checking the same story over and over again, a practice that continues to this day.

Like the discrepancy cases, live-sighting reports influenced relations between the United States and Vietnam. In particular, the United States sought a mechanism whereby immediate, in-country investigations of such reports could be pursued. The Vietnamese steadfastly refused this proposal for a number of years, arguing that such reports were fabrications and citing the sovereignty implications that a sustained American presence pursuant to such investigations would raise (Stern, 1995: 49). Nevertheless, as Vietnamese cooperation with the U.S. accounting effort gradually became more earnest, the request was eventually met. Indeed, the 1980s saw Vietnamese cooperation on the issue of unaccounted-for servicemen heightened across the board. At the same time, the United States needed the cooperation of the Indochinese governments, especially Vietnam's, to secure the accounting it sought. Under other circumstances, this might have offered the possibility of rapprochement between the two countries, perhaps even leading to a final resolution of the question of unaccounted-for soldiers and to normalization of relations. Yet the seeds of doubt had been sown by the discrepancy cases and live-sighting reports, and there were significant uncertainties on the home front about the condition of the American body politic in the aftermath of the war. National dialogue on the meaning of the Vietnam War had yet to begin, and there was neither a national memorial nor a tomb honoring an unknown Vietnam War soldier where these issues might be collectively pondered. Further, given the degree to which the national government had been complicit in the materialization of the unaccounted-for body, it was ill-equipped and even less inclined to provide leadership on the issue of missing servicemen, choosing instead to attribute responsibility for resolution of the issue to the Vietnamese.

These uncertain remainders of the Vietnam War proved fertile ground for the continuing formation of the unaccounted-for body. A new genre of captivity literature deployed all the most sordid tropes of the Vietnam War while Hollywood apotheosized the warrior ethic in films in which a brawny hero rescued emaciated POWs, thereby finishing a job the effete American government had been unable to accomplish on its own. Perhaps a still greater influence was exercised during these years by a burgeoning POW/MIA activist movement. Its members leveled numerous allegations of conspiracy and deceit by the United States and Vietnam, launched private efforts to allegedly rescue American POWs thought still to be held in Southeast Asia, and falsified photographs and other so-called evidence in an effort to publicize the "plight" of missing Americans who, they argued, had not only been left behind by their government but forgotten by the American people. These activities had a profound impact on the intelligibility of the body unaccounted-for in Southeast Asia. They largely succeeded in removing the veil of uncertainty that had surrounded these bodies and replacing it with certainty—certainty not that they might be dead or that their remains were unrecoverable, but that they were still alive and in captivity in Southeast Asia. As a result, to paraphrase the Senate select committee charged in 1993 with analyzing the accounting effort, the dead and missing soldiers of the Vietnam War took on a life of their own (U.S. Congress, Senate, 1993: 44). Indeed, this much was confirmed during the committee's deliberations by a poll conducted in August 1991 by the *Wall Street Journal*/NBC News in which 69 percent of respondents believed that Americans were still POWs in Southeast Asia and 52 percent thought the government was not doing enough to get them back (Franklin, 1993a: xv).

PRIVATE RESCUE MISSIONS AND FRAUDULENT EVIDENCE

By the 1980s, the above factors had long since combined to make it abundantly clear that the aftermath of the Vietnam War would look nothing like that of prior wars, in which unaccounted-for bodies were an accepted, if unwelcome, side effect. These bodies were to be the subject of controversy to a degree unheard of in American history, and the pursuit of an accounting for them only drove the United States further into the arms of its former enemy. Some observers have suggested it was precisely the threat of this sort of reconciliation with Vietnam that inspired much of the POW/MIA activism that took place during the 1980s (Franklin, 1993a: 197). For present purposes, however, the primary issue is the degree to which such activism affected the ways in which the unaccounted-for soldier came to be known. Through diligent exploitation of the doubt and mistrust created when the numbers of returned American prisoners failed to match the inflated figures of the Go Public campaign, the activists ensured that the matter of the unaccounted-for body would be indicative of larger questions about governmental honesty and candor in the post–Vietnam War era. The absence of the body would thus become synonymous with the absence of principles that characterized the war itself.

Perhaps the most far-fetched exploits of the POW/MIA movement in the early 1980s were private forays into Southeast Asia to rescue living prisoners of war thought to be held still by Southeast Asian Communists. Organized by a variety of individuals, not one of these expeditions ever resulted in the return of a living POW to American control or even produced credible evidence that any existed. Among the most notorious of these private mercenaries is the retired army colonel and former Green Beret James "Bo" Gritz, who in the early 1980s undertook the first of several incursions into Laos, one of which, known as Operation Grand Eagle, enjoyed at least some support from the U.S. government.[3] Although Grand Eagle never took flight, a subsequent Gritz-led foray, Operation Lazarus, did succeed in at least getting to Southeast Asia. What ensued, however, was a farcical combination of errors, incompetence, and fanciful imaginings. Having been spurned by both the DIA and the CIA because of his earlier efforts, Gritz concluded he needed direct support from the president of the United States, Ronald Reagan. To facilitate contact Gritz enlisted the support of the actor Clint Eastwood, who contributed thirty thousand dollars to the adventure. Eastwood also averred that, upon receiving confirmation that Gritz was in possession of American POWs, he would alert the president, who would then send American rescue helicopters. Upon reaching Thailand, where he intended to base his foray, Gritz found he had been swindled out of nearly thirty-three thousand dollars by his Lao comrades, that a small army and a boat he had earlier arranged to rent were no longer available, and that a contact who was supposed to supply the mission with guns had lost the key to the locker in which they were stored. Gritz elected to continue anyway, leading his followers on a sixty-five-mile trek during which they were ambushed by Lao forces, who captured one of the team members. Although he now had a confirmed prisoner to rescue, Gritz ordered a retreat and the team returned in haste to Thailand (Keating, 1994: 136–38).

Gritz was hardly alone in his efforts to rescue American POWs believed to be held against their will in Southeast Asia. All share the same basic outlines of Gritz's failure in Operation Lazarus. Confirmation of the existence of live prisoners would be claimed, and a rescue of some kind would then be launched, only to be foiled at the last minute by some unforeseen twist of circumstance. At a minimum, such missions had a deleterious effect on relations between the United States and the governments in the region, particularly that of Laos. Paul Mather (1994: 108–09), a longtime member of the U.S. military's Joint Casualty Resolution Center, succinctly summarizes the situation:

> On the diplomatic front, the communist governments of the Indochinese states, always paranoid and particularly willing to believe the United States is intent on overthrowing their regimes, have seized upon these private forays, whether actually carried out or only threatened, as evidence of US ill will toward them. In their society, where governmental control of the individual citizen is so complete, they find it difficult to comprehend that a US citizen could conduct a foray on his own volition without the US government both condoning and sponsoring it. Further, to them it is unimaginable that the US government is relatively powerless to halt this activity. Consequently, when private forays by American citizens have resulted in accusations that the United States is sponsoring raids into their sovereign territory, US denials have generally fallen on deaf ears.

Additionally, such missions ensured the further materialization of the unaccounted-for body as a figure in a conspiracy featuring the Vietnamese on one side and the U.S. government on the other. Since the U.S. government had proved too effete to win the war in Southeast Asia, the task of liberating America's prisoners would have to be taken up by the few true warriors who could operate outside its constraints.[4]

Another example of influential, if somewhat less spectacular, POW/MIA activism has been the dramatization of fraudulent photographs depicting American POWs still held in captivity. Like the private raids, none of these photos has ever correlated to a living American, and all have proven to be deliberate frauds. Three incidents, all of which occurred within a short time span in the early 1990s, are notable. In mid-1991, a photo of three middle-aged Caucasian men standing near some trees began appearing on the front pages of newspapers across the

United States. Lending credibility to the photos were claims by family members that the men depicted were American POWs John Robertson, Albro Lundy, and Larry Stevens. The photo caused an immediate uproar, not least among government officials in the United States who, given how the issue of missing Vietnam War soldiers had come to be articulated, had little choice but to take it seriously. Soon enough, yet another picture made the front pages, this one claiming to show Navy Lieutenant Daniel Borah, who had been shot down over Vietnam in 1972. Like the families of the men in the first picture, Borah's parents claimed with certainty that Daniel was staring back at them from the celluloid. Senator Bob Smith (R-NH), himself long involved in the search for missing American soldiers, immediately drafted a resolution calling for the creation of the Senate Select Committee on POW/MIA Affairs to look into this and other issues related to missing soldiers—a motion that was passed with little hesitation. Before long, a third photo made the headlines, this one allegedly showing Donald Carr, an army captain who had gone missing in Laos. Carr's family too was convinced of the photo's veracity. Suddenly, all the years of conjecture and rumor about American POWs in Southeast Asia seemed to be true. Perhaps the United States really had forsaken the missing (Keating, 1994: 221–37).

Once again, ensuing developments followed a predictable pattern. Each of the three photos was determined to be a fraud produced by well-known activists in the now-heady POW/MIA movement, some of whom had actually begun making a living collecting money in support of this or that organization that would soon be freeing some number of Americans imprisoned in Southeast Asia. The Robertson, Lundy, and Stevens photo had been concocted in Cambodia with a picture of three Russian farmers that had appeared in an issue of *Soviet Life* magazine from 1923. Considerably modified, the image came into the hands of the POW/MIA activist Eugene "Red" McDaniel, who took it upon himself to publicize its existence after numerous congressmen refused to take the bait. Daniel Borah turned out to be a half-French, half-Lao hill tribesman in his mid-70s, whose image came to the United States via Lao refugees and eventually ended up with Senator Smith, who introduced it as evidence in support of his resolution creating the select committee. Finally, Donald Carr turned out to be none other than a rare bird smuggler who posed for the picture at the behest of Jack Bailey, another longtime POW/MIA advocate who broadcast the photo in a bid to outdo the Robertson, Lundy, and Stevens photo then being hawked by his rival activist McDaniel (Keating, 1994: 221–37).

For some, of course, the mindset to debunk had struck again, a crime for which American POWs would pay with continued detention in Southeast Asia. For others, the photos were simply more proof of the lunacy that animated belief in living American POWs. Either way, the deliberate fabrication of fraudulent evidence of the existence of live American POWs in Southeast Asia must be regarded as one of the most cheerless elements of the Vietnam War's contentious legacy. At the very least, such events further poisoned relations between the United States and the Indochinese, put the families of missing servicemen through untold additional anxiety, and contributed to a wide perception of the possibility of living prisoners that substantially disregarded both the odds and the evidence of their survival. Yet herein lies the point: the ground upon which truth claims about the missing are constituted had by this time been tilled and retilled to such a degree that, for some anyway, virtually anything would grow. Such events are vital to the genealogy of the unaccounted-for body because they create conditions under which the materiality of the absent body becomes indicative of both truth *and* falsity, depending on the division between those who believe the Vietnamese are holding American prisoners and those who see in such belief nothing but myth. This duality, in turn, greatly hinders the effort to achieve a satisfactory accounting of the missing because that effort must contend with a body of deliberately false but still intelligible information about the absent soldier. However improbable such information may be, it nevertheless revivifies a body that has been intelligible since before the end of the Vietnam War, that of the live prisoner still held in Southeast Asia. As we will see in the next chapter, this circumstance has dramatic implications for the materialization of the *accounted*-for body. Accounting for the missing now requires not merely determining that the missing are in fact deceased, but also adducing verifiable proof in the form of identifiable remains.

COOPERATION, NORMALIZATION, AND THE BODY OF THE UNACCOUNTED-FOR SOLDIER

The final element in this genealogy of the unaccounted-for body is the lengthy process of normalization of diplomatic and economic relations between the United States and Vietnam. With the North Vietnamese victory on April 30, 1975, American attempts to gain an accounting of its soldiers still missing in Indochina reached their nadir. Opportunities to address the problematic nature of the prisoner lists furnished by the DRV and the paucity of names on the Laos list of February 1 vanished, and the JCRC was forced to relocate to Thailand. Furthermore, because the United States had been obliged to accept the adequacy of the prisoner return, the MIAs and the KIA/BNRs became the primary focus of American accounting efforts in the years after 1975. While the question of American prisoners remained unresolved in the minds of many, from a military and practical standpoint it had been resolved upon the completion of Operation Homecoming in March 1973. At the very least, these outcomes meant that any accounting of missing Americans would be achieved only with the cooperation of the Southeast Asian governments in question. Ideally, such cooperation was to be governed by the terms of the Paris Peace Accords, in particular Article 8(b) requiring the signatories to assist each other in obtaining information about those listed as missing in action and Article 21 obliging the United States to grant economic assistance to repair the damages of war.

Yet herein lay the crux of another debate that would also greatly hinder U.S.-Vietnamese relations in the immediate postwar years. The liberation of Saigon proved to the world that North Vietnam had violated virtually every aspect of the peace agreement of 1973 ending the war in Southeast Asia, not least the prohibition against infiltration of men and materiel into South Vietnam. On this basis, the United States argued it was no longer bound to fulfill its obligations under Article 21. The Vietnamese responded by claiming it would therefore no longer be obliged by Article 8(b). The United States found itself in a bind. It could no longer lay claim to the validity of the peace accord as a means of achieving an accounting of missing Americans since this would require the provision of reconstruction aid to Vietnam. Yet even had the administration agreed to supply such aid, a series of congressional resolutions had decisively prohibited any assistance to Vietnam. Such prohibitions in turn clearly meant that the United States was also in violation of the Paris Peace Accords. Moreover, in yet another twist of the Vietnam War's legacy, it is not unreasonable to suspect that such noncompliance was deliberately built into the U.S. understanding of Article 21. In exchange for the list of American prisoners held in Laos, President Nixon had given a letter to North Vietnam outlining $3.25 billion in American grant aid to be given over the next five years. Characteristically, Nixon kept the letter secret. A congressional delegation visiting Hanoi in December 1975 was stunned to learn of the letter from the Vietnamese themselves despite extensive pretrip briefings in which the delegates specifically asked Kissinger for any additional information related to Article 21 (Clarke, 1979: 62). Significantly, the letter included a codicil added by Kissinger subjecting any form of aid to each country's "own constitutional provisions" (Clarke, 1979: 64–65). This clearly meant that congressional approval would be required before any aid went to Vietnam; given the climate of opinion at the time, this virtually ensured that no aid would be forthcoming.

Secret codicils notwithstanding, the body of the unaccounted-for soldier would from this point on be inextricably intertwined with tit-for-tat negotiating, especially over the issue of the normalization of relations between the United States and Vietnam. The materiality of the unaccounted-for body was no longer the effect just of the Go Public campaign and the uncertainty occasioned by discrepancy cases, live-sighting reports, and fraudulent evidence. It also became an effect of confrontations over the political and economic issues of the postwar years, particularly as it became obvious that Vietnam needed to normalize relations with the United States as a way of lessening its diplomatic and economic isolation. The United States, for its part, was contending with family organizations that continued to press the government for an accounting of the missing. Compounding this pressure was the lingering disorientation of the Vietnam War and the wounds to the body politic caused by the absence of these individual bodies. As the Senate select committee was to remark in 1993. "the questions of whether American prisoners were left behind and, if so, whether they remained alive somewhere in captivity . . . haunted America" (U.S. Congress, Senate, 1993: 44). Thus, while the Vietnamese sought resolution of the diplomatic and economic differences between the two countries, the United States sought resolution of the deep ontological and corporeal rift produced by the Vietnam War. While the matter of the unaccounted-for body was for one side a prerequisite for fuller participation by Vietnam in world politics, for the other it was a condition of the possibility of resolving the war's many ambiguities.

As a means of contextualizing the debate over normalization, it is helpful to examine in more detail two analyses of the issue of missing soldiers undertaken by the U.S. government in the years after the Vietnam War. The analyses' assessments of the prospects for an accounting of American soldiers are pivotal in view of the subsequent salience of the issue and its centrality to the question of normalized relations. The first is the aforementioned House Select Committee on Missing Persons in Southeast Asia (U.S. Congress, House, 1976). Although the committee began its investigation a mere seven months after the Communist victory of April 1975, its final report reached some exceedingly sobering conclusions as to the likelihood that American service personnel were still alive in Vietnam and cast great doubt on the prospects for repatriating the remains of soldiers KIA. On the question of prisoners, the committee stated unequivocally its belief that "no Americans are still being held alive as prisoners in Indochina, or elsewhere, as a result of the war in Indochina" (U.S. Congress, House, 1976: vii). By the same token, the question of repatriation of remains was different in that one could accept the committee's findings regarding prisoners and still believe that every effort should be made to repatriate the remains of KIAs. Thus, the committee was meticulous in its assessment of this issue as well, noting that because of improvements in search and rescue techniques during the Vietnam War, all but twenty-eight—or 5/100 of 1 percent—of the bodies recovered at the time of death had been positively identified (U.S. Congress, House, 1976: 169). As to the recovery and identification of additional bodies, the committee concluded that "because of the nature and circumstances in which many Americans were lost in combat in Indochina, a total accounting by the Indochinese governments is not possible and should not be expected" (U.S. Congress, House, 1976: vii).

The select committee's findings, while hardly optimistic, nevertheless held out the possibility of at least some accounting of the missing. Thus, the Woodcock Commission was sent to Vietnam in fulfillment of a campaign promise by President Jimmy Carter to take the issue of missing soldiers more seriously than previous administrations. While the commission's final report was certainly no more sanguine than the House committee's had been, its recommendations were notable because of the emphasis placed on normalized relations with Vietnam. The commission argued that "normalization of relations affords the best prospect for obtaining a fuller accounting for our missing personnel and recommend[ed] that the normalization process be pursued vigorously for this as well as other reasons" (U.S. Department of State, 1977: 374). The commission also noted that "it impressed upon the Vietnamese and Lao our realistic attitude on the MIA issue and our intention to resolve it on a reasonable basis in order to remove it as an obstacle to normalization." (U.S. Department of State, 1977: 373).

From a contemporary standpoint, the views of both the House select committee and the Woodcock Commission are nothing short of extraordinary. For a brief moment in the mid-1970s, it appeared as though the aftermath of the Vietnam War might resemble those of prior American wars, in which the unaccounted-for body was accepted, though certainly not welcomed. That the two investigations failed massively to foresee the impossibility of this circumstance can be viewed cynically or charitably depending on one's assessment of the likelihood of a full accounting. Either way, the discourse of the unaccounted-for soldier in the immediate postwar years meant that statements in favor of normalization of relations with Vietnam would remain largely incomprehensible, while those which found in the materiality of the absent body an expression of Vietnamese or American culpability would be authorized. This disjuncture would not only delay normalization for another two decades but also come to play a large role in the continuing materialization of the unaccounted-for body. As it turned out, the road to normalization was littered with the bodies of missing soldiers whose materiality now became the effect and gauge of Vietnamese "cooperation" in resolving the issue of unaccounted-for Americans.

Such cooperation gained momentum during the 1980s as the Vietnamese economy began to falter and Soviet patronage became increasingly unable to make up the difference. Noteworthy during this period was a mutual shift away from any language of obligation like that contained in the Paris Peace Accords. This enabled the United States to replace the stick of Article 8(b) with the carrot of normalization as a means of pressuring the Vietnamese to account for missing Americans, thereby warding off Vietnamese claims regarding Article 21. Still, this development did not necessarily mean discussions between the two sides were exactly harmonious. The Vietnamese believed their willingness to cooperate with the United States meant that resolution of unaccounted-for cases should not be a precondition to normalized relations but rather one among many issues mutually affecting the two countries. In particular, Vietnam sought assistance from the United States with "problems concerning wartime orphans, amputees, victims of chemical weapons, and Vietnam's own wartime missing" (Stern, 1995: 37).

Like the discourse on normalization, however, that of the unaccounted-for body had so calcified as to prohibit even minimal consideration of assistance for Vietnam. This circumstance had much to do with events in the United States, particularly Reagan's assumption of the presidency in 1981. Committed to increasing public awareness on the POW/MIA issue, President Reagan declared to a meeting of the National League of Families in 1983 that the fate of American missing was now a matter of "the highest national priority" (U.S. President, 1983: 131). Statements like this, along with a sizable increase in resources devoted to the accounting agenda, resulted not in an expansion of the discursive parameters of the unaccounted-for body but in their contraction around a peculiarly American understanding of the matter. Not unexpectedly, the Vietnamese took exception to many of the demands placed upon them even as they agreed in 1988 to a long-standing American proposal for joint field searches of graves and aircraft crash sites. Vietnam also agreed to provide additional information on discrepancy cases, to arrange for more rapid investigation of live-sighting reports, and to increase American access to wartime documents and witnesses who might assist in the resolution of cases. Vietnam agreed even to cooperate in resolving cases which occurred in those parts of Laos that had been under North Vietnamese control during the war (Stern, 1995: 41). Despite the increased levels of cooperation, the Reagan administration concluded in 1989 that "we must operate under the assumption that at least some of the missing could have survived until we can jointly conclude that all possible efforts have been made to resolve their fate" (in Stern, 1995: 42).

That such a conclusion ultimately dictated the nature of American relations with Vietnam—especially given the evidence in question and the passage of sixteen years since the withdrawal of American forces from Southeast Asia—suggests how much strength the unaccounted-for body had acquired since the end of the Vietnam War. As had been the case during the war, when absent bodies were produced as a rationale for the United States to continue fighting, the factors surrounding normalization of relations suggest that, far from being destined to become the central feature in U.S.-Vietnamese affairs, the absent body had to be produced as such. During the 1980s especially, that body increasingly became a precondition for the normalization of relations. Normalized relations thus came to simultaneously produce and be produced by the absent body since normalization of relations required the

Vietnamese to produce the body and production of the body required the United States to normalize relations.

This, at any rate, was how Vietnam saw the issue, which explains to a great extent their long-standing enmity for the U.S. economic embargo. Calling it "abnormal and inhuman" and arguing that it had "worsened the destruction wrought by the war," Vietnamese leaders pointed out that U.S. efforts "were not equivalent to Hanoi's attempts to resolve the MIA issue and 'not proportional to the grave consequences of the economic embargo'" (in Stern, 1995: 77). Yet in the United States during the 1980s statements in favor of normalization continued to be not only largely unintelligible but practically nonexistent. In view of this, U.S. requests for further cooperation in the accounting effort raised serious questions in Vietnam about precisely how "to respond to what they saw as infinitely escalating American demands for 'cooperation' on the MIA issue" (Stern, 1995: 78). Vietnam's mistrust was accompanied by increasing pressure from American business interests to lift the embargo, pressure the Vietnamese were quick to argue demonstrated the decreasing legitimacy of U.S. policy toward Vietnam. These developments led the United States in 1993 to tentatively consider lifting the embargo. As a condition, however, four specific areas of cooperation were cited in which Vietnam would be expected to provide 'tangible progress" prior to any further steps in improving relations between the two nations. These included the repatriation of remains, the resolution of discrepancy cases, further assistance in resolving cases along the Vietnam–Laos border, and increased access to all Vietnamese archives that might contain information relating to missing American soldiers (U.S. Department of State, 1993b: 534).

Here again the materiality of the body makes an appearance, this time in conspicuous relation to the possibility of normalized relations between the United States and Vietnam. Indeed, the stipulation of "tangible progress" marks the further commitment of the United States to the discourse of the unaccounted-for body in which materiality serves as the only means of determining the truth of the missing. Vietnam was not overly enthusiastic about these new requirements, but again they were not unaware that their fulfillment held out the prospect of securing a lifting of the economic embargo and the normalization of diplomatic relations; accordingly, they once again endeavored to make the improvements required by the United States. At the same time, however, it became increasingly clear that such indices as "tangible progress" were primarily designed to placate domestic constituencies, above all the families of the missing and the POW/MIA activists, who had recently been whipped into a frenzy by the fraudulent photographs discussed above as well as by the steady stream of live-sighting reports that seemed still more proof of the existence of living American POWs. The Senate Select Committee on POW/MIA Affairs had only recently concluded its work, having disbanded with the somewhat ominous conclusion that "there is no proof that U.S. POWs survived, but neither is there proof that all of those who did not return had died" (U.S. Congress, Senate, 1993: 7). Public opinion on the matter was largely predictable. A CBS–*New York Times* poll in January 1994 indicated that more than half of Americans believed missing soldiers were still alive in Vietnam (Lesinski, 1998: 56).

Despite these hurdles, on February 3, 1994, President Bill Clinton lifted the trade embargo and agreed to expand the official American presence in Vietnam to a liaison office. By way of clarification, of course, Clinton stressed that "these actions do not constitute a normalization of our relationship. Before that happens, we must have more progress, more cooperation, and more answers" (in Stern, 1995: 125). What he meant, of course, was that the United States needed more bodies. However, given its accounting protocol requiring identifiable remains to remove a name from the list of the missing, the United States had placed itself in an inescapable conundrum. On the one hand, the repatriation of bodies could be held up as evidence of Vietnamese cooperation and of the elimination of the state of ambiguity in which the families of the missing lived. On the other hand, the continued existence of unaccounted-for bodies could also signal either more Vietnamese obduracy or, since it had long argued that many more would likely not be forthcoming, further conspiracy by the U.S. government to obscure the existence of bodies. This was a new quagmire, one in which every effort at extraction drew the United States further into the muck. As in the Vietnam War itself, it seemed further (already dead, it was hoped) bodies would have to be produced if the United States was finally to make it out of Southeast Asia.

It was hardly a surprise, then, that when President Clinton finally chose to normalize relations with Vietnam on February 11, 1995, the decision was met with a chorus of strident objections. By this time, however, various influences had created the space necessary for a rearticulation of statements about the missing. John McCain, an Arizona senator and former Vietnam War POW, remarked, "For the sake of America, maybe it's time we ended the war. I believe normalization would be an important part of the healing process" (Greenhouse, 1995: A4). Further, American business interests had begun clamoring for the right to establish themselves in Vietnam. The discourse of the unaccounted-for body was again altered as prominent Vietnam veterans were finally able to assert the legitimacy of their views on this issue and as the dictates of international capital began to take precedence over the parochial concerns of the families of the missing. This, however, was far from the end of the effort to account for the missing. As President Clinton said, "Normalization of our relations with Vietnam is not the end of our [accounting] effort" but rather "the next appropriate step" (in Lesinski, 1998: 134).

COUNTING THE UNACCOUNTED-FOR

This genealogy of the unaccounted-for body has traced the political, cultural, and epistemic conditions that, despite the very small number of absent soldiers when compared to those of previous American wars, enabled that body to emerge as the most material effect of the U.S. defeat in Vietnam. At the very least, these conditions ensured that the Vietnam War would retain its status as a war like no other in American history, that its aftermath would be characterized by the endless replay of many of the most sordid elements of the war itself, and, ultimately, that the search for missing soldiers would delay the healing and reconciliation such a pursuit is allegedly intended to achieve. Each of these factors has to do with how *unaccounted-for* is defined in the first place, namely, as the absence of the body rather than the absence of information concerning the fate of the missing soldier in question. The departure this definitional decision represents from other possible means of accounting is noteworthy to say the least. At a minimum, circumstantial evidence is invalidated as a stand-alone means of accounting for the missing, and this despite the admission by the United States itself that every unaccounted-for soldier is deceased and the existence of often overwhelming circumstantial evidence in support of this assertion. That the passage of time brings no new information on the soldiers in question, although it may permit a presumptive finding of death under the Missing Persons Act, means nothing to the accounting. Finally, the information gathered from the incident of loss that led to the initial KIA classification is insufficient in and of itself to close an unaccounted-for case. The body and only the body is what matters, which means that removing names from the list of the missing is a very difficult task.

One senses there is much going on here—indeed, that missing Vietnam War soldiers are much more intimately implicated in the lingering ontological and corporeal uncertainties occasioned by wartime defeat than their relatively small numbers might suggest. Perhaps this ambiguity helps explain the decision in 1980 by the Department of Defense to add the names of soldiers originally listed as KIA/BNR to the total of Americans unaccounted-for in Southeast Asia (U.S. Congress, Senate, 1993: 158). The result, as would be pointed out in 1993 in the final report of the Senate Select Committee on POW/MIA Affairs, was "the anomalous situation of having more Americans considered unaccounted for today than we had immediately after the war" (U.S. Congress, Senate, 1993: 164). This "anomalous situation" is even more consequential given that the KIA/BNR category required evidence of death so convincing that no plausible alternative could be considered under the circumstances. Put simply, the fate of these soldiers was never in doubt despite the absence of their bodies. Their addition to the list of the unaccounted-for, therefore, marked yet another change in the official discourse of the unaccounted-for body and entailed a correlative transformation in how that body would be counted. This, by extension, meant that the counting of *accounted*-for servicemen would require a tangible presence that might replace a material absence. Anomalous though this situation may be, it is also quite instructive. If the post-Vietnam War era is a time of corporeal ambiguity, then perhaps the search for the missing is better viewed as an effort to resolve that uncertainty by replacing it with the certainty of the identified body, whose materiality might put to rest the concerns and doubts comprised in the contentious legacy of the Vietnam War. As we will see in the next chapter, however, things are not quite so simple as this, especially if— as sometimes happens—the materiality of the body results in still more uncertainty.

chapter three

The Body of the Accounted-For Soldier

Never before in the history of mankind has any nation done what we're doing. The effort of Joint Task Force-Full Accounting to honor the U.S. commitment to our unaccounted-for comrades, their families and the nation is unprecedented.
—Douglas "Pete' Peterson, U.S. Ambassador to Vietnam
  ("Joint Task Force-Full Accounting: Fiscal Year 1999")

Having examined the materialization of the unaccounted-for body in Southeast Asia I turn to an analysis of the practices through which that body is located, excavated and identified, and thereby becomes accounted for. Evaluating the emergence of the accounted-for body requires the simultaneous analysis of the practices which enable that emergence—including archival research, archaeological excavation of grave and aircraft crash sites in Southeast Asia, and forensic identification of recovered remains—along with the epistemic conditions upon which these practices depend. First, however, I stress that the materialization of the body of the accounted-for soldier begins with what at face value appears to be its most basic element: the list of the missing. As it was during the U.S. withdrawal from Vietnam in 1973, the list is contentious, though for reasons that have less to do with suspicions about its numerical accuracy than with the ways in which it frames the effort to account for missing soldiers. Because that effort has been tied to the resolution of the many ambiguities occasioned by the loss in Vietnam, some measure of success must be in place so that progress, or the lack thereof, might be effectively gauged. The list of the missing thus figures prominently in assessments of the accounting endeavor because it implies that nothing more complicated than removing names over time ensures the success of the search. Finding bodies, repatriating them, linking them to names, and then returning them to their families become the mission.

The issue, however, is not nearly so simple, precisely because there are no bodies to repatriate, at least not in the sense implied by the list of the missing. At the outset, then, the list often complicates the quest for closure and certainty that informs the search: for the body contemplated by the families of the missing and listed by the U.S. government is not the same body as that examined by forensic scientists charged with making a positive identification of repatriated remains. The first body is the fully formed human who left for Vietnam and failed to return in any form, whereas the second body is any quantity of biological evidence with physical characteristics sufficient for identification purposes. In an attempt to account for this dichotomy, the U.S. government has devised a two-part accounting protocol by which names can be removed from the list. The first requires the return from Southeast Asia of a living American whose status is not already known to the United States, an event that has yet to occur since the repatriation of 591 POWs during Operation Homecoming in 1973. The second method, which forms the subject of this chapter, is the recovery and repatriation of what the U.S. government terms identifiable remains, meaning human remains of sufficient size and quantity as to be useful in the range of sophisticated techniques employed in the identification process (Command Briefing, JTF-FA, 2000). This, of course, implies there must be enough of the soldier's remains to be subjected to the various scientific procedures used to make a positive identification. Given the time elapsed since the end of the war and the circumstances of a soldier's death, satisfying this requirement is often close to impossible. After the crash of a fighter jet at five hundred miles per hour followed by thirty years during which the remains are lying in acidic tropical soil, there simply is not much body to bring back, for identification purposes or for anything else. Quite often, all that remains of the body fits in an envelope or perhaps a shoe box.[1]

The radical fragmentation of the absent soldier's body is thus an obstacle to the success of a search conceptualized in terms of nameable, identifiable bodies in that it simply will not be possible to account for every soldier still missing as a consequence of the war in Southeast Asia. Responding to this problem, the United States pursues what it calls "the fullest possible accounting," by which it "acknowledge[s] that we may not solve all cases due to the horrific realities of war' ("Personnel Recovery and Accounting: POW/MIA Accounting": 5). The government even goes so far as to specify the number of soldiers for which it believes it will never be able to account, a figure that currently stands at 663. Officially referred to as "no further pursuit" cases, these identifications are not pursued for lack of information on the missing soldier in question, hazardous recovery conditions, and instances in which a pilot was lost over water (DPMO Website, 2004). The phrase "fullest possible accounting" thus acknowledges the impossibility of solving all outstanding cases because of the practical difficulties that beset the search and also gestures at the difference between the body that once left for Vietnam and the one that (sometimes) returns to the United States in the form of so many shards of bone.

In addition to the practical dimension, the locution "fullest possible accounting" makes a statement about the anxieties that animate the attempt to repatriate missing bodies in the first place. After all, the Vietnam War is the only American war that has seen anything approximating a systematic accounting of the missing. The repatriation and identification of the remains of American war dead have been official military regulations since the Civil War (Anders, 1983), but prior to the Vietnam War it was also recognized that many bodies would forever remain unrecoverable precisely because of the same horrific realities of war cited in the current accounting protocol. The shift in emphasis from "unrecoverable" to "unaccounted for" in the years following the U.S. loss in Vietnam can thus be said to reflect the absence of an interpretive structure within which the Vietnam War might be rendered intelligible. To list those missing as unrecoverable leaves defeat intact, while unaccounted for suggests that at least some elements of that defeat might in time be redeemed. The fullest possible accounting thus seeks not merely to mollify family organizations and members of Congress who have long been critical of the government's effort to account for missing soldiers, but also to redress the remnants of the loss in Vietnam embodied by those still missing. At the same time, the fullest possible accounting serves political purposes in that it acknowledges the impossibility of a full accounting while allowing the U.S. ambassador to Vietnam to boast, "Never before in the history of mankind has any nation done what we are doing" ("Joint Task Force-Full Accounting: Fiscal Year 1999").

Acknowledging that not every soldier will be accounted for, however, generates its own share of political anxiety, especially with respect to the search's role in the pacification of Vietnam War ambiguities. In particular, the United States tacitly admits it cannot end the war in Vietnam in the view of those for whom "the war won't really be over until they're all accounted for" since that war is now waged on an interpretive terrain in which the objective has become a reconstituted sense of ontological and corporeal coherence achieved solely through the ever-deferred project of "bringing them all home" (Dillow, 1995). Practically and politically speaking, this circumstance creates enormous pressure to positively identify remains recovered in Southeast Asia. Since the accounting protocol is ultimately based on nameable, identifiable bodies, identification must eliminate the uncertainty contained in the phrase "fullest possible accounting" by providing absolute certainty of the identity of those soldiers whose remains are recovered. This is all the more important given the relationship between the (possibly) live body and its definitively dead counterpart (see chapter 2). Remains identification here becomes the only way of assuring that the recovered soldier in question is not a prisoner of the Vietnamese. Finally, identification must effect a reconciliation between the body contemplated by forensic science and that awaited by the families of the missing, since the accounting effort is, in one sense at least, not an exercise in scientific cunning but a means of giving closure to the families and restoring a sense of ontological and corporeal coherence for the nation. Hence the search for the missing embraces identifiable remains because only they offer the certainty that can compensate for the uncertainty indicated by the materiality of the absent body.

This chapter is divided into four sections, beginning with an overview of the structure of the U.S. personnel recovery apparatus. The second part is an analysis of the materialization of the accounted-for body, with consideration of the archival research work used to assemble background information on the unaccounted-for soldier in question and the circumstances of his loss. The significance of such work is not limited to maximizing the possibility of locating and then recovering the remains of the soldier in question. Of equal importance is the creation of the epistemic conditions that will eventually enable the removal of a soldier's name from the list of the missing. Here again, we encounter an oddity written into the protocol requiring positive identification of remains. Though circumstantial evidence does not suffice as an independent means of accounting for the missing, the body identified in the laboratory must nonetheless correspond with a body of circumstantial evidence about the missing soldier in order for the identification to be valid. That requirement underscores the degree to which the intelligibility of bodies is not discovered but produced. In this case, the intelligibility of the accounted-for body begins with the compilation of archival data about the absent soldier—data which begin the process of establishing the conditions required for his being accounted for.

The third section turns to the excavation work undertaken in Southeast Asia. Such work is meticulous in the extreme and follows all of the standard procedures used in archaeological digs. Here, the above-noted protocol requiring identifiable remains takes on special significance given that the eventual materialization of the accounted-for body—that is, the moment at which its name can be removed from the list of the missing—depends at the outset upon remains being recovered. Identifiable remains then combine with the above-noted preexcavation procedures in the continuing formation of the epistemic conditions within which the accounted-for body will (hopefully) emerge. As with archival data, items recovered at excavation must correspond with those data and with the identity of the remains in question if a name is to be removed from the list of the missing.

The fourth section of the chapter explores the process of identification of remains. Undertaken at the Central Identification Laboratory (CIL) at Hickam Air Force Base in Honolulu, identification is determined by procedures that are frequently even more sophisticated than those employed at an excavation site. Like the excavation itself, remains identification is subject to the rigorous requirements of science and makes use of mitochondrial DNA (mtDNA) analysis. As indicated, identification of remains is crucial to the accounting since it is only at this stage that identifiable can finally become identified—that, in other words, the materialization of the body of the soldier can eventuate in an accounted for designation and permit the removal of the soldier's name from the list of the missing. Here again, the government's protocol requiring identifiable remains plays a large role in establishing the conditions under which those remains can meet the demands made of them. Not simply part of what constitutes the intelligibility of objects recovered at excavation, that protocol also suggests the terms under which the materialization of the accounted-for body will proceed. In the absence of identification, repatriated remains continue as so many disparate, fragmentary data that cannot positively resolve the status of the soldier in question. The materialization of the soldier's body remains incomplete, unaccounted for despite the ostensible recovery of the remains that have become so important in the post–Vietnam War era. Remains may provide indisputable circumstantial evidence that, for example, the pilot of a particular aircraft went down at said location on a given date, yet that evidence cannot lead to an accounted-for body—cannot, in other words, permit a change in status from absent to present. The name in question thus remains on the list of the missing.

As will be seen, however, the certainty allegedly offered by forensic science and by other means used to identify recovered remains is far from a pre-given fact. In some cases, for example, identification of remains is made via such a small fraction of the body that relatives are left wondering whether the rest of their loved one might still be alive somewhere in Southeast Asia. An example comes from the identification in 1993 of the remains of Navy Captain Harley Hall by means of three of his front teeth. Hall's wife found this insufficient proof of death. As she remarked at the time, "After 20 years of almost unbearable uncertainty, I now face the worst possible scenario: still not knowing" (Cary, 1994b: 22). In other cases, the identifications made by CIL scientists have seemed arbitrarily imposed rather than achieved in accordance with standard forensic scientific procedures. Not surprisingly, this has created the impression that the accuracy of CIL identifications is subordinate to their political utility. Finally, and still worse, identification at times fails to generate the identity of the body in question because of the practical difficulties occasioned by its fragmentation. Given that the accounting effort has long been defined as an attempt to return the missing to the United States, failed and unsatisfactory identifications not infrequently invite the charge that the government is forsaking the missing. They are forsaken, in other words, because the U.S. government has failed to secure their return, that is, failed to generate via the identified body the certainty of the soldier's return home which that government has taken upon itself as a sacred obligation to unaccounted-for servicemen, their families, and the nation.

It is at this moment that the initially understandable desire for certainty as to the fate and whereabouts of unaccounted-for soldiers becomes a logic with insidious political consequences. This logic derives its force from the two bodies discussed in chapter 2, the (possibly) live body left behind in Southeast Asia and its dead counterpart whose remains have yet to be recovered. Within this conceptual dualism, the certainty of the repatriated, identified body indicates one more incremental step toward a successful outcome of the accounting effort. On the other hand, the logic of certainty often leads to the assumption of continued life when proof of death in the form of the identified body cannot be provided. Hence highly compelling circumstantial evidence about the fate and whereabouts of the missing is denied or portrayed as a conspiracy to conceal living American prisoners in Southeast Asia. Perhaps worse, the failure to achieve certainty transfers responsibility for missing soldiers from the horrific realities of war to the U.S. government or to the Vietnamese. Certainty, in other words, has become a weapon used to perpetuate the material and interpretive hostilities which the search for the missing was designed to appease. An analysis of the specific means employed to account for the missing must therefore be attentive to the political consequences it entails. Certainty is not necessarily the panacea it is portrayed to be, but indeed something which does much to ensure that the missing will never be fully accounted for.

The materialization of the accounted-for body—when it happens—refutes the claim that the absence of the body endures as the result of Vietnamese deception and obstinacy. Indeed, the United States and Vietnam have largely succeeded in creating an atmosphere of trust in which practices oriented toward the transparent exchange of information can flourish. Consequently, as virtually everyone involved with the accounting effort now acknowledges, much of the success of the search is due to the willingness of the Vietnamese to cooperate with the U.S. government and with individual search teams. So great has this cooperation been that it is not inappropriate to suggest that the very possibility of accounting for the missing as currently construed is the result of Vietnam's assistance. One could imagine, for example, an accounting process restricted to document and archival analysis or to excavations performed solely by the Vietnamese themselves. Thus, in opposition to the claims of those who believe that Vietnam owes the United States a full accounting of the missing must be placed the recognition that the American presence in Vietnam is an intrusion on Vietnamese sovereignty, one that must be earned and negotiated rather than expected and taken for granted. It should in turn be recognized that it is through the consent and cooperation of the Vietnamese that the ambiguities of the Vietnam War may be overcome at all.

THE STRUCTURAL ORGANIZATION OF THE ACCOUNTING EFFORT

The U.S. effort to account for missing personnel has become a global endeavor encompassing both military service members and civilians, and it includes those missing from World War II, the Korean War, the Vietnam War, the Cold War, and the first Persian Gulf War. Responsibility for overall recovery policy falls to the Department of Defense Prisoner of War/Missing Personnel Office (DPMO), whose primary function is to establish policy requirements and to coordinate efforts with the case resolution of other groups, including the U.S.-Russia Joint Commission on POW/MIA Affairs.[2] A further task of the DPMO is file research and case analysis for each soldier listed as unaccounted for ("Joint Task Force-Full Accounting: The Fullest Possible Accounting"). Such research is an absolute precondition to the success of any search. In addition to helping locate sites for later excavation, preexcavation case file analysis supplies a great deal of the antemortem information required to make a positive identification of the remains of an unaccounted-for soldier.

The organization charged with conducting personnel recovery operations in Southeast Asia is the U.S. military's Joint POW/MIA Accounting Command (JPAC).[3] Based at Hickam Air Force Base, JPAC is composed of over four hundred investigators, linguists, scientists, and other specialists from all four branches of the military as well as Department of Defense civilian employees (JPAC Website, 2004). JPAC is divided into three detachments. Detachment One, located in Bangkok, serves as a staging area for recovery teams from the United States; in addition, it coordinates the resolution of cases in Cambodia, for which it was determined that a separate detachment was unnecessary given the relatively small number of personnel unaccounted for in that country. Detachment Two is located in Hanoi and Detachment Three in Vientiane (JPAC Website, 2004). Like that of the DPMO, the work of JPAC includes extensive file research and document analysis in preparation for missions in the field. Within JPAC is the CIL, whose primary job is to identify remains recovered in the field. To facilitate that effort, CIL personnel deploy to Southeast Asia during recovery missions to ensure the scientific integrity of the excavation site.

On the basis of archival research and negotiations with the host country in question, JPAC then organizes remains recovery missions to Southeast Asia to carry out research and excavation activities. The fieldwork is called Joint Field Activities (JFAs) to designate the cooperation between the four branches of the U.S. military and that between the government of the United States and those of the host nations. Each mission commonly lasts between thirty and forty days and is made up of anywhere from forty (in Laos) to one hundred people (in Vietnam) ("Joint Task Force-Full Accounting: The Fullest Possible Accounting"). Vietnamese assistance under the auspices of the Vietnam Office for Seeking Missing Persons (VNOSMP) includes logistical support and hiring of indigenous personnel to assist JPAC recovery teams during the excavation process. Since the creation in 1992 of JPAC's predecessor, JTF-FA, seventy-eight JFAs have been conducted in Vietnam, eighty-five in Laos, and thirty-one in Cambodia (as of July 2004). The total number of positively identified remains repatriated from Southeast Asia during that time stands at 734 (DPMO Website, 2004).

In October 2003, a reorganization combined the formerly independent JTF-FA with the CIL to create the Joint POW/MIA Accounting Command. Predictably, certain family organizations stridently denounced the proposed reorganization, believing it to signal the imminent demise of the effort to account for Vietnam War soldiers and thus the moment at which the U.S. government's forsaking of the missing would reach its apotheosis. In June 2002, for example, when plans for the merger were announced, the National Alliance of Families said, "Today, we will go out on a limb and predict that once the merger of CIL-HI and JTF-FA occurs, eventually, CIL-HI will become the dominate [sic] organization and JTF-FA will eventually fade away, as will the investigations into the fate of our Prisoners and Missing. This, we are sure, will be denied. Just as it was denied that JTF-FA, as we know it, would disappear by 2004" (Bits n Pieces, 2002). Sentiments like these have become common in the context of missing Vietnam War soldiers and have done much to condition the intelligibility of the unaccounted-for body. Combining an almost limitless reservoir of resentment and a continuing sense of victimization over a lost war and lost bodies, such beliefs have erased the possibility that the U.S. government might ever do right by the missing or might be genuinely concerned with their eventual return. At one level, then, the following overview of American efforts to account for soldiers missing in Southeast Asia—and the extraordinary attention to detail on the part of the government it reflects—is presented as something of a corrective to this point of view. At another level, the very existence of such detail makes manifest the degree to which the families' view of the issue of missing servicemen has prevailed—an interpretive possibility they seem all too willing to ignore.

ARCHIVAL RESEARCH AND CASE FILE ANALYSIS

The methodical, painstaking work of DPMO and JPAC reveals a high sensitivity to the need for the indisputable evidence required in the post–Vietnam War era to support the removal of a soldier's name from the list of the missing. Accordingly, the accounting process begins with the gathering of archival information in the United States, a task normally pursued jointly by the DPMO and JPAC. JPAC maintains files on all American soldiers whose remains have yet to be recovered and identified. The information includes maps, casualty reports, search and rescue reports, line of duty investigations, witness statements, and all files from the two mortuaries operating during the Vietnam War at Da Nang and Tan Son Nhut (Command Briefing, CILHI, 2000). The archives also contain the missing service member's medical and dental records (Heussner and Holland, 1999). Other organizations, including the National Archives and the Library of Congress, also provide assistance at the information gathering stage.

Of utmost importance at this stage is a review of the circumstances surrounding the incident in which the missing soldier was initially lost. In many cases, eyewitness reports and extensive records such as Search and Rescue logs kept by the U.S. military during the war have yielded a surprising amount of information. If, for example, two planes were flying in the same area over North Vietnam and one of them was shot down, perhaps crew members from the other aircraft observed whether anyone had ejected from the damaged plane. The crew members might have observed whether those who ejected had deployed their parachute and, if so, whether they appeared to be alive. A missing soldier's case file also normally contains other details about the incident of loss, including the date of the incident, the specific coordinates of the operation in which he was participating, and factors surrounding that operation. So, for example, the case file of a foot soldier who failed to return from a night patrol should reveal roughly where he might have been at the time of loss, the nature of the operation in question, whether hostile forces were present in the region, and whether any combat occurred.

In addition, research is conducted outside the United States in the archives of Southeast Asian nations to determine if any information therein can be correlated with that already uncovered. The DPMO and JPAC identify archival facilities in other countries and the type of information to be collected. Once obtained, these data are copied and furnished to family members if it pertains to a specific individual and to either the National Archives or the Library of Congress, where it is open to public review ("Archival Research: Our Role in DPMO"). Archival information obtained both at home and abroad is vital. In November 1998, for example, DPMO completed the seventeen-month Cambodia Archival Research Project involving the review and translation of over sixty-five thousand pages of military dossiers from 1970 to 1975. The documents were then used to develop a database containing information correlated to missing American soldiers from the Vietnam War ("Archival Research: Highlights and Activities").

On the basis of information gleaned from archival research, other leads can be pursued, among them interviews with members of the missing soldier's unit and with veterans of the North Vietnamese Army (NVA) who may have been in the area at the time of the soldier's loss. To facilitate this element of the accounting process, the Oral History Program was created. Based with Detachment One, the program seeks to identify and interview Vietnamese who were of senior rank or status during the war and who, owing to their experience or position, might have knowledge of unaccounted-for American personnel or of a specific incident of loss. Interviewees may also be able to shed light on crash or burial sites or point to potential sources of additional information ("Joint Task Force–Full Accounting: Fiscal Year 1999").

In addition to the Oral History Program, the governments of Laos, Cambodia, and Vietnam participate in the Trilateral Witness Program, which brings former Vietnamese soldiers and other witnesses into Laos or Cambodia to assist in the investigation of incidents in which they were involved during the war. The program has occasionally led to the recovery of remains believed to be those of unaccounted-for American personnel. Unilateral investigations by the governments of Laos, Cambodia, and Vietnam are also performed periodically, and all three governments encourage their citizens to report any information they may have about potential American aircraft crash sites or ground battle loss sites ("Joint Task Force-Full Accounting: Fiscal Year 1999"). Here, the central importance of cooperation by Vietnamese and other Southeast Asian villagers must again be underscored. In many cases, grid coordinates and other techniques for recording the location of a particular incident of loss are not sufficiently precise. The assistance of local villagers who may have witnessed the incident can lead investigators to the site in question. On still other occasions, local villagers may be in possession of remains believed to be American. Though it is the official policy of the U.S. government not to pay for the remains per se, they will reimburse the possessor for the cost of transporting them (Command Briefing, JTF-FA, 2000).

Yet another element in the information gathering process is the resolution of live-sighting reports. Given the large number of such cases, the DIA decided in 1987 to augment the efforts of existing search personnel through the creation of a group known as Stony Beach (Mather, 1994: 175). Based with Detachment One, the Stony Beach group coordinates the investigation of all live-sighting reports by interviewing anyone who claims to have seen a living American POW or unaccounted-for soldier in Southeast Asia. Live-sighting reports have long played a leading role in keeping alive the belief that Americans are being held against their will in Southeast Asia (see chapter 2). In an attempt to assuage this concern, the U.S. government, through the offices of DPMO, JPAC, and the Stony Beach group, places special emphasis on the immediate resolution of live-sighting reports. Searchers anywhere in Southeast Asia drop their work on a moment's notice to pursue a live-sighting report, however circumstantial or anecdotal it may be.

The final element of JPAC's accounting process prior to excavation work relates to the resolution of what are known as either discrepancy cases or last-known-alive cases. These cases involve currently unaccounted-for American service personnel who were last known to be alive in Vietnamese custody but who were not returned to the United States at Operation Homecoming in 1973 and whose remains have never been repatriated. The United States has reason to believe the governments of either Vietnam, Laos, or Cambodia might reasonably be expected to have information regarding these cases. Given the contentiousness of this issue in the postwar era, resolution of last-known-alive cases forms another element in the accounting process to which JPAC must devote attention. A special Research and Investigation Team

(RIT) operates within Detachment Two in Hanoi and focuses exclusively on resolving discrepancy cases. RIT, which includes a member from the Stony Beach group, travels extensively throughout Vietnam pursuing various leads, investigating general information, and, in some instances, conducting limited excavations of alleged loss locations. RIT also investigates leads that may result in the resolution of cases in Laos and Cambodia ("Personnel Recovery and Accounting," 2000: 58).

FIELDWORK AND SITE EXCAVATION

Basing itself on the findings of archival research and case file analysis, the Joint POW/MIA Accounting Command determines whether accounting for the missing service member in question warrants a JFA. To proceed with fieldwork, of course, implies that the host countries in Southeast Asia agree to the presence of American search teams. Owing to the high level of cooperation established between the United States and Vietnam, especially since the lifting of the economic embargo and the normalization of diplomatic relations in 1995, investigators from JPAC are allowed to choose which sites in Vietnam they would like to investigate and are allowed to move freely about the country; they also benefit from the extensive good will and assistance of the Vietnamese. Cambodia also allows JPAC to choose sites for investigation and to move freely. In contrast, the United States generally enjoys far less autonomy in its fieldwork in Laos. Many restrictions govern the locations at which search teams can conduct excavations, and numerous bureaucratic hurdles at both the national and provincial levels must be cleared before recovery and investigation teams can begin their work. Search teams are limited to forty members, no American can remain stationed in Laos for longer than one year, and the five missions permitted annually must proceed sequentially from north to south. In addition, Laos often seeks reciprocal benefits from the United States such as infrastructure improvements and other forms of compensation in return for granting the privilege of conducting excavations and other in-country investigations (Command Briefing, JTF-FA, 2000).

Once permission to undertake fieldwork in a given country has been secured, recovery operations can commence. Each JFA is divided into two groups, an Investigative Element (IE) and a Recovery Element (RE); normally, the IE work occurs first. One task of the IE is to continue the process of information gathering begun at the archival research stage.

It gathers additional circumstantial evidence and interviews any local villagers who may have witnessed an aircraft crash or who may know of a burial site containing American remains. Like the earlier methods of gathering information, these interviews are sensitive to the need for the independently verifiable information required to remove a name from the list of the missing. When investigating an aircraft crash site, for example, members of the IE pose both open-ended and case-specific questions about when the aircraft went down, what the aircraft looked like, what the Americans in the aircraft looked like, and what events led to and immediately followed the crash (Heussner and Holland, 1999). At this point, continuity between archival information and the early evidence collected in the field is required if the recovery mission is to proceed to the excavation stage. The work of the IE thus not only contributes to the archival research performed in the United States, but also serves to verify the accuracy of that information. The IE determines whether the site under consideration for excavation is indeed the place where a plane was known to have crashed or where bodies were known to have been buried and, further, whether such information correlates to the missing soldier(s) under investigation during that JFA.

All of these initial judgments and the decision to proceed to excavation depend on the IE's knowing with some precision the location of the site to be excavated. Hence, to the gathering of information is added the IE's second function, that of pinpointing the coordinates of the site in question. This element of the search often presents some of the greatest difficulties in the accounting process. In many cases the extremely rugged nature of much of the terrain in Southeast Asia and the dense jungle foliage complicate the search. Indeed, even during the war itself it was very difficult, despite almost immediate search and rescue missions, to locate the site of an aircraft crash or other incidents of loss. A gap of thirty years obviously compounds these initial difficulties. In other cases, trouble locating a site for excavation stems from the inadequacy of information about where the incident of loss occurred, and this despite the extensive research that occurs even before a search and recovery team deploys to Southeast Asia.

An example illustrates these difficulties. On March 20, 1968, an Air Force pilot took off from Thailand bound for Khe Sanh in South Vietnam. The last radio contact with the pilot occurred at 2:35 P.M., and radar contact was lost twenty-five minutes later. At no point did the pilot indicate he was experiencing either mechanical difficulty or coming under enemy fire, and no Mayday! signal was broadcast. When the pilot failed to report to his intended position above Khe Sanh or return to base in Thailand, an electronic search was conducted over his planned flight path, which included part of eastern Thailand, the Lao panhandle, and western South Vietnam. Nothing was found. Given that his last radio contact occurred when he was over Laos, it would appear his plane crashed in that country, though he might just as easily have ventured into Vietnamese airspace or been over Thailand before experiencing difficulty (U.S. Congress, House, 1976: 200–201). Even if archival research could determine the region of this aircraft's loss with some specificity, the IE would still have a considerable task before them in locating the actual crash site for excavation.

A further difficulty in locating aircraft crash sites derives from errors in the coordinates of a particular incident of loss. In some cases, such mistakes were made by other pilots in the area at the time. Upon witnessing the crash of an aircraft, these other pilots would often attempt to mark their position, sometimes by placing their index finger directly on a map as they continued to fly. Needless to say, this method of recording the location of an incident of loss has not always proved to be especially accurate, particularly for purposes of locating a crash site on the ground. While attempting to mark his position, the pilot may himself have been flying a damaged aircraft, might have been attempting to avoid antiaircraft fire, or was perhaps simply mistaken as to where he was at the time of the incident. As a result, a second pilot's report of where he thought an incident of loss occurred is not always sufficiently accurate for subsequent accounting efforts (Command Briefing, JTF-FA, 2000). Furthermore, while specific grid coordinates do exist for a vast number of wartime aircraft losses in Southeast Asia, problems arise when these coordinates represent nothing more than the last-known or best-known position of the missing aircraft—for example, the end of the runway from which a fighter jet last took off—rather than the site of the crash itself. Such obstacles have long been recognized as endemic to any accounting effort that might be undertaken on behalf of missing personnel in Southeast Asia. As noted in the final report of the House select committee in 1976, "Sites listed as unknown are not likely to be found except in those cases where indigenous persons witnessed the crash or later observed the crash site" (U.S. Congress, House: 207). Understandably, the passage of decades between the date of the incident and the arrival of search teams not only magnifies the problem but makes American reliance on the knowledge of Southeast Asian villagers even greater.

At one level, of course, the work of the IE ensures the efficiency of the search effort in Southeast Asia, given that it would be an obvious waste of resources to send an excavation team to a site at which there were, in fact, no recoverable items. Additionally, however, the IE continues the process of specifying the conditions required for the materialization of the body of the accounted-for soldier. Research and investigative work in-country ensures that clues discovered in the field correspond with the information gathered in the archival research process, all of which, as will be seen, make a unique contribution at the identification stage. More precisely, the body of the missing soldier comes to be more clearly formed as the IE becomes more accurately informed as to the particulars of the terrain and the location of the site. By the time a JFA deploys to Southeast Asia, they know exactly who it is they are looking for and a great deal about the additional information that will most likely be discovered when they get there. If the discoveries made by the IE were to prove to be totally at odds with the archival research that brought them to the site in the first place, the materialization of that missing soldier's body would of necessity come to a halt because of the inadequacy of the knowledge produced by the two processes. While such knowledge might eventually prove useful in the resolution of other unaccounted-for cases, the missing soldier in the case under consideration could not but remain missing.

Should the IE succeed in locating the site under consideration and recommend that it be excavated, JPAC then makes a final determination to proceed based on weather conditions, safety considerations, and the availability of equipment and personnel. An RE is then sent to the excavation site. A typical recovery team in Southeast Asia is composed of a team commander at the rank of captain, an anthropologist who supervises all excavation activity, a noncommissioned officer in charge at the rank of sergeant first class, various mortuary affairs specialists, medics, and a photographer. Additional personnel, such as an explosive ordnance technician, a linguist, and an aircraft wreckage analyst may augment the team when deemed necessary by JPAC ("Not to be Forgotten": 6; Heussner and Holland, 1999). In early 2003, likely in response to the increasing difficulty of finding anything at all during the excavation process, dogs trained to detect human remains were added to the recovery teams (Redmann, 2003). The team commander is responsible for training, preparation, deployment, operation, and the return to the United States of the RE; further, he is the senior person in-country responsible for interacting with foreign government officials, ambassadors, and members of the press (Heussner and Holland, 1999). The noncommissioned officer in charge ensures that the RE deploys with the proper equipment and coordinates the procurement of necessary personnel, which for virtually all excavations includes local civilians, who help excavate the site and sift through the soil. The senior anthropologist ensures the scientific rigor of the excavation conducts spot checks at various points during the excavation, and ultimately determines where to dig and when to stop (Heussner and Holland, 1999).

In many cases, once the difficulties of locating a site have been resolved, a new obstacle arises: getting the RE to the site. Sometimes, especially in Laos where infrastructure is poor, transportation by helicopter is the only means of reaching a site, and even that option may leave searchers still a distance from the excavation. Other sites require lengthy expeditions across rugged terrain or climbs up steep, mountainous terrain.[4] Arrival at the excavation site, however, does not necessarily bring an end to the hazards faced by members of the RE. Searchers must also be wary of venomous snakes and tropical diseases like malaria and other water- and food-borne ailments. Jet fuel sometimes lingers in the soil surrounding a downed aircraft, requiring searchers to climb out of the excavation pit periodically to rinse off their skin (Butler, 1995: 62). Live ordnance in and around the excavation site, including unexploded bombs, shells, grenades, mines, and rockets, poses a special danger. In Vietnam, the RE must negotiate financial compensation in return for permission to excavate (Heussner and Holland, 1999). In Laos, the RE must make arrangements with the village shaman, including sacrifices and other offerings, to clear the ground of spirits prior to an excavation ("Laos-MIAS," 1999).

Like any archaeological dig, the excavation itself is an exercise in scientific precision, one that requires carefully coordinated efforts. Before the digging begins, the site is marked off in a grid system of four-meter squares with pegs and twine so as to record the specific location of any recovered items. Excavation of the soil by hand then begins.[5] Workers dig each grid down to a predetermined depth, place the soil in buckets, then pass the buckets one by one to the screening stations. At the screening stations, all soil from the buckets is poured onto a wire-mesh rack and sprayed with a jet of water to rinse away the earth from any human remains or other valuable debris. The screens are replaced if they develop a hole larger than one quarter of an inch; a larger hole could mean the loss of a tooth, which could in turn make the difference between identifiable remains and mere bones (Sheehan, 1995: 81). RE searchers also record the location of any recovered object that might prove useful for identification.

What begins to emerge from the excavation, under ideal circumstances at least, is an even more detailed picture of the incident of loss under consideration and, consequently, a more precise correspondence between archival evidence and evidence discovered in the field. If, for example, a pilot lost in an aircraft crash was thought to have gone down with the plane, then searchers expect to find not only human remains but also pieces of the cockpit, articles of clothing worn close to the body, the parachute harness, and wreckage from the ejection system. The absence of such clues might suggest an entirely different set of circumstances than those believed to be pertinent to the case. If, for example, searchers lack any prior knowledge of whether a missing pilot ejected from his aircraft before the crash, the absence of ejection system parts in the excavation pit suggests he did, in fact, eject and, further, that his body may have ended up a great distance from the site of the crash. The careful cataloging of the location of items recovered from the excavation pit affords a clearer picture of the missing soldier, but their spatial distribution in the soil is also important. If the pilot was believed to have been in the aircraft at the time of the crash, then the discovery of pieces of fabric from a pilot's suit suggests areas within the excavation pit that might yield human remains. Under the guidance of anthropologists and other experts, searchers will thus carefully excavate the areas around a discovery of this kind until no more items of significance are found, a technique designed to minimize the possibility of missing an item that could prove crucial to an identification. RE specialists stationed at the screening stations are the only ones authorized to discard items left on the screen after the rinsing process. Given the length of time between the incident of loss and current recovery efforts, separating human bone from animal bone, for example, is not always a simple task. Anything that looks even remotely like human remains is therefore returned to the laboratory in the United States for further analysis (Command Briefing, CILHI, 2000).

In general, the quantity of items recovered from a given excavation is quite small, in part because the ideal conditions that permit an accurate picture to emerge from the excavation pit are only rarely present in Southeast Asia. Such difficulties are the result of several factors. First, the effects of time and climate are significant. Monsoon rains and ensuing shifts in the soil, the spread of root systems, and the scavenging of human remains by animals over a thirty-year period conspire in many cases to displace both wreckage and human remains over a wide area (U.S. Congress, House, 1976: 204). Soil in Southeast Asia is more acidic than soil in temperate climates, thus hastening the decomposition of bone, fabric, and metal. A second difficulty, and still more troublesome from the standpoint of forensic science, is the extensive prior scavenging by humans of aircraft crash sites and other locations possibly containing the remains of unaccounted-for soldiers. The reasons for such activity are numerous, but in a great number of cases stem from the awareness of Southeast Asian people of the strong desire of the United States to repatriate the remains of its KIA. Virtually all sites pertaining to unaccounted-for Americans have thus been extensively scavenged. Remains are then offered for sale either directly to the United States or to Vietnamese boat people by remains traders who convince them that possession of such remains will gain them automatic entry into the United States.[6] Aircraft crash sites present an additional bonanza because pieces of the downed aircraft can be sold as scrap metal.

Other motives for disturbing a site are commendable. For example, local villagers may wish to give the dead a decent burial regardless of nationality or wartime circumstances. No matter the reasons, such problems make an already difficult job infinitely more complicated. As one searcher remarked after enumerating these sorts of difficulties, "It's a wonder that we find anything" (in Sheehan, 1995: 82). Yet the significance of scavenging is not limited to its impact on the quantity of items recovered at excavation. Scientifically speaking, each site has its own story to tell, the interpretation of which depends not only upon the quantity and type of items in the excavation pit, but also upon their spatial distribution and the extent to which they can be correlated with information already known about the missing soldier in question. Disturbances of the site disrupt the chain of evidence and potentially impact the chances of a positive identification.

Given an accounting protocol that requires identifiable remains in order to remove a name from the list of the missing, by far the most important items recovered during any JFA are obviously human remains. Yet this objective foregrounds what is often the largest obstacle to the success of the accounting effort: the extreme fragmentation of the missing soldier's body. Virtually all excavations in Southeast Asia share this trait in their failure to yield bodies in the sense presupposed by a list of names. Further, in the vast majority of cases (particularly as the effort to account for the missing continues and the easier cases are resolved), the amount of human remains recovered during any given JFA is decidedly small. These circumstances raise some not insignificant issues within the conceptual commitments of the accounting protocol. As indicated earlier, an accounting for missing Americans in Southeast Asia can be obtained either through the return of a live body to the United States or through the repatriation of identifiable remains. Given that no living soldier whose fate was not already known to the United States has returned from Southeast Asia since the end of hostilities in 1973, the return of identifiable remains is of absolute centrality to the accounting process. Consequently, despite their fragmentation the remains recovered at excavation make a tremendously important contribution to the body of information being assembled about the missing soldier. They mark the most important indication yet that said soldier crashed or was buried at this particular spot. Almost by definition, the discovery of remains means that the RE has found the soldier for whom they were looking. Yet the word *almost* simultaneously takes up an enormous amount of space within the politics of the U.S. post–Vietnam War accounting effort. Given that removal of a name from the list of the missing requires a positive identification, no matter how substantially these fragmented remains contribute to a body of evidence about a particular missing soldier, that body cannot be the same body that appears on the list of the missing. The remains discovered at excavation remain only so many disparate, conclusive-yet-inconclusive indications of the return of the soldier whose long absence has occasioned so much anguish and grief. The body in question is so close and yet so far.

Consequently, despite the strong circumstantial evidence provided by the recovery of remains, additional laboratory procedures are required in order to unify the body of evidence with the body of the soldier on the list of the missing. Only at this point can the missing soldier be considered officially accounted for. Further, only then can the fragmented remains of the body discovered at excavation become the same body mandated by an accounting effort based on a list of the missing. Should the remains prove unidentifiable, they are remanded to their original status as so many undifferentiated and ultimately inconclusive artifacts recovered at excavation. Accordingly, to identification is left the task of transforming these diverse and uncertain fragments of a body into one that functions intelligibly within the conceptual commitments imposed by a list of names. Only then can the search be considered a success.

IDENTIFICATION OF REMAINS

Upon recovery in Southeast Asia, all human remains plus related personal effects, wreckage, and other debris are turned over to the CIL. Thus begins the often lengthy and frequently uncertain process of affixing a name to the fragmented remains discovered in the field. CIL anthropologists and odontologists analyze skeletal and dental remains and other repatriated artifacts and then correlate their findings with information obtained from archival research. For all identifications, CIL requires that the anthropologist attempting identification in the laboratory be different from the one who worked on the case in the field. This precaution is designed to eliminate bias that may incline the anthropologist toward an identification not supported by scientific evidence. As a result, laboratory scientists begin their analysis with a set of remains about which they know nothing in advance, including the number of bodies represented thereby. Only later in the identification stage will their findings be compared with previously gathered information on the missing soldier in question.

From a forensic standpoint, positive determination of the identity of human skeletal remains usually proceeds through a combination of three analyses: skeletal, dental, and DNA. Many of the same problems encountered at excavation are present at the identification stage as well. The extreme fragmentation of recovered remains renders skeletal analysis inordinately difficult. Put differently, problems in identifying skeletal remains have to do not merely with quantity but also with quality. Roots from tropical vegetation bore their way through the porous bone tissue, causing premature decomposition, while insects and gnawing by animals also speed the breakdown of bone matter. Bones become extremely fragile because of surface flaking, pitting, natural weathering, and other types of erosion, further complicating analysis of their unique characteristics (U.S. Congress, House, 1976: 204–05).

Nevertheless, analysis of recovered bone fragments is a vital part of the identification process. To begin, CIL anthropologists prepare a biological profile for the remains that seeks to establish certain basic facts about them, including the number of individuals represented in the set, their age, race, sex, muscular structure, and stature. The biological profile also includes indications of antemortem, postmortem, and perimortem injuries (that is, those suffered during the actual death-causing incident) and any characteristic abnormalities ("Not to be Forgotten": 10). Antemortem injuries can be especially useful for identification purposes. If a missing soldier's medical record contains X rays of a broken bone and that same bone is recovered at excavation, scientists are that much closer to establishing identity. Long bones are helpful in reconstructing data on height, weight, and anatomical structure, while vertebra and even ribs can offer clues because of their uniqueness. Ribs may be useful because routine antemortem lung X rays taken by the military provide crucial points of comparison (U.S. Congress, House, 1976: 170). Once this profile is completed, the anthropologist compares the characteristics to known information about the individual contained in CIL's archives.

Occurring simultaneously with the study of skeletal features is analysis of recovered teeth. CIL forensic odontologists begin by examining and taking X rays of all recovered dental remnants and documenting any restorations or other unusual characteristics. These findings are entered into a computer program called Computer Assisted Post-Mortem Identification, or CAPMI, system, which contains the dental records of all unaccounted-for U.S. service personnel from the Vietnam War. The computer then compares the dental profile of the recovered remains with all profiles in the database and generates a rank-ordered list of names whose dental profile matches that of the missing soldier. Using this information, the odontologist then consults the original dental records from the archives and physically compares the records to the recovered dental remains ("Not to be Forgotten": 10). Despite the increasing use of DNA analysis to make identifications, teeth remain the holy grail of remains identification (Smiley, 1996: 21). Teeth are the most indestructible parts of human anatomy and thus retain their unique characteristics the longest, and these same characteristics are almost always found in the missing soldier's antemortem medical record. This is especially true if X rays and other records exist for dental work the soldier may have had during his lifetime. A filling in a recovered tooth, for example, presents a precise profile under X ray examination, a profile that can be compared to the antemortem record. If a sufficiently unique characteristic exists, positive identification can be made with a single tooth (Command Briefing, CILHI 2000).[7]

The final method through which positive identification of remains can be made is through mitochondrial DNA (mtDNA) analysis, a process used in an increasing number of identifications. While analysis of human DNA has proved extremely useful in determining the identity of Vietnam War remains and has also been used in a number of high profile criminal cases, contrary to widespread belief it is not the answer to all problems of ancient and fragmented remains identification. Why not? First, because there are two types of DNA in the human body, nuclear DNA (nucDNA) and mtDNA. NucDNA is found in the nucleus of human cells, and there is one nucleus per cell. Akin to a fingerprint, it gives a profile unique to the individual in question when extracted and sequenced. MtDNA, on the other hand, is found in the mitochondria of the cell, of which there may be hundreds or even thousands per cell. MtDNA is passed down through the generations and is thus not quite like a fingerprint in its uniqueness. Consequently, even though it is easier to extract a profile of mtDNA from a small quantity of tissue or fragmentary skeletal remains (simply because there is more of it), nucDNA analysis is preferable as an identification technique because of its fingerprint-like uniqueness. Both mtDNA and nucDNA analysis, however, require an antemortem DNA sample from the dead person in question to which they can be matched. Since there are no antemortem DNA samples for Vietnam War soldiers, nucDNA cannot be used in any identification regardless of the quantity or quality of the skeletal remains retrieved at excavation.

MtDNA is passed through the generations on the maternal side of an individual's family. The genetic profile obtained from a sample of recovered remains can thus be compared to that determined from a tissue or blood sample provided by someone on the maternal side of the missing soldier's family. Problems arise, however, when no maternal relative from the missing soldier's family exists or when a relative is unwilling to give a sample. Accounting for missing soldiers who came from small families and may no longer have relatives on the maternal side or— more difficult still—for adopted soldiers for whom no information of biological parentage exists cannot be achieved through mtDNA analysis because no definitive comparison can be made. Nevertheless, owing to greater awareness of the need for samples from family members, CIL can proceed with mtDNA analysis on an increasing number of remains of unaccounted-for service members, including those from the Korean War and World War II.

To perform mtDNA analysis, laboratory scientists cut a six- to eight-gram sample of bone from the recovered remains. The sample is sent to the Armed Forces DNA Identification Laboratory (AFDIL) in Rockville, Maryland, for extraction and sequencing, a procedure that determines the genetic profile of the remains (Gromer, 1994: 45). However, still another difficulty with DNA analysis presents itself at this point. The extraction and sequencing procedure requires that the bone sample be ground to a fine powder, meaning, of course, that it is a destructive process. As a result, there will always be at least some cases in which DNA analysis cannot be considered as an identification technique because it requires destruction of recovered remains, a circumstance quite at odds with the U.S. desire to repatriate the remains of its missing service personnel. To ensure there will be something left of the remains after removal of the bone sample, CIL will attempt DNA analysis only in cases for which a sufficient quantity of remains have been repatriated.

When the genetic profile of the sample is compared to that of the family member, a final problem occurs. Because mtDNA is passed maternally, it does not, like nucDNA, function like a fingerprint. Unavoidably, then, scientists cannot be 100 percent certain that a profile confirms identity simply because it matches the profile of a family member. In one case, for example, genetic scientists at AFDIL extracted an mtDNA profile from a missing soldier's remains that matched the genetic profile of 13 percent of the population (Command Briefing, CILHI, 2000). While almost indicative of identity, DNA analysis by itself is not quite indicative enough. Like the uncertainty encountered at the excavation site, that of DNA analysis forces its way into the space between unaccounted-for and accounted-for, between the body in the laboratory and the body named on the list of the missing. This is why DNA analysis is not the solution to all remains identification problems, and why teeth are considered the "mainstay of the identification process" ("Not to be Forgotten": 10). Highly scientific though it may be, DNA can only make a circumstantial contribution to the identity of a missing soldier.

Upon completion of laboratory analyses of the remains under consideration, the anthropologists who performed the work present their findings to the CIL scientific director, who compares them to the archival information ("Not to be Forgotten": 11). The scientific director decides whether the evidence supports a conclusive determination of identity, a determination that will in turn be subject to numerous levels of review to verify both the accuracy of the scientific findings and to combine those findings with archival data so as to build as conclusive a case as possible in support of a positive identity. If the evidence supports identification, the scientific director compiles an identification case file. That file is sent first to the commander of CIL and then to the director of the Casualty and Memorial Affairs Operations Center (CMAOC) for administrative review and comment. The CMAOC director in turn sends the file to the Mortuary Affairs Office of the branch of service in which the now-identified soldier served, which in turn notifies the family of CIL's findings. For reasons that will be seen below, the family is under no obligation to accept CIL's findings and has the right to select an outside laboratory to review the determination of identity. Should this occur, the case is sent to the Armed Forces Identification Review Board (AFIRB), composed of senior military officers from each branch of the service who decide either for or against CIL's findings. Upon acceptance of the remains by the family, they are transferred to a location selected by the family for burial with full military honors ("Not to be Forgotten": 12).

Or at least hopefully. While this overview of the remains repatriation and identification process suggests an impressive amount of attention to detail and an almost obsessive preoccupation with the accuracy of the identities arrived at thereby, no discussion of CIL can be complete without discussion of the political and historical circumstances that have dramatically affected its procedures and personnel over the years. Not surprisingly, the body has been at the center of what have often been exceedingly fervent debates over the accuracy of identifications and, by extension, over what constitutes a body in the first place. On the one hand, the problems have stemmed from the fragmentation of the remains recovered in Southeast Asia. Simply put, complete skeletons are never recovered at excavation, meaning the issue concerns bodies that are only relatively present at best. Even with this recognition in place, however, the magnitude of the difficulties imposed by fragmentation is imposing. According to testimony of the CIL before the Senate Select Committee on POW/MIA Affairs in 1992 (U.S. Congress, Senate, 1993: 295), a mere 1.3 percent of the sets of remains in their possession were more than three-quarters of a full skeleton; 23.9 percent were less than one-quarter of a full skeleton, and 4.5 percent were between one- and three-quarters complete (oddly enough, no mention is made of the condition of the other 70.3 percent of remains in their possession). Accordingly, what counts as a body from the perspective of the CIL scientific staff is any part of the remains that enables identification to be made. This can, as noted, amount to a single tooth or a similarly small fraction of recovered remains.

On the other hand, however, is the body which the families of the missing ideally want to return alive, or failing that, the dead body subsequently to honor and bury. As one military officer long associated with the accounting effort testified before Congress, "[Families] want them to walk out of the jungle and come home, but they will tell you very quickly that 'if that can't be the case, please end the uncertainty for me. Give me something so that I can put this to rest, I've been with it so long'" (U.S. Congress, Senate, 1993: 286). Obviously, a single tooth might not be exactly what the family had in mind when the remains of their loved one were identified, even if they admit that the alternative something might be a quite paltry quantity of remains. Worse, in the poisoned interpretive atmosphere of the U.S. efforts to account for its missing soldiers, identifications made on the basis of such a small quantity of the body have in some cases left families wondering whether the other parts might still be alive somewhere in Southeast Asia. The certainty allegedly provided by the materiality of the body is not always so straightforwardly achieved as the identifications supplied by forensic science might suggest, and that materiality does not necessarily result in the something desired by the families "so that I can put this to rest." Indeed, that materiality has long produced still more anxiety and has further complicated the question of what constitutes a body in the context of the accounting effort. Paradoxically, the massive effort at remains identification has, in some cases at least, done much to ensure that even the identified body will disable the quest for certainty which animates that effort in the first place.

The reasons for such undermining can be partially traced to CIL and its scientific procedures, which, during the 1970s and 1980s above all, were considered by some to be insufficiently rigorous and therefore not of the sort that could generate remains identifications of the desired certainty. At the center of these controversies was Tadao Furue, for years CIL's only physical anthropologist. A Japanese national with a bachelor's degree in science from the University of Tokyo, Furue came to Honolulu in 1977 and became a full-time civilian employee of the U.S. Army, a position in which he was more or less single-handedly responsible for determining the identity of remains recovered from all American wars. Furue's lack of either an M.D. or a Ph.D. in an appropriate scientific field—an issue that would later loom large in the eyes of those charged with evaluating CIL's scientific standards—was, at the time of his hiring, balanced by his broad experience identifying the remains of soldiers killed in action, something he had been doing for the United States since the early 1950s. So wide was his experience and so renowned had he become that "one physical anthropologist who has worked with Furue says that many members of their profession have far greater experience in other realms of knowledge—such as assessing the antiquity of remains dug up on archaeological sites—but that no one can hold a candle to Furue in identifying remains from the country's last three wars" (Sheehan, 1986: 91). Furue's skills were further attested by an absence of controversy surrounding his identifications. Indeed, "no relative of a Second World War casualty had ever questioned a Furue recommendation, and although the families of a number of Vietnam servicemen had asked to have his work reviewed by dentists or physical anthropologists, no dentist or physical anthropologist had ever overruled Furue" (Sheehan, 1986: 90).

Of course, it is hardly insignificant that families of Vietnam War missing were the first to question identifications performed by the Furue-led CIL, nor, in some respects at least, is it especially surprising. As we saw in chapter 2, the politics surrounding the issue of the missing have always been animated by the distinction between the (possibly) live body left behind in Southeast Asia and its dead counterpart whose remains had yet to be recovered. On these terms, the distinction between the two can be resolved only if either a fully formed American soldier walks out of Vietnam under his own power or if the remains of that soldier can be positively identified. That families presented with a single tooth were ever in a position to hold out hope that the remainder of the body to which that tooth belonged might still be alive somewhere in Southeast Asia is therefore very much a consequence of the contorted logic of the issue of missing American soldiers in the post–Vietnam War era. Moreover, the request by families of Vietnam War missing for verification of Furue's findings was invited by the language in which CIL has always articulated them. Presented as precise indications of the identity of the body thanks to the rigidly scientific nature of the process, identifications are eligible for outside review as little more than a matter of standard scientific protocol. Nonetheless, even the apparently innocuous practice of scientific peer review in the context of remains identification ran its share of risks. In those cases in which Furue's identifications were called into question, peer review was an example of the logic of certainty returning to haunt a process whose veracity had come to depend in the last instance on that certainty, the absence of which keeps the remains in question in that indistinct zone between the (possibly) live body and the dead one left moldering in Southeast Asia.

One example illustrates the tension over what constitutes a body in the context of Vietnam War remains identifications and the complexities that accompany a logic in which the certainty of those identifications is the sole standard by which their adequacy is judged. The case concerns the recovery and identification in 1985 of remains from a site in Pakse, Laos, where an American AC-1304 Spectre aircraft crashed in December 1972. Sixteen crew members were aboard when the plane took antiaircraft fire in its forward fuel tank and exploded in midair. Two men near the rear of the plane parachuted and were rescued; the arm and hand of a third were found by friendly Laotian forces and later identified as belonging to Captain Joel Birch, who was thus classified as KIA. The remaining thirteen crew members were listed as MIA. Significantly, in view of later events, a captured Laotian enemy soldier reported having found a pile of bloody bandages, five deployed parachutes, and the remains of five or six individuals near the crash site, remains which were later buried in a common grave. Of equal note was the discovery five months later of a symbol tamped down in the grass approximately three hundred miles from the crash site and reading either "1573 TH" or "1973 TH." The military believed at the time that this symbol was a code of the kind given to all American pilots to facilitate their rescue if they were shot down; further, they believed this code correlated to Lieutenant Colonel Thomas Hart, a crewman on the downed Spectre. However, all information about the bloody bandages, the five deployed parachutes, the common grave, and the symbol in the grass was classified (*Hart v. United States*, 1990).

In 1978, upon resumption of status reviews following the legal challenges mounted against presumptive findings of death, the thirteen crew members listed as MIA were reclassified as KIA/BNR, a finding with which Anne Hart, Colonel Hart's widow, agreed at the time. In keeping with procedures at the time, however, the classified information in the government's possession was not made available to either family members or the review panel. In 1985, CIL excavated the Pakse crash site, recovering over fifty thousand bone fragments as well as aircraft parts, personal effects belonging to the crew members, and other identification media. Four months later, primarily thanks to the work of Furue, CIL announced it had identified all thirteen crew members, in some cases via process of elimination and in combination with the circumstantial evidence, which suggested that no one other than the two crew members who parachuted to safety could have survived the crash. The review board from the Armed Services Graves Registration Office (ASGRO, the predecessor to today's AFIRB) accepted CIL's recommendation, and Anne Hart was notified that the remains of her husband had been positively identified. Hart, however, had bothered to do something which apparently no one in the U.S. government had, namely, the math. Sixteen crew members minus the two who parachuted to safety equals fourteen identifications required to account fully for the crew on board the AC-1304 that day. The missing man in this instance was Birch, whose arm and hand had been found the day of the crash. Hart reasoned that the other parts of Birch's body should also have been recovered at the time of CIL's excavation, thus generating fourteen rather than thirteen positive identifications. Further, the report concerning the five bodies buried in a common grave after the crash had not been considered when the identifications were made (largely because it was still classified), a fact Hart took as further evidence of the scientific and logical shortcomings of CIL's findings.

Suspecting that the identifications were arbitrary and by this time in possession of the government's classified information, which she had obtained through other channels, Hart filed suit to prevent the remains from being returned to their respective families until they could be examined by an outside source. The court granted a temporary injunction until the remains could be reexamined, this time by Dr. Michael Charney, a forensic anthropologist from Colorado State University. Contrary to CIL's findings, Charney concluded that, given the fragmentation of the remains, it was impossible to tell whether they were those of Colonel Hart or anyone else. Based on these findings, Anne Hart refused to accept the remains. In the meantime, the army decided to convene a civilian inquiry into CIL's identification of the remains recovered at Pakse. Three well-known forensic anthropologists, Lowell Levine, Ellis Kerley, and William Maples, spent three days at CIL reviewing Furue's work on a wide range of cases. Although the three scientists were able to conclude that "the administration of CIL was excellent and that CIL's personnel were dedicated, well-trained, and experienced" (*Hart v. United States*, 1990), they were more circumspect regarding the Pakse remains. In their words, "two of the bodies were acceptably identified, and there is no real reason to doubt any of the others. However, we did not feel that there was sufficient evidence to establish the other identities either" (in Sheehan, 1986: 92). In particular, they felt that Furue's identifications in this case "did not appear to be justified according to standard forensic methods and could not withstand scientific scrutiny" (*Hart v. United States*, 1990). Furue, for his part, stood by the identifications. Nonetheless, in view of the panel's findings the Air Force offered to reconsider the Pakse identifications, an offer accepted by Hart. ASGRO rescinded the identification of Colonel Hart on June 10, 1986.

At this point, the conflict between the body contemplated by the knowledge practices of forensic science for purposes of remains identification and the body required by family members in order to achieve certainty about the loss of their loved one comes fully into view. In other words, despite the painstaking, meticulous efforts made to recover and identify remains it is still possible that the body named on the list of the missing and that which later materializes in the identification laboratory may not be the same. The ambiguity occasioned by the bodies of missing soldiers remains. To make matters worse, CIL identifications that cannot be supported by prominent members of the forensic scientific establishment contribute much to the vitriol that has come to characterize that conflict. Indeed, the appearance of arbitrariness makes it seem that even the identified body is little more than a scientific conjuring trick designed to satisfy political imperatives rather than the needs and wishes of families of missing soldiers. Having said this much, however, these same forensic anthropologists did conclude there was "no real reason to doubt" the identifications of the Pakse remains. In other words, given the circumstances of the crash and the extensive commingling and fragmentation of the remains, it's a wonder any satisfactory identifications were made at all. There simply were no bodies available, at least not in the day-to-day phenomenological sense that animated those bodies when they left for Southeast Asia so many years ago. On this basis, it becomes clear that the occasional and often rancorous disagreement between the CIL and the families of the missing has less to do with the truth of the identified body (or lack thereof) than with conceptions of that body embraced by each. To put those conceptions altogether too simply, CIL is committed to discovery of who that body *could* be and no more, while the families of the missing are committed to an understanding of who that body *should* be and no less. These understandings, moreover, are an effect of the contentious legacy of the Vietnam War and the highly charged interpretive atmosphere that enables the (possibly) live body embraced by families of the missing and the body recovered at excavation in Southeast Asia identified by CIL.

Not surprisingly, the competing bodies featured in the U.S. effort to account for missing soldiers occasionally lead to behaviors that would otherwise be difficult to imagine. Further developments in the Hart case are again instructive. Given the government's accounting protocol, one might have expected that Colonel Hart's name would be returned to the list of the missing following the decision to rescind the identification of his remains. It was not, and no official explanation for the refusal was provided. Apart from whatever else was indicated by this decision, it created the impression that the government simply wanted the situation over with, a sense that dovetailed altogether too nicely with the possibility that CIL was offering up arbitrary identifications as a political expedient. That much of the information related to the Pakse crash remained classified until Anne Hart pursued legal action also fueled suspicion that the government had something to hide, in particular the possibility that Colonel Hart might have survived the incident and thus been left behind in Southeast Asia. The decision to keep him in the ranks of the accounted for despite having rescinded his identification thus seemed to confirm the worst as far as the families of the missing were concerned.

At the same time, many of Anne Hart's decisions in the aftermath of the rescinded identification speak to the flip side of the interpretive coin, the side exposed when the absence of certainty in the form of the identified dead body is taken as evidence of continued life despite substantial and compelling evidence to the contrary. Revealing here is Hart's decision to file a second lawsuit against the U.S. government, this time for intentional infliction of emotional distress brought about by CIL's knowing false identification of her husband's remains and by the government's refusal to return Colonel Hart to unaccounted-for status. Hart also asserted—though she was unable to prove so—that her husband was still alive, and she expressed her belief that the government's decision to retain Colonel Hart's accounted-for status would encourage his captors to kill him. The district court found in favor of Hart, a decision the United States elected to appeal. Significantly for Hart's claim that her husband was still alive, the appellate court took up the issue of the formerly classified material concerning the parachutes, the bloody bandages, and the pilot rescue symbol discovered in the grass. In particular, they pointed out that in 1976 the House Select Committee on Missing Persons in Southeast Asia had analyzed the Pakse crash and determined, first of all, that it was not clear either that the parachutes discovered at the site were flare chutes, personnel chutes, or drogue chutes or that they may have been deployed by the force of the crash. Second, the committee discovered that the bloody bandages were found ten kilometers from the crash site in an area where rival Laotian factions had recently engaged. Third, the DIA revealed to the committee their eventual determination that the symbols in the grass more likely originated with victims of a crash that occurred only five miles away rather than with those of the Pakse crash at a distance of more than three hundred miles (*Hart v. United States*, 1990).[8]

In spite of these findings, which were a matter of public record in 1976, Anne Hart not only chose to persist in her belief that her husband was still alive, but also leveraged it in her damage claims against the U.S. government, particularly its decision to consider her husband accounted for despite the rescinded identification of his remains. The irony here, of course, is Anne Hart's distress over the government's refusal to return Hart to the category of ultimate *uncertainty*, that of unaccounted for. At the very least, this circumstance is an instructive, if somewhat extreme, example of what can happen when certainty becomes the dominant epistemological and ontological orientation within the effort to account for missing American soldiers. Put forth as a matter of honor, duty, and principle, the United States offers the certainty of the identified body as a matter of humanitarian importance to the families of missing soldiers. In addition, certainty is presented as something which not only *should* be achieved but something which *can* be achieved if appropriately rigorous methods of forensic science like those detailed in this chapter are employed in the identification process. Articulated in this way, failure to produce the positively identified body quickly becomes a failed obligation, one that compounds the many failures that allegedly produced absent bodies in the first place. For their part, families of the missing are then quick to embrace the conclusion that the missing are being forsaken, since failure to produce the identified body must mean the missing are still alive. Given the conceptual underpinnings of the accounting process, no amount of circumstantial evidence can suffice for purposes of resolving the ambiguity of loss and absence. In this atmosphere, one final episode in the contentious history of the Pakse case seems almost perversely inevitable, a report that "Hart was captured alive in 1988, and a sighting of a 'Tommy Hart' was reported in Laos in the same year" (*Hart v. United States*, 1990).

As it happened, CIL did implement a number of procedural and personnel changes in the aftermath of the Pakse controversy. Although Furue was kept on as senior anthropologist, the army hired a board-certified forensic anthropologist to validate CIL's findings and a dentist with expertise in forensic odontology. Upgrades were also made to the laboratory's facilities and record-keeping capabilities (Sheehan, 1986: 92; U.S. Congress, Senate, 1993: 294). For present purposes, such changes are notable for the commentary they offer on the changing nature of the identified body. As the quantity of repatriated remains becomes ever more paltry and fragmented, the body in question becomes increasingly susceptible to either misidentification or failed identification altogether. As we have seen, this circumstance not only is inevitable as easier cases are resolved, but also has been widely recognized as endemic to the accounting effort practically since the beginning. Nevertheless, guided as that endeavor is by the quest for certainty, the options for the repatriated body are limited indeed, a factor that is only exacerbated when families of the missing refuse to accept circumstantial evidence as a determination of fate. The allegedly neutral epistemological posture of CIL's forensic science becomes enslaved to a set of political commitments with which it is ill-equipped to cope, namely, the quest to produce an outcome to the Vietnam War that resolves the many ambiguities to which that war gave rise. A vicious cycle is instituted, one that is impelled by the political agitation of families of the missing and fueled by the commitment of both the U.S. government and the forensic scientific establishment to assist in the resolution of those ambiguities. Depending on one's view of the effort to account for missing Vietnam War soldiers, the results are open to interpretation. What cannot be denied is that there is no longer any such thing as an identified body apart from the ontological requirements which compel its existence in the post–Vietnam War era.

Such requirements confirm this book's larger premise that the attempt to account for missing American soldiers goes well beyond the event of their absence and extends to broader political and cultural issues related to the defeat in Vietnam. Indeed, it is hardly coincidental that such an extraordinary effort to account for such a relatively small number of missing soldiers follows the only war the United States has ever lost. The exclusion of circumstantial evidence as a means of accounting, the enormous emphasis on the certainty of the identified body to remove a name from the list of the missing, the recriminations, accusations, and vitriol that ensue when such certainty is not forthcoming—all of this implies needs that can no longer be fulfilled by the pronouncements of those in positions of authority or, as arguably occurred following previous American conflicts, by simple acceptance of the inevitability of absent soldiers in the aftermath of war. After all, loss of the Vietnam War was due in large measure to the deceits and failures perpetrated by those very same authorities, a circumstance continually signified by the lingering absence of some number of soldiers. Accordingly, agents must be found, responsibility apportioned, guilt assigned, until—or even beyond the point at which—each and every absent soldier has returned home from the war in Vietnam. The quest for certainty, in other words, is now a war unto itself, a condition which has unavoidably resulted in additional casualties in the years since the withdrawal of American forces from Southeast Asia. As we shall see in chapter 4, those casualties are in many ways registered in the bodies of the soldiers who went to Vietnam and managed to make it back alive. As in the cases of the unaccounted-for body and the identified body, certainty remains a principle of intelligibility, though in a manner which suggests the Vietnam veteran will likely not assist us in our efforts to redress the many ambiguities of the post–Vietnam War era.

chapter four

"Our Stateside MIAs"

The Body of the Vietnam Veteran

This is probably the most capable and highly educated generation of veterans in history, with powerful latent motivation to contribute to the rebuilding of America, and their own society thinks of them as dregs and dropouts, dehumanized killers and drug addicts or pitiful victims of a hated war to be avoided and shunned.
—Quoted in Starr 1973: 32

In turning to the Vietnam veteran, I want to devote explicit attention in this chapter to a body that has not played anywhere near the same role as the repatriated and identified body in the post–Vietnam War United States. Indeed, the body of the Vietnam veteran has been largely excluded from the discourse of recovery and certainty which animates the effort to account for missing American soldiers and, by extension, the attempts by the United States to come to terms with the contentious legacy of the war in Vietnam. This is not to suggest, however, that the veteran has completely disappeared from view. As will be seen, the Vietnam veteran has been extensively analyzed, classified, and represented in the years since the end of the war. The difference lies in the nature of the analysis to which the body of the veteran has been subjected and, more precisely, in the degree to which that body has been deemed undeserving of the kind of solicitude extended to the unaccounted-for body.

The exclusion of the Vietnam veteran is therefore not a complete expulsion but a form of cultural degradation and a denial of entry into the realm of postwar politics within which the body of the unaccounted-for soldier is deemed eminently worthy.

Such exclusion, as we shall see, is not merely an incidental feature of the accounting for American soldiers missing in Vietnam but instead one of its constitutive elements. Because it bears traces of the wounds, divisiveness, and loss of the Vietnam War, the body of the veteran has become one over and against which both the body of the missing and that of the accounted-for soldier are defined. In particular, because the materiality of the accounted-for body is a definitive indication of one more returned soldier and, along with that, a certainty that one more step has been taken toward the cessation of the Vietnam War, the materiality of the veteran body offers certainty of a far different sort, namely, that which reinforces the loss of the war by indicating its continuation in the often maimed and dysfunctional bodies of its combatants. Nevertheless, I am not asserting that the accounting effort *causes* the exclusionary status of the Vietnam veteran. Rather, what I offer here is the more limited claim that meaning is derived from oppositions. Those oppositions are not discovered in nature but are a consequence of the struggle that accompanies the production of comprehensible statements. At issue on a broad scale is the ability to make sense of the Vietnam War, an event for which the United States lacked and in many ways continues to lack an adequate interpretive structure. Related to this is the intelligibility of the accounted-for body, the materialization of which lends interpretive coherence to the Vietnam War through resolution of one of the war's many ambiguities, that of the missing soldier. The struggle to create viable interpretive possibilities, of which the effort to account for missing American combatants is exemplary, produces as its opposite the body of the Vietnam veteran, that which is excluded as the defining limit of the body of the accounted-for soldier.

Another way to put this is to say that both the unaccounted-for and the identified body materialize within an "exclusionary matrix," one that "requires the simultaneous production of a domain of abject beings" (Butler, 1993: 3). The veteran has typically occupied this domain of the abject both during and after the Vietnam War, whether explicitly in the form of prisons and psychiatric wards or implicitly in the form of so many cultural stereotypes about the "demented vet" who brought the war home with him (Swiers, 1984). Read in this way, the body of the Vietnam veteran functions in the effort to account for missing soldiers by providing the opposition upon which the intelligibility of both the absent and the identified body depends. Production of this difference, furthermore, is not simply one among many moments in the materialization of the accounted-for body. Rather, it operates normatively through the instantiation of interpretive boundaries capable of firmly separating those bodies worthy of solicitude from those which are not.

The significance of such interpretive boundaries to the differential materialization of bodies is vast. As Judith Butler (1993: 8) has argued, "We see this significance most clearly in the examples of those abjected beings who do not appear properly gendered; it is their very humanness that comes into question." Likewise, the very humanness of the Vietnam veteran has itself been called into question. The author John Wheeler has even gone so far as to claim that "the Vietnam veteran was the nigger of the 1970s. You create a nigger by depriving a person of part of his or her personhood. Ignoring that person or inflicting traumatic hurts is the traditional way to treat a nigger" (in Jeffords, 1989: 74). In response, Susan Jeffords (1989: 75) has pointed out that "by translating nigger to include other than blacks subject to racism in America, [Wheeler] is denying the existence of a separation, such as black and white, that could distract from the formation of his collective" (75). The collective in this case is composed of men who, through the experience of soldiering, reaffirm that "there are things worth dying for," an affirmation Wheeler characterizes as "*the* masculine statement" (in Jeffords, 1989: 74). As this chapter will make clear, uncertainty about the ultimate worth of the deaths that occurred in Vietnam is precisely the point so far as the masculinity of Vietnam veterans is concerned. Indeed, a sense of impaired masculinity has informed our understanding of the veteran, tacitly justifying his presence in the psychiatric wards, the prisons, the Veterans Administration (VA) hospitals, and the detox facilities which have become repositories of the abject in the years following the Vietnam War. As a result, Vietnam veterans have often been shunted away from public life and have seen their legitimacy as warriors severely restricted.

Such factors have often led to the further deterioration of the public image of Vietnam veterans. Rather than engendering a national discussion on the deleterious effects of war upon surviving combatants, the discourse of the Vietnam veteran has primarily been framed by the image of the veteran as demented, altered by the experience in Vietnam and therefore unable to rejoin civil society upon the cessation of hostilities. The imagery persists despite the relatively small number of veterans to whom the category of the abject might apply. As a group, Vietnam veterans consist of approximately 3.1 million men and women who served in the Vietnam theater out of roughly 8.2 million people who served in the U.S. military as a whole during the Vietnam era, that is, 1964–75 (Kulka et al., 1990: 21). Of those who served in the Vietnam theater, 14 percent, or roughly 434,000 men, served in a combat capacity (Dean, 1992: 73). The figures are important because the image of the abject Vietnam vet with severe psychiatric and readjustment difficulties is drawn largely from the 14 percent who experienced combat rather than from the 86 percent who did not.

Not only were the vast majority of Vietnam veterans unaffected by the specific horrors of frontline combat, but many have assumed positions of prominence in the United States and, like veterans of previous American wars, have used their war record as a means of securing this legitimacy. Senator John Kerry of Massachusetts, Senator John McCain of Arizona, and former Senator Bob Kerrey of Nebraska (now president of the New School University in New York City) are among the well-known examples. Yet the successful readjustment of some veterans casts further, if tacit, aspersions on those who have been unable to adapt. The abjection of the Vietnam veteran becomes even more peculiar when we recall that unaccounted-for soldiers are veterans, too, as are the returned POWs. Far from being vilified in the manner befitting the stereotype of the demented vet, the POWs were enthusiastically welcomed by President Nixon's administration and by the American public. That such a welcome was an elaborate political exploit designed to consolidate President Nixon's claim to have secured "peace with honor" in Vietnam does not detract from the general observation that the Vietnam POWs have not historically been included among the veterans deemed a problem for the United States. Moreover, as discussed in chapter 3, unaccounted-for veterans are the beneficiaries of a massive publicly funded effort to repatriate and identify their remains. At the outset, then, attention is drawn to these factors to acknowledge that there is no such thing as a "Vietnam veteran" understood as a unitary and fixed body. Instead, the focus here is on when and how the Vietnam veteran is constituted. Such acknowledgment neither diminishes the salience of the abject veteran in the post–Vietnam War era, nor alters the frequency with which the abject veteran materializes in opposition to the body still missing in Southeast Asia. It does suggest that such materializations serve certain purposes and are therefore not just given in the nature of postwar things.

As we will see one of those purposes is intelligibility. In other words, the long-running and often intractable opposition between the body of the Vietnam veteran and that of the missing soldier has contributed much to how each has become known in the postwar era. This phenomenon is captured perhaps most succinctly in the words of one veteran, the founder of a homeless shelter, who claims, "There's half a million vets out there, what I call our stateside MIAs, most of 'em the sick and wounded from 'Nam, [and none of us] is gonna quit until the last one is present and accounted for" (in Solotaroff, 1995: 83). Among other things, this manner of describing the Vietnam veteran suggests the degree to which the intelligibility of the veteran depends on the loss embodied by those still missing in Southeast Asia. Long represented as the primary victims of the war in Vietnam—and in particular of the duplicity and weakness of the U.S. government—the absent unaccounted-for body becomes a heuristic device extended to the Vietnam veteran, an attribution all the more potent since the veteran actually made it back to the United States alive. By the same token, this interpretive possibility also implies that the absence of the veteran must be continually produced in the form of abjection in order to preserve the search for the missing as *the* domain in which the loss of the Vietnam War might be salvaged. To put this convergence slightly differently, the representing of the unaccounted-for soldier as the primary victim of the Vietnam War obscures the role of the United States in the creation and continuation of the conditions under which that soldier became absent and remains absent, while the disparaging of the Vietnam veteran allows him to be seen as the most material expression of the martial, masculine void that produced such absences in the first place.

The task here, then, is to analyze the persistence of the opposition between the debased veteran and the valorized unaccounted-for soldier, especially given the successful readjustment of the vast majority of Vietnam veterans. It also entails inquiry into the purposes served by the production of the Vietnam veteran as a debased remainder of the war in Southeast Asia; further, attention must be paid to how those purposes might be thought of in relation to the unaccounted-for body. No single explanation is available in this context. Consequently, I seek here not so much to determine the laws of the veteran's production but to thin out the now tightly intertwined interpretive thicket that has for so long enabled the body of the Vietnam veteran to achieve cultural intelligibility. This process begins by tracing some of the many representational strategies that have figured in the production of the Vietnam veteran as a means of historicizing the political pressure in the United States to differentiate between the living veteran and its dead, missing counterpart. Of significance here were efforts by the Nixon administration to drive a wedge between antiwar Vietnam veterans and soldiers held prisoner or missing in Vietnam, whom the president was presenting as the latest rationale for continuation of the war. Also of importance are Hollywood films, whose portrayals of Vietnam veterans contributed much to the cultural salience of the "demented vet."

First-person accounts of the war by returning veterans also did much to alter the traditional interpretation of the American fighting man. Significantly, given the political and social consequences that could reasonably be expected to ensue, a substantial number of veterans actively and publicly embraced self-representational strategies by which they located themselves among the barbarians and the imperialists. In particular, these accounts featured veterans *emphasizing* their role in the atrocities and extralegal violence in Vietnam as a means of illustrating what they saw as the essentials of American policy in Vietnam. Especially in light of the gilded narrative of the heroic fighting male of World War II, the image of the Vietnam War soldier could not help but come up short thanks to these accounts and to events like the My Lai massacre, the Tet offensive, and the ultimate loss of the war. As if these weren't enough, veterans' antiwar activism also played an instrumental role in tipping the interpretive balance against Vietnam veterans. Returned veterans joined the antiwar movement in substantial numbers in the late 1960s and early 1970s, even forming their own protest organization, Vietnam Veterans Against the War. These veterans were not reluctant to add their voices to the criticisms of a government in support of whose policies they had recently been sent to fight in Vietnam. However much one might applaud or condemn the antiwar activism of these veterans, there can be little doubt that individual protest events like Operation Rapid American Withdrawal (RAW), the Winter Soldier Investigation, and Dewey Canyon III did much to ensure that the Vietnam veteran would be produced as something entirely different from— if not the exact opposite of—the World War II veteran.

A further factor central to an understanding of the Vietnam veteran is the role of psychology and psychiatry as a means of knowing warriors and veterans and the effect these knowledge practices had on interpretations of soldierly masculinity. Specifically, while the accounted-for body has come to be known largely through the interventions of modern forensic science, the knowledge practices brought to bear on Vietnam veterans have more frequently taken the psyche as their point of departure. As we will see, by the time of the Vietnam War a comprehensive psychiatric discourse handed down from the world wars had become the primary means of interpreting and in many cases of treating the experiences of soldiers both in wartime and afterward. While psychotherapy was no doubt of assistance to many hundreds of thousands of American soldiers throughout various wars its manner of knowing military casualties led to an interpretive framework in which soldiers and veterans with adjustment difficulties were experiencing some deviation from a psychological norm. Whatever else this may have meant, it clearly both borrowed from and contributed to a discursive reservoir filled with such terms as *psycho, demented, crazy,* and the like, terms which could all too easily be marshaled in support of a distinction between the "good vet" who recovered from his wartime experiences and the "bad vet" who did not.

At the same time, these observations are complicated by what we know from World War II, namely, that veterans of that war suffered higher rates of psychiatric casualties and postwar maladjustment than Vietnam veterans. Yet it would be rather incongruous to invoke the stereotype of the demented World War II veteran (especially in the era of the "greatest generation").[1] Accordingly, issues of masculinity will here be proposed as a means of understanding the relationship between the loss in Vietnam and the persistence of the image of the abject Vietnam vet. Construed in this way, the defeat in Vietnam was owing not simply to the pathetically unsophisticated strategies of American policymakers and military planners, but also to a denigrated masculinity registered in the bodies of the soldiers who went to fight but failed to secure victory. As Jeffords (1989: 146) has argued, that failure has been consistently explained through "representations of the feminine, principally the stereotypical characteristics associated with the feminine in dominant U.S. culture—weakness, indecisiveness, dependence, emotion, nonviolence, negotiation, unpredictability, deception. Each of these inhabitants of blame in turn takes on and then repels some of these qualities." Accordingly, the production of the abject Vietnam veteran always includes the tacit ascription of femininity. Indeed, abjection itself acquires a gender, though here that gender refuses to respect the physical characteristics on which such determination is traditionally predicated. Instead, to be a Vietnam veteran of any gender is to be a loser in war, and to be a loser in war is to be emasculated, that is, shorn of those manly traits that had previously combined to produce the victorious American warring body. The feminine thus becomes that which has to be expelled for the war experience—and, by extension, masculinity—to be recouped.

In this light, the effort to account for missing American soldiers in Vietnam can itself be read as an effort to repel incursions of the feminine onto the terrain of the masculine. As he was during the war itself, the unaccounted-for soldier remains the good guy worth fighting for, irreproachable because he is not responsible for the loss—indeed, is one of its victims—and valorized as that which indicates the continued vitality of a body politic able to uphold that manly code whereby no soldier is left behind on the field of battle. Ceremonies that accompany the repatriation of remains from Southeast Asia suggest the point, suffused as they are with symbols of the nation, patriotism, and military honor and thus contrasting with the allegedly cool reception accorded to living Vietnam veterans upon their return to the United States. At the same time, the unaccounted-for body preserves the feminine as the characteristic responsible for the continued absence of American soldiers because that absence is due to the weakness, passivity, and duplicity of the U.S. government or the deceptiveness and treachery of the Vietnamese or both. The feminine becomes something to be overcome, an overcoming that is later registered in the repatriated, identified body that occasionally makes its way back to the United States—not coincidentally as a result of the heroism and soldierly dedication of the military's Joint POW/MIA Accounting Command and the scientists in the identification laboratory. In turn, the discourse of closure is enhanced, invested as it is in the relationship between repatriation of the absent body and cessation of the Vietnam War. The body of the veteran, by contrast, actively complicates such closure because of its implication in the continued presence of the defeat in Vietnam more than thirty years after the signing of the Paris Peace Accords. This departure from what it means to be an American fighting *man* thus stands as yet another principle of the veteran's intelligibility, one rendered all the more salient in the context of the effort to account for missing American soldiers and its status as *the* forum for the resolution of all sorts of post–Vietnam War issues.

The importance of an analysis of the body of the Vietnam veteran in the midst of a study of the effort to account for American soldiers missing in Southeast Asia now becomes more clear. In particular, the body of the veteran confirms the centrality of the epistemic and ontological terms identified in chapter 3. The need for certainty in the aftermath of the divisiveness and loss in Vietnam gives rise to the "fullest possible accounting" and its related epistemic regime in which the identified body functions as the sole measure of success. On these terms, the Vietnam veteran cannot assuage the need for certainty because the presence of its body is the re-presentation of the uncertainty of the Vietnam War. The task here, therefore, is to historicize the materialization of the abject Vietnam veteran and to chart the deployments of his opposition to the body of the absent soldier as a means of further specifying how the differential materialization of bodies contributes to the intelligibility of the post-Vietnam War era.

CONSTRUCTING THE VETERAN, PART I: NIXON AND HOLLYWOOD

As a means of tracing some of the specific ways in which the body of the Vietnam veteran has come to be known, it is helpful to chart the historical opposition between the veteran body and the body missing in Southeast Asia. Such mapping will illustrate the claim that the interpretive possibilities with respect to the veteran body are crucially shaped by their interactions with those of the missing body. As noted in chapter 2, much of how the unaccounted-for body came to be known during the later years of the Vietnam War derived from the Nixon administration's Go Public campaign and its effort to frame the issue of missing Americans as something for which the nation should continue to fight. In addition, the absence of the body became a fact for which some entity was to be held accountable, usually the Vietnamese, though later the U.S. government as well. The result was a body available for use in a number of ways, most immediately in terms of its liberation from imprisonment and return to the United States, later in terms of the repatriation and identification of its remains. More to the point, the absent body remained unsullied by events like the My Lai massacre and the indiscriminate application of technological violence against a dramatically underpowered foe; what is more, it was perhaps the only element of the Vietnam War about which Americans could feel a sense of satisfaction, even pride. Indeed, "neither a traitor nor a war criminal, the POW found himself 'perhaps the only hero of the Vietnam conflict,' and his 'warm and tumultuous welcome,' POW Robert Naughton later observed, created 'a unanimity among Americans which had been lacking during the long years of the Vietnam conflict'" (Howes, 1993: 9).

The welcome accorded American prisoners of war in the spring of 1973 also drew sustenance from the idea that the prisoners—and by extension, the American people—were victims of the cruelty and barbarism of the Vietnamese.[2] In this respect, the Go Public campaign makes yet another appearance, as do the numerous efforts by the Nixon administration to portray the behavior of the Vietnamese as unprecedented and uniquely barbaric. Such images served,

> for the American public at large, as distinctive evidence of the victimization of a segment of the American population. To the extent that the war in Vietnam is seen to be the cause of a general disillusionment with American government and ideals, POWs are taken to be emblematic of the American public as a whole, victims of a war it never understood. . . . Fears about the estimated twenty-five hundred MIAs possibly still being kept in camps create anxieties about the continuation of such victimization. (Jeffords, 1989: 121)

Seen in this way, the body unaccounted for in Vietnam is both an affront to the American sense of itself in the world and a material expression of the disaster that was the Vietnam War. Still more, the uncertain fate and whereabouts of those listed as MIA present the real possibility that that disaster will prolong the victimization of the United States well beyond the cessation of overt hostilities. Hence, a massive effort to ensure the return of the absent body becomes the paramount goal of the postwar years.

During this same period, by contrast, the Vietnam veteran was coming into view as one among many elements of the war which either could not or would not serve the purpose of salvaging a sense of achievement from the remains of the war. As in the case of the unaccounted-for body, however, this emergence was not an expression of antecedent truth about the veteran body, but rather the outcome of how that body had come to be known. Again, foremost among these schemes were efforts by the Nixon administration to actively discredit Vietnam veterans as they began protesting the war in large numbers. Most troubling from the government's point of view was the high level of credibility of veterans' perspectives on the war because of their experiences in Vietnam, along with the willingness of the veterans to lend authority to the antiwar movement through the establishment of such organizations as Vietnam Veterans Against the War. Not surprisingly, this factor presented unique challenges to the interpretive balance sought by the administration. Having seen the war firsthand, many Vietnam veterans concluded that the United States was fighting an immoral, unjust war. At the same time, the Go Public campaign meant that imprisoned soldiers were now the primary rationale for the war, and hence the need to continue fighting was simply a matter of supporting American troops. The latter possibility, however, raised its share of questions, especially with respect to Vietnam veterans who supported the antiwar movement: it was more than a bit difficult to embrace soldiers as something worth fighting for without also taking seriously their critique of the war itself (Lembcke, 1998b: 53).

The Nixon administration responded to this problem by attempting to discredit the antiwar movement by portraying it as alien and un-American and to split Vietnam veterans from the broader antiwar movement. A major part of this campaign was directed by Vice President Spiro Agnew, who routinely likened antiwar sentiment to support of the enemy and who characterized the leaders of the antiwar movement as "an effete corps of impudent snobs who characterize themselves as intellectuals" (in Lembcke, 1998b: 50). Countering antiwar sentiment, the administration proclaimed the week of November 9–16, 1969, Honor America Week, a time during which prowar veterans were to be mobilized in support of the war. The event included demonstrations by the National Guard, conservative organizations, traditional veterans groups, and reservists, all of whose activities were likened to "an atomic explosion of patriotism" (in Lembcke, 1998b: 54). The effect of this strategy was twofold. First, it placed before the American public the traditional image of the patriotic, prowar veteran, an especially trenchant representation given that the standard in question was the victorious World War II soldier. Second, mobilization of a conservative, prowar constituency enabled the Nixon administration to "reframe the debate from this-war-is-about-U.S.-objectives-in-Southeast-Asia to this-war-is-about-the-men-who-are-fighting-the-war" (Lembcke, 1998b: 51). As a result of these efforts, the status of antiwar sentiment was rendered increasingly tenuous. America's true war heroes supported the effort in Southeast Asia, while those opposed somehow fell short of the patriotic mark. Any form of antiwar protest became tantamount to a betrayal of the soldiers who were fighting on the nation's behalf.

A perhaps more telling consequence of these early efforts to garner support for the war and discredit the antiwar movement was the creation of a mythical opposition between the good vet and the bad vet (Lembcke, 1998b: 53). The good vet, of course, was the outwardly patriotic supporter of the war in Vietnam, a soldier who could be a veteran of any war but to whom could be attributed the stereotypically heroic qualities of the World War II soldier. The bad vet, by contrast, was explicitly a veteran of the Vietnam War who opposed continued American involvement in Southeast Asia. Within the good vet/bad vet mythology, disagreement with the Vietnam War was not viewed as a principled political stand reflective of the long-standing American tradition of loyal opposition. Instead, it was seen as a stance approaching a pathological condition afflicting returned Vietnam soldiers, one which called into question their patriotism and suggested that they had not been fit for soldiering in the first place.

Events in Vietnam and the United States alike redoubled whatever credence the image of the bad vet had already acquired. The details of the My Lai massacre, for instance, gained widespread publicity in late 1969. Polls taken in December of that year revealed that 49 percent of respondents believed stories of the massacre to be untrue: "'Our boys wouldn't do this,' said one man who believed America should get out of Vietnam. 'Something else is behind it'" (in Turner, 1996: 41–42). Irrespective of the will to disbelieve, an attitude arose in which "the assigning of 'madness' to and the blaming of veterans for crimes committed in a larger sense by the nation as a whole was to become commonplace" (Turner, 1996: 42). As did the continued absence of the unaccounted-for body, the blaming of the veteran for the crimes of the Vietnam War served certain purposes. Such sentiments "functioned as an alibi for America's political culture. It enabled Americans to feel it was a few 'crazies' who were responsible, rather than their government's policy or themselves" (Lembcke, 1998a: 192). Such arguments are striking because they suggest that, long before the conclusion of the war, the Vietnam veteran had become a site for the displacement of anxieties the war caused the United States. The slide from "our boys" to "crazies" laid much of the groundwork for the later image of the Vietnam veteran.

Hollywood reinforced such messages about the Vietnam veteran through representations that nearly always confirmed the emergent cultural configuration of veterans as crazies. Although the Vietnam War as a film genre is currently most well known for such films as *Platoon* (1986), *Full Metal Jacket* (1987), and *Hamburger Hill* (1987), in which combat scenes are explicitly featured, the first Vietnam War films all centered on the homecoming experiences of veterans. Films like *Taxi Driver* (1976) and *Coming Home* (1978) were two of the first and most trenchant interpretations of the post–Vietnam War experience. Noteworthy in these films is the depiction of the veteran as estranged from countrymen, kin, friends, and self. Early films also introduced Americans to disabled veterans, psychotic veterans at risk of acting out against society without warning, and returned veterans in conflict with the antiwar movement.

While these images play a leading role in the abjection of the Vietnam veteran, the issue is more complex insofar as the encounter between the veteran and the unaccounted-for soldier is concerned. Within noncinematic discourse the materiality of the veteran's body indicates irremediable impairment, whereas that of the unaccounted-for soldier represents the possibility of ultimate redemption. However, this opposition is not so straightforward in films featuring both veterans and missing soldiers. Indeed, many of these films, including *The Deer Hunter* (1978) and *Rambo: First Blood, Part II* (1985), point toward a correspondence of interests between the two in a manner that echoes the veteran shelter founder's likening of veterans to "our stateside MIAS." In implying the existence of a bond between the veteran and the missing soldier, these films reveal the degree to which their opposition within the interpretive commitments of the effort to account for missing soldiers is an enabling construction, one that contributes to the intelligibility of both.

Motor Psycho (1965) marks the beginning of what would become a distinctive disparaging of Vietnam veterans in which they were portrayed as radically altered by their experiences in Southeast Asia. The film's main character, Brahmin, who even at this very early date is shown to be psychologically traumatized by his experiences in Vietnam, terrorizes two couples before being killed by the husband of one of the women he has raped. *Motor Psycho* features Brahmin lapsing into delirious recollections about fighting the Viet Cong, thus prefiguring by fifteen years the flashbacks that would become a central tenet of post-traumatic stress disorder, the primary means of interpreting psychiatric difficulties among Vietnam veterans (Lembcke, 1998b: 149–50). The late 1960s also witnessed the first films about returned soldiers in conflict with the antiwar movement. The B-grade *Satan's Sadists* (1969) depicts a clean-cut Marine veteran named Johnny engaged in desert warfare with members of a motorcycle gang, who are portrayed as "peace-loving long-hairs." The lines of conflict are clearly drawn and yet remain contestable, in part because the technique "(mis)associates the anti-war movement and the violence of the motorcycle gang and (mis)associates the Vietnam veteran with opposition to the anti-war movement" (Lembcke, 1998b: 152).

Filmic confrontations between veterans and the antiwar movement continued in 1972 with the release of films like *Parades*, in which the mythic World War II veteran with no readjustment issues is displaced by "a more structural good vet/bad vet narrative in which the 'bad' identity of Vietnam veterans was developed through story lines that show them in conflict with 'good' veterans of previous wars, often their fathers" (Lembcke, 1998b: 149). At a minimum, such films set the stage for a confrontation over the assigning of responsibility for the loss of the Vietnam War. In addition, they reveal the degree to which Hollywood had begun parroting themes from the Nixon administration's counter-offensive. *Coming Home* is exemplary, featuring as it does the returned veteran who has difficulty adjusting and is in conflict with virtually everyone around him. A winner of four Academy Awards, the film relies on what by then had become customary stereotypes of Vietnam veterans. Bob, the main character, returns to find antiwar protesters awaiting his arrival at the airport; he immediately feels hostile toward them. Bob begins a long spiral into violence, spousal abuse, paranoia, and suicide attempts, the origins of which are implicitly linked to the encounter at the airport. Yet this rendering is substantially at odds with the great majority of Vietnam veterans' homecoming experiences. Further, such depiction skews what was for a long time a very important and close relationship between the antiwar movement and returned veterans (Nicosia, 2001).

Themes like those presented in *Coming Home* recur to varying degrees in many other films about Vietnam veterans, often in extreme form. *Deathdream* (1972), for example, depicts a veteran named Andy who returns from Vietnam as a vampire and brings the war home with him in the form of a killing spree that claims everyone in his family, including the dog. Despite the outlandish nature of the plot, the film did much to reinforce what was gradually becoming one of the dominant ways of knowing the Vietnam veteran. In particular, "The Andy who came home was some*thing* else . . . the incarnation of the political and cultural values of 'the other' that America had gone to war to kill" (Lembcke, 1998b: 155). "Andy was 'living' proof that the reality of this war was going to stalk America long after its end. Worse than the horror of death, Andy represented the living Vietnam veteran who embodied the death of America" (Lembcke, 1998b: 155). The importance of this representation of the Vietnam veteran is not limited to Andy's portrayal as a psychotic mass killer. In addition, it reveals the depth of the cultural compulsion to render the Vietnam veteran in terms that might somehow locate the defeat in Vietnam outside the conventional terms associated with the virtuous American warrior. Faced with a military defeat for which adequate interpretive possibilities were lacking, popular representations of the Vietnam veteran sought recourse in stories in which that defeat was the responsibility of the individual warriors who went to fight. Perhaps worse still, from the standpoint of veterans themselves at least, Hollywood films typically chose to articulate that responsibility in the vernacular of the crazed veteran who returns from Vietnam as "some*thing* else." These early examples suggest that the Nixon administration's distinction between the veteran and the soldier imprisoned or missing in Vietnam had permeated American culture more thoroughly than it could have ever hoped. Indeed, films from this period include virtually no representations of normally adjusted Vietnam veterans who returned from the war without substantial difficulty. Accordingly, although the immediacy of the Vietnam War begins to recede as the 1970s wear on, the effects of the war registered in the bodies of so many deranged veterans increasingly take center stage.

In light of these circumstances, the significance to Vietnam veterans of the political and cultural configurations of American prisoners of war in Southeast Asia can be seen with greater clarity. In particular, the displacement occasioned by placing blame for failure in the Vietnam War on the shoulders of its veterans meant that "when Americans contemplated the suffering wrought by the war, they began to think more of white men (mostly Air Force officers) in cages than of the grunts of all colors slogging through the jungle or of Asians being blown to kingdom come by earth-shattering B-52 raids" (Nicosia, 2001: 156). The overt political value for the Nixon administration was clear, especially since the "difference between the vets and GIs, on the one hand, and the POW/MIAs, on the other, was that the latter group were not in a position, at least for the time being, to gainsay the president's use of them as an excuse to prosecute the war" (Nicosia, 2001: 156). Such opposition between the veteran and the soldier imprisoned and/or missing in Vietnam became one of the means by which the Vietnam veteran would gradually secure intelligibility. The veteran was not only irrelevant to the larger project of securing the repatriation of missing Americans: he was an outright hindrance, opposed as he was to the continuation of a war whose express purpose was now articulated in terms of saving those still missing. This attitude, in turn, would mark the beginning of a general tendency in American political culture to disparage the Vietnam veteran as ultimately unworthy of the solicitude of the nation. From the beginning of veteran antiwar activism until the signing of the Paris Peace Accords, "Nixon would act as if the only players that mattered in the whole Indochina conflict, the only ones he was duty-bound to serve, were the silent figures behind the barbed wire — the 'daddies' who wanted to come 'safe, sound and soon' — the American POW/MIAs" (Nicosia, 2001: 157).

The conception of the unaccounted-for body was simultaneously furthered by representations of the Vietnam veteran, especially to the degree to which the body of the unaccounted-for soldier is seen as amenable to intervention by the nation. Because of the Go Public campaign, the bodies of the POW and the MIA are counted among those for whom the nation can and should act. Their absence constitutes an almost impregnable basis for their lionization, while as justifications for continuing the war they remain largely exempt from the hollow promises which had in earlier years posed so often as predictions of victory. The body of the veteran concurrently begins to materialize at precisely the opposite end of this spectrum. Perpetrator of heretofore unimaginable deeds, publicly opposed to the war, and, it begins to appear, fundamentally scarred by what it has experienced there, the body of the veteran has been consumed by the war and is unable to account for its role within the increasingly urgent need of the American public to salvage something approximating victory from a progressively disastrous, disorienting experience. There is no Go Public campaign on behalf of the Vietnam veteran, therefore, because his materialization as the other within the U.S. experience in Vietnam has rendered him ineligible for the sorts of moral and material concern proposed for POWs and the body unaccounted for.

CONSTRUCTING THE VETERAN, PART II: FIRST-PERSON NARRATIVES AND ANTIWAR ACTIVISM

While the opposition between the Vietnam veteran and the soldier unaccounted for in Vietnam cultivated by the Nixon administration and Hollywood in the later years of the Vietnam War played a crucial role in the production of each, the specifics of Vietnam veterans' opposition to the war were also of moment. In contrast to the antiwar movement generally, the opposition voiced by veterans often took the form of a confessional in which veterans publicly called attention to their personal role in the violence being perpetrated in Vietnam. Politically speaking, of course, this was a powerful strategy, one that highlighted the nature of the policies being implemented in the name of an American people deemed too ignorant to know better. Hundreds of veterans offered personal testimonies of atrocities they had either committed or witnessed in Vietnam, and, further, they insinuated that events such as the My Lai massacre were less the exception than the rule. Other veterans offered critiques of the war effort based less on the commission of atrocities than on the futility of the war's strategic underpinnings, the extent of the apathy among South Vietnamese for the American presence, and the absence of either a consistent or a convincing rationale for that presence. Still other veterans returned from Vietnam to an American people who seemed to them ungrateful, largely unaware of their readjustment issues, or outright hostile. The cool reception too engendered criticism because it accentuated the moral and political bankruptcy of the nation whose interests they had been asked or compelled to defend.

Taken together, the political activism of returned Vietnam veterans and the first-person idiom in which that activism was articulated refined the Nixon administration's characterization of Vietnam warriors as bad vets. For present purposes, however, the role of veterans' self-representations in the perpetuation of the good vet/bad vet opposition is less notable than how it figured the Vietnam veteran both during and after the Vietnam War. Such representations furthered the idea that the men returning from Vietnam were not only damaged by their experiences there, but likely unable to readjust to civilian life in the United States as a result of those experiences. Given the disinclination of Americans to see Vietnam veterans as being worthy of adulation, the self-representations could not help but aid in the production of the abject Vietnam veteran that had already gained such momentum in other areas of American culture.

Among the more consistent self-representations have been first-person accounts of combat experience. Such accounts often locate veterans' subsequent estrangement from postwar civilian norms in the disregard for life they were forced to adopt as a survival strategy in Vietnam. The difficulty of describing that disregard in terms intelligible to those who have never been in armed combat tends to structure veteran-civilian interaction in a manner that provokes mutual misrecognition. As a result, Vietnam veterans feel spurned by the very people whose interests they were asked to defend in war, while these same people see soldiers as little more than butchers who, for whatever reason, fell short of the standards of just belligerence that allegedly govern American warfare. This dynamic has become a standard means of characterizing the experience of Vietnam veterans and their relationship to the civilian world to which they returned. In this way, first-person accounts often complicate the effort to achieve critical distance on the veteran/unaccounted-for opposition by obscuring the successful readjustment of the majority of veterans and by confining abjection to the veteran and heroism to the accounted-for soldier. The following discussion of first-person accounts of combat in Vietnam and return to civilian life is therefore not meant to convey the truth of those experiences, whatever that may mean. Rather, it is intended to highlight how first-person narratives affect the formation of the Vietnam veteran in the years since the end of the Vietnam War. Just as the good vet/bad vet opposition cultivated by the Nixon administration helped produce the veteran as such, so the cultural intelligibility of the body of the Vietnam veteran derives much from how the experience of combat in Southeast Asia has come to be known.

Vietnam War stories begin with the subjects that accompany virtually all wars: the rites of initiation, the camaraderie, the fear and anxiety of battle, and coming to terms with killing another human being. Vietnam-era soldiers fresh out of basic training were no different from their forebears when it came to feeling prepared to meet the challenges of combat. In the words of one, "By the time you get to the end of that whole process, you feel like you're the baddest thing that ever walked the earth. When they call you Marine in the graduation ceremony, there's tears in your eyes. You are thoroughly indoctrinated" (in Baker, 1981: 22). Nevertheless, that indoctrination was of a kind, namely, it was that of the military and its peculiarly regimented lifestyle rather than of an ideological orientation in which soldiers marched off to a war whose mission was understood and interiorized. As one observer writes,

> The American soldier was not an ideological soldier. If he enlisted, he enlisted for primarily personal reasons. But beneath his lack of a specific commitment to the aims of the war lay a basic faith in the legitimacy of American institutions and a deeply ingrained sense of obligation. Although he typically knew very little and cared less about Vietnam beforehand, he took it on trust that he would be fighting with the "good guys" against the "bad guys." This trust sustained most of the drafted men as well as the enlistees. And it was this basic trust that would be severely tested, and in many cases shaken, by the war experience. (Starr, 1973: 9)

In the standard telling, then, the soldiers who went off to fight in Vietnam lacked what for their counterparts in World War II had been a sine qua non of the fighting experience: a readily identifiable enemy and clearly defined goals.

The above account points up an initial difference between the Vietnam War and others, but such divergences were not limited to ideological backing for the war in Southeast Asia. At issue too was the day-to-day experience of fighting the war. First-person narratives cite the difficulty of distinguishing friend from foe and stress that a basic confusion thus reigned in the American mission in Vietnam. As one combat veteran remarked, "You can't tell who's your enemy. You got to shoot kids, you got to shoot women. You don't want to. You may be sorry that you did. But you might be sorrier if you didn't. That's the damn truth" (in Baker, 1981: 193). As the line separating friend from foe began to blur, so too did the line delineating right from wrong. Soldiers were mystified by orders that prohibited them from returning fire or from firing on the enemy without first securing command-level permission. The idea that a military presence in a given area might at least render it secure for those who lived and operated there seemed laughably inapplicable in Vietnam, with consequences that were often nothing short of deadly. Even the search-and-destroy missions that formed the basis of the U.S. offensive strategy engendered acute feelings of vulnerability, especially among individual infantry soldiers: "In the search and destroy tactic he is, strictly speaking, the bait to catch the enemy. According to plan, he is intended to be a target, a sitting duck for the other side to attack at their ultimate cost. But the cost of action from the American perspective is inevitable casualties among GIS" (in Starr, 1973: 15). Again, the war story of the Vietnam combat soldier departs from the mythical version handed down from previous American wars. Soldiers in Vietnam were not defenders of liberty and freedom against the advances of an evil enemy, but cannon fodder. This impression became increasingly palpable as the war dragged on with no clear end in sight.

Another factor in the narrative of Vietnam War combat soldiers is race. In and of itself, the experience of fighting either among or on behalf of people of different races was far from unique in American military history, as the examples of the Philippine Insurrection and the Korean War amply demonstrate (Fleming, 1985). Still, in the standard telling, the racial animosities that animated the American reaction both to the enemy and to the people on whose behalf they were allegedly fighting were significantly more difficult to resolve in Vietnam than they had been in previous conflicts. The result is the enduring impression that American soldiers in Vietnam operated with a disregard for life that seemed to transcend the process of merely becoming hardened to war. As one American soldier would recall, "I don't understand when they talk about prisoners and stuff. We didn't go through that nonsense. I used to shoot them. We'd stand them up against the wall, put a gun to his head and say, 'Talk. If you don't talk, we're going to pull the trigger.' Or they take the man's wife or daughter and screw his daughter in front of him. And made him talk. If he didn't talk they would shoot the woman. Then shoot him. Taking a life was nothing. It was customary" (in Baker, 1981: 65).[3]

Such attitudes found their most horrific expression in the My Lai massacre of 1968, in which a unit of the Americal Division killed several hundred Vietnamese civilians. Although Lieutenant William Calley was later convicted of premeditated murder in connection with the killings, the incident created the indelible image of American soldiers gone crazy, literal monsters operating in a zone beyond law and morality. Still, Calley's conviction did much to reinforce the already powerful tendency of the American people and government to interpret the events of the war in terms of the shortcomings, depravity, and outright psychosis of individual soldiers. In turn, the U.S. government could deny responsibility for such events and the relative purity of the unaccounted-for soldier could be preserved. My Lai thus moved quickly from being an event to being a defining characteristic, one that assimilated the depravity of American conduct in Vietnam with the spoils of a lost war to produce the demented veteran detached from all societal moorings. Speculating on the reasons behind the events at My Lai is, of course, a delicate enterprise. What is certain is that the growing disillusionment with the American project in Southeast Asia at all levels of the military cannot have helped prevent such incidents. Apart from whatever effect the impact of declining morale had on the frequency of atrocities, there was the abiding sense that the war was no longer winnable and that the cause to which the United States had staked its claim in Southeast Asia was no longer valid. This, in turn, signaled the further deterioration of the heroic narrative as one of the war's interpretive possibilities. As one GI put it, "One of the first things you realized when you got to Nam was that you weren't going to win this war. There was no way we could win doing what we were doing. After the first month, me and everybody else over there said, 'I'm going to put in my twelve months and then I'm getting the fuck out of here. It's not worth it'" (in Baker, 1981: 95).

Not surprisingly, the combined effect of such circumstances greatly undermined the sense of meaning that might have alleviated the suffering and deprivation that are the concomitants of war. In addition, their subsequent effect upon those who fought in Vietnam and upon the United States as a whole can hardly be overestimated. The United States was faced with its first outright military defeat, an experience for which legitimate interpretive possibilities were lacking, while the nature of that failure and the reasons behind it meant that the need for some sort of interpretation was all the more urgent. Furthermore, the American people had long since reached a point of exhaustion with the war, meaning that the sort of national dialogue required to make sense of it would, at the very least, be delayed. Perhaps most important with respect to Vietnam veterans, the search for why the United States lost in Vietnam had many Americans on the lookout for scapegoats. The Nixon administration's enthusiastic embrace of the POWs and those unaccounted for, along with its efforts to separate returning veterans from the antiwar movement as a means of disparaging veterans' contributions to that movement, made it all the more effortless to see the Vietnam veteran as the embodiment of all that had gone wrong in Vietnam. As the political activism of Vietnam veterans became more vocal and more strident, the options for understanding the veterans and their experiences became decreasingly sophisticated and tended to coalesce around the unitary image of a soldier whose departures from the codes of American military honor were ultimately unredeemable.

These factors make the participation of Vietnam veterans in the antiwar movement all the more vital in that such activism deliberately assumed some of the most sordid elements of the first-person narratives and then put them on a national stage to challenge the American people, whom the veterans saw as too complacent to act to stop the war. The value of this tactic to the political effects of the antiwar movement was great, yet there can be little doubt that events such as Operation RAW, for example, presented a version of the Vietnam veteran for which many Americans were in some sense too well prepared, conditioned as they were by the Go Public campaign and Honor America Week. Organized by VVAW and conducted over Labor Day weekend, 1970, Operation RAW consisted of two hundred Vietnam veterans marching from Morristown, New Jersey, to Valley Forge, Pennsylvania. Along the route, veterans dressed in combat fatigues and actors hired for the purpose staged mock search-and-destroy missions in which the actors were subjected to the same treatment meted out to Vietnamese peasants who refused to cooperate with American soldiers. The actors were shoved, screamed at, trussed up by their wrists, and even held at knifepoint. Although no real weapons were involved, the scenes were vivid enough to distinguish unequivocally between the images of heroic warfare received from World War II and the unidealized, day-to-day nature of the fighting in Vietnam. Yet Operation RAW was not just shock theater. It was a critique of U.S. war aims designed to call attention first to the tactics employed by American troops (and, by extension, to the policies of the U.S. government), and second to the responsibility for such tactics and policies shared by every American who chose to remain silent. A typical speech following a day's march emphasized to spectators that such events were "something the Vietnamese experience every day—absolute repression, an infringement of all civil liberties—and it's done in your name. They're murdered and butchered by guys like us, who are carrying out the policy of this government, that you are allowing to continue. If you continue to remain silent, *you* are responsible" (in Nicosia, 2001: 65–66).

The march was a trenchant form of activism—indeed, it looks both courageous and ingenious over three decades later—but Operation RAW's critique of the Vietnam War took material form in the bodies of veterans who quite readily presented themselves as perpetrators of heretofore unimaginable deeds. Emphatic political critique was easily assimilated into the growing opposition between the veteran and the soldier unaccounted for. It was not at all clear whether the VVAW's message was received in the manner intended. Predictable reactions came from World War II veterans, for example, who taunted the marchers with cries that they join the Communists in Hanoi (Nicosia, 2001: 64). At this point, at least, Vietnam veterans were (probably unconsciously) paying a heavy price for their activism since in the process they so often confirmed the representation of Vietnam veterans being pedaled by the Nixon administration. In this light, the Winter Soldier Investigation of 1971 is another milestone in antiwar activism. Again, Vietnam veterans actively represented themselves in ways designed to stir revulsion rather than adulation. Held in Detroit in January, Winter Soldier featured more than a hundred veterans who gathered to testify about atrocities they had either witnessed or participated in in Vietnam. The investigation was designed not so much to determine guilt as "to take the all-too-available atrocity stories coming out of Vietnam and show their direct relationship to American policies" (Crandell, 1994). Americans became still more familiar with the tactics employed by American soldiers as "veteran after veteran described the training and orders that led to the murder of civilians" (Crandell, 1994).

Although the Winter Soldier Investigation was, like Operation RAW, an important instance of veteran antiwar activism, its litany of atrocities ran the risk of portraying such events as the fault of a few crazies rather than a direct result of American policy in Vietnam. The prevalence of one or the other of these interpretive possibilities notwithstanding, the Winter Soldier Investigation had a lasting effect on how the Vietnam veteran would come to be known. In one sense, of course, the idea articulated so commonly in the aftermath of the My Lai massacre to the effect that such crimes were committed by a handful of crazed soldiers could no longer be so innocently sustained. The Winter Soldier Investigation was instrumental in this change, being organized into "panels arranged by the combat units in which [veterans] fought so that it [would be] easy to see the policy of each division and thus the larger policy" (Crandell, 1971). By the same token, if atrocities were a direct result of policy and all soldiers were the executors of that policy, then each and every veteran had been an instrument of civilian death whether he had committed a crime or not. Accordingly, those who wished to preserve the sanctity of the American fighting man from previous wars and align themselves with the Nixon administration's bad vet from the Vietnam War were free to continue doing so. Indeed, "the picture that the Winter Soldier Investigation painted of 'our boys' was not pretty. These were not embraceable 'good veterans.' And because they weren't, the picture painted by Winter Soldier closed the gap between 'us,' the good guys, and 'them,' the evil-incarnate Asian others" (Lembcke, 1998b: 61).

Of the many events staged by antiwar veterans, perhaps the one that achieved the highest profile, was Dewey Canyon III. Dubbed "a limited incursion into the country of Congress" in sardonic reference to American operations in Laos and parts of Vietnam which bore the name Dewey Canyon, it was held in Washington, D.C., in April 1971 and featured massive demonstrations by veterans and civilian antiwar activists. The most powerful effect of the march, however, was not the number of protesters but the images of decorated Vietnam veterans throwing their medals and ribbons over a fence onto the steps of the Capitol. Some veterans declared their medals "a symbol of dishonor, shame, and inhumanity." Others dedicated the junking of their medals to fallen comrades, while still others used the occasion as a means of apologizing to the Vietnamese (Nicosia, 2001: 141). The act was simultaneously one of defiance, both of the military and the nation, and a further attempt to get the attention of the federal government and the American people. And while these objectives were arguably accomplished with greater success at Dewey Canyon III than at any previous moment of veteran activism, the event, like those before it, sharpened the opposition between the veteran and the soldier unaccounted for in Vietnam.

Taken together, Operation RAW, the Winter Soldier Investigation, and Dewey Canyon III provided numerous opportunities for the marginalization of the Vietnam veteran. In particular, "the grisliness of their testimony, combined with their willingness to indict their own government for war crimes, produced the ultimate 'otherization': these were not veterans, at least not *our* veterans. *Our* veterans were 'good' veterans" (Lembcke, 1998b: 62). The body of the veteran thus began to emerge in the late 1960s and early 1970s in opposition to the body of the unaccounted-for soldier, the foundational repudiation over and against which the *accounted*-for body would later assume such importance.

KNOWING THE VIETNAM VETERAN:
PSYCHOLOGY AND IMPAIRED MASCULINITY

Although much of the salience of the abject Vietnam veteran can be traced to the representational strategies of the Nixon administration, to the first-person narratives of veterans themselves, and to veterans' antiwar activism, the staying power of the abject Vietnam veteran also finds roots in historically constituted knowledge practices that have been brought to bear on the bodies of warriors generally and on those of Vietnam veterans specifically. The most prominent of these are psychology and psychiatry, disciplines whose commitment to the medicalization and treatment of the human mind have contributed much to the marginalization of Vietnam veterans. This is not, of course, to say the sciences of the psyche have not played a beneficial role in the lives of veterans and nonveterans alike, and even less to insinuate the existence of a conspiracy whereby analysts and clinicians are arrayed against Vietnam veterans. Rather, my focus on psychology and psychiatry serves as another contextual element adding to one's understanding of how the Vietnam veteran has secured cultural intelligibility during and since the Vietnam War. Once again, the contrast with the unaccounted-for body and the identified body is stark. As we saw in chapter 3, the intervention of forensic science in the unaccounted-for body enables the identification of fragmentary remains in the production of a body that can at last be heralded as having come home from the Vietnam War. In the process, discourses of closure and healing rooted in the ontological fragmentation occasioned by the loss in Vietnam are advanced since the absence of American bodies has long been articulated as the most material example of a war without end. Technically difficult, to be sure, the accounting effort nonetheless offers a solution that is seductive in its conceptual simplicity.

Psychological discourse, by contrast, has long been caught in something of a double bind. On the one hand, psychology has aspired to all kinds of remedies at both the individual and societal levels. As Ellen Herman (1995: 12) has argued,

During and after World War II, social engineering was not a slur but a mission proudly embraced by experts active in the civil rights movement as well as by those involved in the Cold War military. Behavioral scientists who devised technologies to predict and control the behavior of populations abroad and at home were not entirely unlike clinicians who heralded the healthy personality as the basis for democracy, insisted that mental health could be mass-produced and purchased, and welcomed psychotherapy as a strategy for the manufacture of normality.

Mediating the human mind thus became not simply the goal of clinicians but a means of addressing personal and communal problems in a manner formerly performed primarily by the church and the family. Riding the momentum gained from the treatment of wartime psychiatric casualties, psychology began a rapid postwar expansion into something of a pansocietal heuristic, a development hastened in no small part by the federal government's gradual embrace of psychology as a tool for social policy. The result was little short of dramatic. By the time of the Vietnam War, "popular perception no longer tied clinicians to their historic charges: the institutionalized insane. Perfectly normal (if painfully maladjusted) individuals had become appropriate participants in clinical exchanges, and healing complex social environments had been gathered under the mantle of clinicians' ever-expanding list of therapeutic chores" (Herman, 1995: 223).

Herman's impressive chronicle of the cultural and professional development of psychology in the United States following World War II points to but does not engage with a side effect of that development that ultimately advances the present argument about the role of psychological discourse in the abjection of the Vietnam veteran. That side effect is expressed most patently in the failure of psychology to banish fully the popular wartime belief that "perfectly capable men were using the excuse of mild or nonexistent maladjustment to remain safe at home" (Herman, 1995: 89). During World War II, for example, that belief most often took the form of an accusation in which "war neurotics were yellow cowards and malingerers" whose "disorders were for the most part invisible and depended for their detection on the diagnosis of psychiatrists. Such disorders could not be 'measured' or confirmed by laboratory tests or 'objective findings'" (Hale, 1995: 201). From this standpoint, all the psychoanalysis in the world would not help these soldiers because they either were faking it or were simply not cut from the same cloth as the standard American fighting male. Apart from one's take on this question, the normative force of the distinction between those who suffered from war neurosis and those who did not was enormous. The neurotics were failures in the worst possible sense of the term, unable to endure the trials and tribulations of warfare and therefore to uphold the codes of the heroic and victorious warrior. And while psychotherapy was no doubt of great assistance to many American servicemen, its cultural prominence as the latest and greatest cure meant that war-related anxieties were pathologized rather than seen as a largely unavoidable result of modern warfare. There was just something wrong with these guys.

In the context of the defeat in Vietnam, the cultural stigma attached to war neurosis both during the war and afterward in the form of readjustment difficulties was all the more intense. Or so we have been led to believe anyway, not least by the first-person accounts of Vietnam veterans. Although I don't imply that these accounts are wrong, a comparison of psychiatric casualties and problematic readjustments from World War II and the Vietnam War reveals more similarities than divergences. Perhaps an explanation of the cultural salience of the demented Vietnam vet lies not with the prevalence of psychiatric issues among Vietnam veterans but elsewhere. I will take up one possible alternative in detail below, but here it can be briefly characterized as an issue of masculinity, one which proposes a link between the loss in Vietnam and the failure to achieve true manhood, of which war neurosis has long been a tacit indication. This connection, in turn, engenders two consequences. First, deviation from the psychological norm becomes a principle of the Vietnam veteran's intelligibility regardless of the incidence of psychiatric difficulties among veterans as a group. Second, war neurosis as an explanatory link between failed masculinity and defeat in war preserves the unaccounted-for body as a domain of embodied existence unsullied by the loss in Vietnam. In a bizarre, yet all-too-logical twist, the distinction between the Vietnam veteran and the soldier unaccounted for originally proposed by the Nixon administration is reinforced by the simple act of veterans seeking treatment for war-related psychiatric difficulties.

Before moving to a more detailed treatment of this argument, however, I want to discuss briefly the alleged uniqueness of the Vietnam War vis-á-vis the psychiatric effect on those who fought it and the maladaption that accompanied the return of its veterans. The intent is to situate the repeatedly heard but often underanalyzed claim that the experiences of Vietnam warriors differed markedly from those of their World War II counterparts. The importance of doing this is once again found in the persistence of the image of the abject veteran from the Vietnam War. If that abjection can be traced neither to the war itself nor to a disparity in the psychiatric difficulties experienced by those who fought it, then the failure of masculinity as a principle of the Vietnam veteran's intelligibility might emerge as a more valid insight into how the veteran has come to be known in the post–Vietnam War era; and, by extension, into the interpretive gulf that separates the veteran from the soldier unaccounted for in Southeast Asia.

The very possibility of such a comparison is derived from the prominence psychology had acquired by the time of World War II as a means of understanding and treating maladies that were not caused by any obvious physical injury. This, in turn, was a legacy of World War I, a conflict in which soldiers first experienced in large numbers what eventually became known as shell shock. Characterized by "staring eyes, violent tremors, a look of terror, and blue, cold extremities," among other things, physicians at the time initially suspected that "the symptoms of shell shock might result from concussion which caused minor damage to nervous tissue" (Hale, 1995: 14–15). The absence of any signs of physical damage, however, eventually inclined physicians toward a psychological explanation for shell shock. Neuropsychiatrists achieved positive results by temporarily removing the sufferer from battle, forcing him to rest, and giving him the opportunity to talk about his anxieties. Nonetheless, the worst cases were stigmatized as "emotional [and] 'hysterical'" and were treated accordingly: "Patients were told that such symptoms as trembling, paralyses, and deaf-mutism were failures of will and character, not symptoms of disease. They were treated by denial of leave, solitary confinement, persuasion, [and] painful electric shocks" (Hale, 1995: 17). Two approaches to war neurosis developed early on. The first was a tendency to see sufferers as people with character flaws that disqualified them from entering the realm of normative masculinity. The second was an embryonic awareness that the psychological wounds suffered in war might persist following the cessation of hostilities. Various civic organizations made it their mission to supply information that might assist relatives of returned veterans and to provide opportunities for convalescence to veterans who had not yet fully recovered (Hale, 1995: 21).

Military planners were well aware of the extent to which psychiatric casualties could hinder a military, and so they were transformed during the interwar period into a problem to be solved. By the beginning of World War II, researchers in the United States had developed a battery of emotional and intelligence tests designed not only to screen out soldiers unfit for the psychological rigors of warfare, but also "to establish a clear-cut working knowledge of the American soldier, his educational background, his likes and dislikes, opinions, attitudes and ambitions; and so to furnish a scientific basis either for the correction of Army maladjustments, or for explaining to the soldier the reasons back of particular policies" (in Herman, 1995: 57). The findings, however, were not always quite what researchers had expected, a situation that complicates the usual opposition between the idealism of the American soldier in World War II and those who would fight in Vietnam a generation later. In particular, researchers discovered that

> U.S. soldiers had no meaningful understanding of why they were fighting or what the war was actually about. Worse, they did not seem to care. According to the Research Branch studies, the number of men who viewed the war "from a consistent and favorable intellectual position" was somewhere between 10 and 20 percent. "Why we are fighting the war" was typically on the bottom of the list of things that soldiers wanted the army to teach them (Herman, 1995: 69).

Researchers were thus forced to conclude that "hatred for the enemy was easier to manufacture than genuine enthusiasm and respect for U.S. institutions" (Herman, 1995: 70). Yet this finding meshed in an unsettling yet entirely logical way with other findings from the time, in particular the conclusion that "U.S. soldiers were motivated by the same primitive feelings and loyalties, the same absence of conscious and reasonable motivation, the same ominous emotional attachments to authority figures, that had been identified as such alarming traits in the German and Japanese national characters" (Herman, 1995: 71). The American soldier was not only not so virtuous as had been previously imagined, but likely not impervious to combat-induced psychological breakdown either, and this despite the massive efforts in the interwar period to solve the problem of war neurosis.

This fear of psychiatric weakness among American soldiers was borne out both immediately prior to and during World War II itself. Prewar screening and evaluation resulted in neuropsychiatric discharges of 1,845,000 recruits, or 12 percent of those recruited and 38 percent of all rejections. An additional 550,000 men who passed their initial entry exam were later discharged for neuropsychiatric reasons before ever seeing combat (Herman, 1995: 88). During the war, psychiatric casualties again constituted a major share of personnel losses. At Guadalcanal, for example, 40 percent of casualties severe enough to require evacuation were neuropsychiatric. Combat divisions in Europe experienced psychiatric casualty rates of 26 percent, a figure which increased to 75 percent during intense combat (Herman, 1995: 89). In the North Africa campaigns of 1942, neuropsychiatric casualties composed 20 to 34 percent of personnel losses (Hale, 1995: 189). Soldiers were "fatigued to the point of exhaustion," "unshaven, dirty. . . . Their faces were expressionless, their eyes blank and unseeing, and they tended to go to sleep wherever they were" (in Hale, 1995: 197).

And matters were not automatically resolved simply because the war ended—not for veterans, at least—despite the common rendition of the aftermath of World War II as a time of happiness, tranquility, and prosperity. The number of psychiatric cases in VA hospitals doubled between 1940 and 1948. By April 1946, some 60 percent of all VA patients suffered from some neuropsychiatric disorder, while 50 percent of disability pensions were being paid to psychiatric casualties, the monthly cost of which approached $20 million (Herman, 1995: 242–43). As had been the case in World War I and as would be the case during the Vietnam War, the effects of combat in World War II were registered at least as much in the psyches as on the bodies of those who fought it. War neurosis appeared to be unavoidable, one of the many nonnegotiable consequences of mechanized warfare apparently not unique to any single conflict or amenable to prevention on the model of the medical sciences. It was, rather, a contingency for which the military had to be prepared, and it had to be dealt with through the latest neuropsychiatric treatment techniques.

In view of the high psychiatric casualty rates from the world wars and the increasing awareness that such difficulties were part and parcel of warfare in the modern era, it is striking that the Vietnam War is so commonly articulated as a uniquely problematic psychological experience for those who fought it. The first-person narratives discussed above are instructive in their suggestion that Americans fighting in Vietnam had little of the sense of pride in country and certainty of purpose from which soldiers in World War II had allegedly, though apparently not all that often, benefited. Other conventional explanations locate the psychological problems caused by the Vietnam War in the difficulty of distinguishing friend from foe, the nonterritorial objectives of a war in which during the day soldiers died to take a hill which was then left for the Communists to reclaim that night, and the feeling that the American military was fighting with one hand tied behind its back. Yet in the Vietnam War, rates of personnel loss for psychiatric reasons were the lowest of any previous U.S. fighting experience in the twentieth century. Whereas the overall psychiatric discharge rate for World War II was 33.1 percent and for the Korean War 23.9 percent, it was 13.7 percent in Vietnam (Tucker, 2000: 261). Some of the decrease may be attributable to the changing nature of psychiatric diagnoses: ailments considered psychiatric in World War II were no longer defined as such in Vietnam. Nevertheless, the overall ability of U.S. forces to minimize and treat casualties of all kinds was greatly enhanced by the time of the Vietnam War. Even allowing for definitional changes, it seems plausible to suggest that psychiatric difficulties during the Vietnam War were no higher than those for other American wars.

The post–Vietnam War experience is also widely believed to have been unique. The readjustment of Vietnam veterans is conventionally thought to have been dramatically different and more troublesome than was the case following previous wars. Yet while World War II veterans with psychiatric diagnoses were filling VA hospitals in the years following that conflict, only 15.2 percent of Vietnam veterans suffered post-combat war neurosis, or what was by then called post-traumatic stress disorder (PTSD) (Tucker, 2000: 335). Further, Vietnam veterans took enthusiastic advantage of such benefits as the GI Bill to defray the costs of higher education. By 1977, over 64 percent of Vietnam veterans had used the GI Bill, compared to 55 percent of World War II veterans and 43 percent of Korean War veterans (Dean, 1992: 64). In an article that from the present vantage point appears almost unbelievable, the *New York Times* reported in 1968 that "returning servicemen were finding jobs faster than at any time in the past 10 years, and some were even worried that the Vietnam veterans would not utilize the GI Bill for education since jobs were so easy to find" (Dean, 1992: 61).[4] Another *New York Times* article from a year earlier speculated that "the Vietnam veteran may be lured instead into the labor force; even in an economy which has softened somewhat, he is much sought after by business and industry . . . since he cannot be drafted!" (in Dean, 1992: 61).[5] In 1968, an article in *The Nation* described the Vietnam veteran as "'knowing exactly what he wants' compared to the veterans of the Korean War who were characterized as 'quiet, apathetic young men who shuffled aimlessly about,' with a 'glassy faraway look . . . staring nowhere'" (in Dean, 1992: 61).

Certain changes to these perceptions were ushered in between 1970 and 1972 because of the large-scale withdrawals of American forces from Southeast Asia. The approximately one million Vietnam veterans discharged from military service combined with a declining economy made for increasing levels of unemployment, a circumstance which initially affected Vietnam veterans disproportionately. News accounts at the time put the jobless rate for Vietnam veterans at 12.4 percent, compared to a national unemployment rate of 6 percent (Dean, 1992: 62). By 1973, however, these problems had largely been resolved, and the unemployment rates for Vietnam veterans were mirroring those for the population at large. Nevertheless, "the indelible impression had been created that Vietnam veterans were unemployed or even unemployable" (Dean, 1992: 62). Stories about high levels of drug use and addiction among Vietnam veterans also became common, despite studies showing that rates were similar to those in the civilian population. Finally, the return of American POWs in the spring of 1973 was accompanied by wide publicity from the Nixon administration as it attempted to put a positive spin on the resounding defeat in Southeast Asia. The publicity naturally called attention to the absence of welcoming celebrations for veterans who had not been POWs. Vietnam veterans "were called 'unheralded, even unwanted,' and 'the most alienated generation of trained killers in American history'" (Dean, 1992: 63).

Belying these headlines were a number of indicators that the readjustment of the Vietnam veteran was at least equal to, if not in some senses more successful than, that of veterans of prior American wars. As noted, use of the GI Bill by Vietnam veterans was higher than for veterans of either World War II or the Korean War. A study in 1977 showed that Vietnam veterans enjoyed a higher median income than their civilian peers (Dean, 1992: 66). A Harris poll taken in 1971 revealed that 94 percent of Vietnam veterans felt their peers had given them a friendly reception on their return. A mere 3 percent said their homecoming was "not at all friendly" (Lembcke, 1998a: 47). Another Harris poll taken in 1979 asked people to rate their feelings toward various groups of people. On a ten-point scale, "veterans who served in Vietnam during the war received an average of 9.8, somewhat above veterans of World War II or Korea (9.6)" (Jeffords, 1989: 126). The late 1970s and early 1980s were marked nonetheless by repeated public invocations of the idea that the homecoming experience of Vietnam veterans was inadequate or failed to measure up to that of other veterans. This, in turn, led to several belated attempts to welcome home Vietnam veterans. Presidents Nixon, Gerald Ford, and Jimmy Carter all declared a Vietnam Veterans Week, and in 1979 Veterans' Day was dedicated to Vietnam veterans Congress declared April 25, 1981, to be Vietnam Veteran Recognition Day, and the Vietnam Veterans Memorial was dedicated in Washington on November 11, 1982 (Dean, 1992: 65).

What is one to make of this disjuncture between the statistical representation of the Vietnam veteran and his readjustment, on the one hand, and the image of the abject veteran forgotten and scorned by his country, on the other? Certainly the very public efforts by the Nixon administration to enforce a distinction between the returning, antiwar veteran and the soldier imprisoned or missing in Vietnam strongly shaped the perception that the Vietnam veteran was less than worthy of the nation's admiration. Yet in spite of widespread recognition that Nixon's intentions were entirely impeachable, the abject veteran persists as one of the Vietnam War's primary interpretive categories. Accordingly, alongside the distinction between the stateside veteran and his unaccounted-for equivalent must be located the continued presence of the defeat in Vietnam as registered in the body of the living Vietnam veteran. As indicated earlier, that defeat has been frequently, if tacitly, ascribed to the impaired masculinity of the soldiers who fought in Vietnam, an impairment implied partly by the presence in veterans of combat-induced psychiatric difficulties which retain certain of their historical linkages to cowardice and malingering. As a clinician at the VA once described it, "There was a bias toward Vietnam veterans, especially after the My Lai massacre broke. It was so much easier to blame the Vietnam veteran, to romanticize the World War II veterans and say they were cut from sterner stuff" (in Scott, 1993: 5). In spite of the relatively small numbers of Vietnam veterans who suffer from postwar psychiatric trouble and of the readaptation often enabled by psychiatric treatment of war trauma, a primary principle of the Vietnam veteran's intelligibility has been deviation from psychological normalcy. A condition of comparatively little moment in the civilian world, psychological impairment in the realm of warfare becomes a commentary on the soldier's qualifications for successful masculinity.

While certainly popular among those who wished to denigrate antiwar Vietnam veterans, characterization of them in the idiom of impaired masculinity was a strategy employed even by those who worried about the veterans' less than honorable standing in the immediate postwar years. Writing in *Harper's* in July 1978, the psychiatrist Jeffrey Jay observed sympathetically that Vietnam veterans "never became the men they hoped to be when, as adolescent recruits, they believed themselves and America invincible. Marked as losers, they feel constantly challenged to prove their manhood" (18). Jay then links this loss of masculinity to the nation as a whole when he asks, "Is the profound inadequacy felt by these veterans theirs alone, or does it reflect a less acute but similar public sentiment?" (18).[6] The question barely seems to require a specific answer, rooted as it is in the premise that the loss in Vietnam was as much an emasculation of the American body politic as it was a failure of masculinity on the part of veterans. So much worse, then, for the Vietnam veteran, saddled in both an individual and a national sense with the failure of his duty as a man to win the war in Vietnam. He must occupy the realm of the abject as that feature of the Vietnam War whose repudiation permits other elements of the war, few though they may be, to remain unblemished. So much better, then, for the soldier unaccounted for in Southeast Asia, whose venerable position as the body worth fighting for is tacitly reinforced by each set of repatriated remains and with each subsequent American military victory that suggests his living counterpart really did manage to blow it in Vietnam.

As does the incidence of combat-induced psychiatric difficulties, the compulsion to revivify American masculinity in the aftermath of warfare finds antecedents in World War II. Kaja Silverman (1992) elaborates this point in her discussion of cinematic representations of American soldiers returned from battle. She reveals that masculinity was very much at issue in the years following that war despite conventional narratives of victorious American soldiers returning home, going back to work, and helping to found the era of prosperity and tranquility that marks the pre–Vietnam War period. In these films,

> the "hero" returns from World War II with a physical or psychic wound which marks him as somehow deficient, and which renders him incapable of functioning smoothly in civilian life. Sometimes the veteran also finds himself strangely superfluous to the society he ostensibly protected during the war; his functions have been assumed by other men, or—much more disturbingly—by women. These texts thus dramatize the vulnera-

bility of conventional masculinity and the larger dominant fiction to what I will call "historical trauma" (53).

That trauma, Silverman argues, is any historical event "which brings a large group of male subjects into such an intimate relation with lack that they are at least for the moment unable to sustain an imaginary relation with the phallus, and so withdraw their belief from the dominant fiction" (55). The dominant fiction, she continues, "neutralizes the contradictions which organize the social formation by fostering collective identifications and desires, identifications and desires which have a range of effects but which are first and foremost constitutive of sexual difference" (54). Sexual difference, of course, is precisely what is called into question by warfare, given the extent to which protection of the home front is given over to women while the men are engaged in battle.[7]

Silverman's analysis thus suggests that in spite of warfare's status as *the* forum for the achievement of normative masculinity, it just as often reveals masculinity's vulnerability to the feminine, expressed as the "death drive" or "the compulsion to repeat experiences of an overwhelming and incapacitating sort—experiences which render the subject hyperbolically passive" (Silverman, 1992: 58–59). The convergence here with contemporary definitions of combat-induced psychiatric illness is striking. According to the American Psychiatric Association, PTSD includes "persistent reexperiencing of the stressor event. The individual is subject to vivid and uncontrollable memories and/or recurrent dreams of the event and may lose track of his or her current surroundings entirely, in what has come to be called a 'flashback'" (in Tucker, 2000: 334). The repetition of war-related experiences thus renders the soldier not more masculine/active but hyperbolically feminine/passive as a result of the overwhelming power of the flashback. The dependence of masculinity on a rejection of passivity is revealed, and this in a manner that disables the afflicted male's ability to continue effecting this rejection by rendering him helpless and limp before the world. Masculinity, therefore, "is particularly vulnerable to the unbinding effects of the death drive because of its ideological alignment with mastery. The normative male ego is necessarily fortified against any knowledge of the void upon which it rests, and—as its insistence upon an unimpaired bodily 'envelope' would suggest—fiercely protective of its coherence" (Silverman, 1992: 61).

In light of Silverman's analysis, the vulnerability of masculinity to incursions by the feminine can no longer be seen as unique to the Vietnam War: it is a historically pervasive phenomenon that has, irrespective of the incidence of postwar psychiatric stress among veterans, long helped govern the American experience of warfare. Masculinity as a defining characteristic of embodied personhood is never capable of prevailing simply on its own terms but is always exposed to and must therefore renounce its opposite as a condition of its continued viability. In this light, it is not difficult to see that failure in the realm of masculine experience par excellence, warfare, combined with episodes in the realm of feminine experience par excellence, passivity in the form of postwar psychiatric flashbacks, makes for an especially potent amalgam when it comes to embodied intelligibility in the aftermath of a military defeat such as that the United States experienced in Vietnam. The failed masculinity that allegedly produced the lost war lives on as the persistent realization of the death drive, a passivity so all-encompassing as to threaten the very existence of masculinity as traditionally conceived. Worse still, warfare itself is called into question (if only momentarily) as a path to masculine virtue, thereby creating an identity crisis for a body politic long dependent on the commission of acts of violence as one of its most sacred prerogatives. On these terms, the successful postwar readjustment of Vietnam veterans is entirely beside the point. Rather, what matters most about these bodies that don't seem to matter all that much is the void they represent at the center of American masculinity's encounter with warfare, a void that must be consistently denied if masculinity as an organizing principle of the warring experience and the warring body is to remain intact.

Little wonder, then, that so many aspects of the post–Vietnam War era have been directed toward what Jeffords (1989: 51) has called "remasculinization," that is, "a regeneration of the concepts, constructions, and definitions of masculinity in American culture and a restabilization of the gender system within and for which it is formulated." And little wonder, furthermore, that remasculinization is so often staged on the body of the soldier missing in Southeast Asia. Much like Nixon's efforts to drive a wedge between Vietnam veterans and imprisoned or missing soldiers, efforts to retrieve the missing reanimate the virility of the body politic by again giving it something to fight for. Equally important, accounting for the missing actively confronts the passivity and weakness of the U.S. government that allegedly produced such absences in the first place. That POW rescue narratives so often feature a Vietnam veteran in the role of liberator thus makes perfect sense in that the act of rescuing imprisoned soldiers both redresses impaired masculinity and partially resolves one of the most vexing issues of the Vietnam War's contentious legacy.[8] The bare-chested, hypermasculine figure of Johnny Rambo, to cite but one well-known example, is cultural shorthand for a whole series of redemptions related to the failure of American masculinity and the continued imprisonment of American soldiers. Starring Sylvester Stallone as the scorned Vietnam veteran, *Rambo: First Blood, Part II* shows the veteran atoning for the range of feminized sins that produced and sustain American POWs. Significantly, with respect to the recuperations carried out by the film, Rambo's primary enemy is not the Vietnamese but Marshall Murdock, a U.S. government bureaucrat sent along to supervise Rambo's activities; Murdock attempts to kill the rescue mission when, to his surprise, evidence of POWs actually surfaces. With even less subtlety than we've come to expect from Hollywood depictions of male warriors, Rambo succeeds not only in rescuing the prisoners but in pinning the blame for their imprisonment on a government too weak and pathetic to ensure their return, as if the nation itself remained in the grip of the hyperbolic passivity occasioned by combat-induced psychiatric trauma. One of the central messages of the film, therefore — and one of the pillars of the rehabilitation of masculinity it undertakes — lies in the fact that that Rambo "defeats his own government, retrieving the very men the government has denied for years" (Jeffords, 1989: 129).

The thrust of *Rambo* is that the exclusion of the Vietnam veteran in his guise as the passive, psychiatrically wounded remainder of the Vietnam War is a functional requirement of the viability of American masculinity. And the force of this requirement is not mitigated by circumstances in which both exclusion and rehabilitation of Vietnam veterans can be observed occurring simultaneously, as in *Rambo*. Indeed, this is precisely the point insofar as remasculinization is indispensable if the Vietnam veteran is to assert and legitimize his claim to membership in the realm of normative masculinity. For present purposes, however, the more important point concerns the larger cultural significance of the effort to account for American soldiers missing in Southeast Asia and the extent to which the unaccounted-for body conditions the intelligibility of the body of the Vietnam veteran and vice versa. In this interpretation, if there were no feminized lack and no weakness and passivity materialized in the body of the Vietnam veteran, there would be no unaccounted-for soldiers because the United States would have succeeded in liberating all the prisoners and recovering all remains during the withdrawal of forces in 1973. Conversely, if there were no unaccounted-for soldiers, the most tangible consequence of the loss in Vietnam would no longer exist, that is, there would be no body whose recovery could stand in as a metaphor for the recovery of lost masculinity. The cultural intelligibility of each thus requires the constant production of the other. The substantial difference, of course, lies in the consequences of that production. As indicated, repudiation of the feminized, abject Vietnam veteran is required to sustain dominant narratives of martial virtue and heroic masculinity. The unaccounted-for soldier, by contrast, must be embraced, and his recovery must be insistently pursued as an act indicative of the restoration of the very masculinity whose failure led to his absence in the first place.

In light of these observations, the persistence of the abject Vietnam vet despite the successful readjustment of the majority of Vietnam veterans becomes more clear. To be precise, that persistence can be traced to the ontological purposes served thereby. Because the United States had not suffered a dramatic military defeat like that experienced in Vietnam, the postwar interpretive structure that greeted returning veterans was without precedent. Meanwhile, the winning of World War II still loomed large in the national imaginary, a fact which invited comparisons between veterans of that war and those returning from Vietnam. It was, perhaps, inevitable that the respective combatants would come to be known for whether they fought in the "good war," on the one hand, or in the "bad war," on the other. In addition, Vietnam veterans' widespread maladjustment was taken as confirmation by some that they were somehow weaker than their World War II counterparts. More important from an ontological perspective, however, is the way in which the body of the veteran enables the Vietnam War to be known. The veteran, in other words, still serves, only this time as a principle of intelligibility for a lost war and a blighted masculinity. Intelligibility itself becomes a form of certainty, and the materiality of the body of the veteran becomes the index by which the anguish and fragmentation produced by the Vietnam War can be consistently affirmed. Materiality confirms what everyone knows about the Vietnam veteran, namely, that he is crazy, demented, psychiatrically unstable, and therefore must be refused the status of the unaccounted-for body in the rehabilitations of the post–Vietnam War era.

THE ABSENCE OF THE VIETNAM VETERAN

Given the expansive attention devoted to Vietnam veterans in journalistic accounts, filmic representations, and scientific literature, to name but a few sites, is it not a misnomer to call the veterans, as the founder of the homeless shelter did, "our stateside MIAS"? For all intents and purposes it appears the Vietnam veteran is quite present. Yet such a claim would be insufficiently attentive to the interplay of presence and absence that characterizes much of the post–Vietnam War era. The serviceman still missing in Vietnam, for example, is both absent in a corporeal sense and present in the form of a specter that haunts the United States and troubles its efforts to come to terms with the Vietnam War. Further, both the absence and the presence of the unaccounted-for soldier find material expression, the former as that which cannot (yet) be accounted for in terms of an identifiable body, the latter in terms of the "Vietnam syndrome" that saps American confidence abroad and generates endless domestic debates on the propriety and morality of the U.S. intervention in Southeast Asia and subsequently

On this reading, the Vietnam veteran is likewise both present and absent. His presence is most clearly registered in the VA hospitals, psychiatric wards, prisons, and homeless shelters that have become his primary residences in the years since the Vietnam War. The practices of exile-enclosure which constitute the American response to pathology have encircled, delineated, and distributed the Vietnam veteran so that his presence in these venues is not only assured but indeed one of his most potent signifiers. At the same time, the Vietnam veteran is missing from the discourse of heroism and valor that has traditionally underwritten the American military experience and from the effort to come to terms with the Vietnam War. Finally, Vietnam veterans are largely absent from public life. Perceived as having failed to qualify for responsible citizenship through successful appropriation of and participation in the martial ethic, many Vietnam veterans have returned to civilian life as quietly and inconspicuously as possible. Indeed, successful readjustment in the post–Vietnam War era has itself become a form of disappearance. Even in these cases, the materiality of the veteran's body signifies an irremediable stigmatization and becomes the occasion for his marginalization; not open to him are the loci in American society where the challenge of how to get beyond the Vietnam War is confronted.

Two striking examples of the veterans' standing in post-war America can be cited. The first occurred on May 7, 1985, in New York City when twenty-five thousand Vietnam veterans marched in a ticker tape parade attended by one million people, many of whom held signs reading, "You're Our Heroes, Vietnam Vets." The explicit intent of the parade was to welcome home the Vietnam veterans, and the celebration was punctuated by veterans who said they had never received such recognition before and were "finally being welcomed home." Similar parades were held in other American cities, including Chicago and Houston (Dean, 1992: 65). Where had these veterans been if not at the margins to which they had been relegated after the war? The presence of Vietnam veterans in the streets of New York in May 1985 gave high resolution to their absence and called attention to the rejection of veterans from American society during the previous ten years. As noted, however, this phenomenon had been observed during the repatriation of POWs in 1973, a return commemorated by extensive publicity and a lavish White House dinner. Observers remarked on the disparity between these blandishments and headlines that read, "The Forgotten Veterans," "Will Somebody Please Welcome This Hero Home?" and "The Vietnam Vet: 'No One Gives a Damn'" (in Dean, 1992: 63). At this early date, however, calling attention to the marginalization of Vietnam veterans failed to produce the outpouring of public sentiment that would occur twelve years later.

The second example occurred in late April 2001 when Bob Kerrey, former governor and U.S. Senator from Nebraska, admitted that he had led a raid in Vietnam in 1969 in which thirteen civilians were killed. Occasionally angry but mostly contrite in the days before the appearance of a feature-length article on the raid, Kerrey claimed full responsibility for the incident and acknowledged he did not consider himself a hero despite having received numerous citations for valor in his career. He further conceded that his guilt over the civilian deaths had been the reason he had never discussed the raid in public (Vistica, 2001). As far as this analysis is concerned, the pivotal elements of the story lie not so much in the revelation that a decorated, obviously well-adjusted veteran was responsible for civilian deaths in Vietnam. More noteworthy, rather, is the degree to which the discourse available to both Kerrey and his numerous interlocutors had been predetermined by the events of both the Vietnam War and subsequent years. That discourse means that even a Vietnam veteran who has managed to travel successfully the martial path to public leadership can be easily and explicitly linked to the crazed, civilian-slaughtering grunt in Vietnam. Such linkage no longer requires even the most minimal articulation, and there is no recognition of the degree to which it functions to scapegoat individual veterans and thus obscure the ways in which American policy in Vietnam compelled the sorts of war crimes of which Kerrey believes himself guilty.[9] This does not mean that Kerrey is not still a successfully readjusted veteran of the Vietnam War. It does mean that to be a Vietnam veteran is to be a certain kind of nonsoldier, always one step away from the bad vet who forever tarnished the reputation of the American fighting man.

The ethos surrounding the New York veterans' parade and Kerrey's admission of guilt reveal much about the materialization of the Vietnam veteran. As the process by which bodies assume cultural intelligibility—indeed, by which bodies as such become possible in the first place—materialization in this context refers not to intelligibility through reference to "identifiable remains" so much as through reference to the various events by which the Vietnam War itself has come to be understood. As we have seen, these events include the campaign by the Nixon administration to discredit antiwar veterans, first-person accounts of the war in Vietnam, including atrocities and other examples of wanton disregard for life, and the veterans' experience with psychiatric problems that were interpreted as an explicit commentary on their masculinity or the lack thereof. What this means is that there is no preconceived Vietnam veteran who is shunted off to the margins of American society upon his return to the United States. Equally, there is no preconceived margin to which abject bodies are banished by the commandment of law. Rather, the two materialize interconstitutively. The body of the Vietnam veteran materializes *as* the margin or, perhaps more accurately, as the margin of corporeal intelligibility in the post–Vietnam War era. As in the case of the body of the accounted-for soldier, that materialization occurs in response to particular norms and within particular epistemic configurations which are themselves dependent upon historically specific ontological conditions.

The ontological conditions are not difficult to identify, having to do mostly with the need to render the Vietnam War intelligible and, by extension, to pacify the ambiguity occasioned by such a disorienting experience. The Vietnam veteran functions in this context precisely because his experiences are so widely believed to be unique. The idea that Vietnam veterans suffered more in the war itself, experienced greater readjustment difficulties upon return, and were shunned to a degree unprecedented in American history enables intelligibility by compartmentalizing the Vietnam War and its veterans and by providing the interpretive boundary markers by which the exceptionality of the Vietnam War can be reaffirmed. That the vast majority of Vietnam veterans readjusted well is, in a somewhat paradoxical fashion, precisely the point insofar as it suggests the intensity of the need in the postwar period for some*thing* that might serve as the interpretive crucible of the Vietnam War. The veteran has become that crucible; or, more accurately, its materialization as the abject remainder of a lost and divisive war satisfies the need to believe that the Vietnam War was the exception rather than an accurate representation of the American fighting man, the way he conducts himself in combat, and his ability to readjust afterward.

The body of the Vietnam veteran thus constitutes the defining limit of the body of the accounted-for soldier by offering unambiguous interpretive possibilities for another of the war's ambiguous elements, namely, the conduct of the war in Vietnam, in which all American bodies seemed defiled, depraved, and corrupted. In this sense, the body of the accounted-for soldier and the body of the Vietnam veteran exist in an uneasy alliance insofar as they both enable the resolution of fundamentally disorienting elements of the Vietnam War. Further, both the accounted-for body and the body of the veteran permit this pacification as the result of a unique confluence of ontological and epistemological circumstances. Both materialize as a result of their encounter with the epistemic regime of modern science, and both fulfill particular ontological requirements. Finally, in both cases various parts come to stand for the whole. Fragmented remains materialize as an identified body, thus enabling the removal of a name from the list of the missing, while the "Vietnam vet" stands as the most material symbol of the U.S. failure in Vietnam. Put differently, the body of the veteran becomes the converse of the accounted-for soldier not because it fails to provide legitimate interpretive possibilities for the Vietnam War but because it provides those interpretations in a way that reinscribes the failures and agonies of the war. Whereas the movement from unaccounted for to identified permits the materiality of the repatriated body to serve as an unambiguous indicator of success within the epistemic terms of the effort to account for missing American soldiers, the materialization of the body of the veteran admits of no such claim. Its materiality enables a different sort of accounting entirely, one which firmly locates the agonies of the Vietnam War within the many bodies of its living combatants.

To say this much, however, still does not engage the specific modalities in which the effort to recover the bodies of missing American soldiers implicates the American body politic to which they are being returned. To do so requires analysis of the accounting effort not merely as a means of redressing the ambiguities of the Vietnam War and of bringing certainty and closure to the families of the missing, but as something integral to the healing of the body politic in the aftermath of a lost and highly divisive war. The body of the Vietnam veteran makes a tacit appearance here as well, of course, since, as I've shown, his abjection makes him ineligible for the sorts of healing which the effort to repatriate the remains of the missing purportedly allows. The discourse of healing that animates the relationship between the unaccounted-for body and the body politic might thus be said to represent the flip side of the discourse of abjection that has contributed so much to the intelligibility of the body of the Vietnam veteran.

chapter five

Practices of Memorialization

The Vietnam Veterans Memorial, the Tomb of the Vietnam War Unknown Soldier, and the POW/MIA Flag

> The ability of a group to think of itself as a nation depends on a consensus existing among its citizens about what it means to be a unified whole.
> —Griswold, 1986: 691

> Vietnam divided us and troubles us still, not only in the hearts and minds of veterans and their families, but in our crippled self-confidence. It is a specter we have to put to rest, a wound in need of healing.
> —Broyles, 1982: 83

In arguing that the bodies at issue in U.S. efforts to account for soldiers missing in Southeast Asia are material effects of the practices that compose the post–Vietnam War era, my analysis has thus far been primarily concerned with the matter of certain individual bodies. The body of the unaccounted-for soldier, for example, was seen to have gained intelligibility in part through efforts by the Nixon administration to reinvigorate public support for the Vietnam War and in part through attempts to resolve live-sighting reports, discrepancy cases, and lingering uncertainties occasioned by the loss in Vietnam. The very desire for an accounting, and the body which served as that accounting's measure, soon had as much to do with these uncertainties as with the resolution of specific cases of unaccounted-for personnel. Likewise, the body of the *accounted*-for soldier can be understood as an effect of the quest for certainty and of the government's accounting protocol mandating identifiable remains as well as of the knowledge practices of forensic science through which the identity of those remains is determined. Finally, the body of the Vietnam veteran was seen to be the constitutive opposition to the body of the accounted-for soldier. Because that body bears traces of failure and loss it has been prohibited from participating in the resolution of U.S. post–Vietnam War anxieties. Its materiality is the all-too-vivid expression of the immutable negative consequences of the loss in Vietnam. While the materialization of the body of the accounted-for soldier fashions a sort of victory from the remains of the war, the body of the veteran is irrevocably lost to the war's history of death and dismemberment.

In this chapter I extend the analysis by exploring the relationship between the bodies of soldiers still missing from the Vietnam War and the American body politic. One venue for discussing this relationship is the various means of memorializing the Vietnam War and participants in it. Three examples are instructive—the Vietnam Veterans Memorial, the Tomb of the Vietnam War Unknown Soldier at Arlington National Cemetery, and the POW/MIA flag. Each is a point of articulation between the individual and the collective body within the Vietnam War's contentious legacy. Clearly, that legacy has made heroic memorialization and iconic monumentalization of the Vietnam War difficult, if not impossible. Marita Sturken (1997: 44) summarizes the problem well when she asks, "How does a society commemorate a war whose central narrative is one of dissent, a war whose history is still formative and highly contested?" The question is even more salient when posed in the context of attempts to account for missing bodies. How ought the body politic commemorate a war in which the lingering absence of the body of the unaccounted-for soldier signifies wounds that have yet to heal? Both questions speak to exceptional difficulties within the post–Vietnam War era, including the contested terrain of remembering and forgetting and the troubled issue of memorialization's role in healing the wounds suffered by the body politic during that war.

Memorials are appropriate for thinking about such issues because they are collective and, in many cases, national projects. In the context of the accounting for missing Vietnam War soldiers, such collective projects are vital because they reinforce a conventional understanding of the body politic as a supraentity comprising so many individual bodies. To perform this role, memorials both draw from and contribute to "cultural memory," or "memory that is shared outside the avenues of formal historical discourse yet is entangled with cultural products and imbued with cultural meaning" (Sturken, 1997: 3). Cultural memory is not concerned with factual representations of the past, but rather must be seen as one among many strategies for the production and maintenance of the identity of a people. On this view, memory, broadly speaking, "is a narrative rather than a replica of an experience that can be retrieved and relived" (Sturken, 1997: 7). As a result, memorials are necessarily a certain representation of the past from the vantage point of a particular present. It is in this sense that memorials can be understood as "entangled with cultural products." They form part of the ensemble of stories a society tells about itself, but they fall outside the bounds of conventional historiography insofar as they do not attempt to produce a history of the event in question in which facts and memory might be indisputably congruent. This is almost necessarily so in that many people who view historical representations at places like national museums and memorials "are not remembering anything at all because they have little, if any, prior knowledge of the subject at hand" (White, 1997: 9). This point suggests a further dimension of cultural or collective memory, namely, that remembering and forgetting are "co-constitutive processes," each essential to the other's existence (Sturken, 1997: 2).

Following on these observations, one must be attentive to "cultural memory's role in producing concepts of the 'nation' and of an 'American people'" (Sturken, 1997: 1). That such concepts need to be produced in the first place implies that they are not things to which we have antecedent recourse but are instead effects of the many varied practices that enable them to secure intelligible meaning. Their coherence derives not from the presence of some stable ontological or cultural core but from textual strategies, identity stories, and the elision of differences and disruptions that challenge narratives of national unity and concord.[1] Monuments and memorials are sites at which these strategies and identity stories are materialized. Indeed, "the architecture by which a people memorializes itself is a species of pedagogy. It therefore seeks to instruct posterity about the past and, in so doing, necessarily reaches a conclusion about what is worth recovering" (Griswold, 1986: 689). As Geoffrey White (1997: 9) argues, "This is especially so for histories of war, with the aura of death and loss that surrounds them, making them prime material for national identity-building projects.' Warfare and the identity building that accompanies both its prosecution and its memorialization are intimately intertwined with the individual body and the body politic alike. As a result, war memorials encompass more than mere commemoration of an event. Especially in national contexts like those under consideration here, memorials consecrate the sacrifice of individual bodies to the nation, while "their histories instantiate the collective, national 'we'" (White, 1997: 11).

It is thus understandable that efforts to memorialize the body politic in the aftermath of war might be complicated by the absence of certain bodies. This is especially true of the United States following the highly divisive and ultimately futile war in Southeast Asia. The lingering absence of the bodies of unaccounted-for Vietnam War soldiers is not merely an unwelcome side effect of the war but, in the interpretation of many, an open wound in the American body politic. On this reading, the American body politic remains uncertain and ambiguous; it requires rehabilitation not through recourse to some allegedly transcendent values and identity configurations but via the various practices that enable the body politic to be regarded as such. Among these practices can be listed memorialization of the Vietnam War and its participants. Indeed, a great deal of Vietnam War commemoration—especially the Vietnam Veterans Memorial—has been described as a process of healing the body politic in the aftermath of this divisive and injurious event. Memorials heal the wounds by remembering and commemorating those who fought and died and by offering a space of reconciliation. Perhaps not surprisingly, the process of accounting for missing soldiers has also been linked to the healing process. As President Clinton once remarked, "For many Americans, the Vietnam War has left deep wounds that have yet to heal. One of the ways to help the process of healing is to help the friends and families of POWs and MIAs to learn the truth" (U.S. Department of State, 1993a: 500). Hence, I want to assert a link between bodies and memorialization, or, more specifically, that memorialization contributes to the emergence of the body politic by forming part of the means by which many bodies are fashioned into one. Memorials link the individual body to the collective body by presenting a set of narratives shared by each. They help form, as it were, the conditions of possibility that enable us to speak of the body politic at all.

To discuss the body politic, however, is to raise a conceptual issue as to the adequacy of this metaphor in light of the advent of democracy and the decapitation of the king that allegedly occurred as a result. The problem is addressed by Claude Lefort (1986: 305–06), who, following Kantorowicz (1957), argues that "the image of the body that informed monarchical society was underpinned by that of Christ." Accordingly, "the society of the *ancien régime* represented its unity and its identity to itself as that of a body—a body which found its figuration in the body of the king, or rather which identified itself with the king's body, while at the same time it attached itself to it as its head" (302). In democratic systems, by contrast, "there is no power linked to a body. . . . [T]here is no representation of a centre and of the contours of society: unity cannot now efface social division. Democracy inaugurates the experience of an ungraspable, uncontrollable society in which the people will be said to be sovereign, of course, but whose identity will constantly be open to question, whose identity will remain latent" (303–04). For Lefort's purposes, totalitarianism responds to this problem through its representation of "the People-as-One" (297). In the context of American efforts to account for and memorialize missing Vietnam War soldiers, however, it appears there is no mechanism to compensate for the dissolution of the body politic. The repatriation of individual bodies is therefore neither necessary nor sufficient to reunify a nation that experienced fragmentation like that which occurred in the United States during the Vietnam War. There simply is no collective body in a sense that might render the repatriation of individual bodies intelligible on a national scale.

Such a suggestion, however, would miss the ways in which the body politic has been reformulated in the age of democracy and the importance it retains as a means of understanding the relationship between the individual body and the body of the nation. Mark Neocleous (2001: 30), for example, has argued that "it is in fact only with the *advent* of the democratic revolutions that the metaphor of the body comes into its own. Far from there being a disincorporation of sovereignty in the late eighteenth century, what took place was *incorporation in a new form*. . . . This was the body of the people, or the social body." Lefort's (1986: 305) point that the dissolution of the body of the king is the orienting principle of the collectivity and that the rise of totalitarianism is "a response to the questions raised by democracy" does not necessarily mean that democracy has dispensed with the body altogether. One might say instead that the democratic social body has replaced the king with individual *names* as a source of interpretive sustenance. Experiencing identity as latent following the disappearance of the body at the center, democratic republics have turned to what they have in abundance: nameable, identifiable, individual bodies whose existence now constitutes both the life and the body of the collectivity. The totalitarian fear that "these individuals might become entities that would have to be counted in a universal suffrage that would take the place of the universal invested in the body politic" is entirely justified (Lefort, 1986: 303). Indeed, the enthusiasm with which democratic republics have embraced such counting intimates that perhaps names now fill the center which, according to Lefort, is vacant.

The reliance of democratic collectivities upon individual bodies may explain why memorial practices following the major wars of the twentieth century, above all those of the World War I, have produced an "explosion of naming" (Laqueur, 1996: 127). That there should be nameable bodies in the first place and that their identity would be so momentous to the nation as to compel it to scrupulously determine and list them on vast memorial walls along the Western Front seems unlikely absent postulation of a collectivity that emphasizes the individual as an indicator of coherence and integrity. One need think only of Edward Lutyens's massive memorial at Thiepval, France, featuring the names of seventy-four thousand soldiers whose bodies were not recovered following the Battle of the Somme in 1916. The individual body, its fate and whereabouts, in death as well as life, has replaced that of the king as indicative of the health and well-being of the society. The chronological listing of just over fifty-eight thousand American names on the Vietnam Veterans Memorial might therefore be seen as an American variant on this uniquely modern and democratic theme, one that not only unites the individual to the collectivity, but also underwrites the discourse of healing that has become the most prominent feature of the memorial since its dedication in 1982.

What are the political implications of conceiving of memorialization in terms of healing the body politic? Still more to the point, what is at stake when the effort to account for missing soldiers through the recovery of their bodies is hitched to that same healing process? At a practical level, the metaphor of healing often complicates efforts to memorialize the Vietnam War and thereby fashion the many into one. In particular, the narrative of healing deployed by the Vietnam Veterans Memorial is thought by organizations composed of family members of the missing to be inadequate precisely because some bodies remain unaccounted for. In their view, to remember the missing at the Vietnam Veterans Memorial is tantamount to forgetting the most important thing about them: their continued absence. Rather than helping to consolidate the body politic, this forgetting in remembering's clothing aggravates the wounds and deepens the divisiveness and controversy over the war itself. This logic has also informed the complicated history of another instance of memorializing the Vietnam War, the Tomb of the Unknown Soldier. Long a symbol of the sacrifice of one for the good of the democratic whole, the anonymity of the unknown soldier in the aftermath of the Vietnam War was no longer the solution but part of the problem, a circumstance which led to the decision in 1998 to exhume the remains for identification. The symbolic reserve of the unknown soldier, so deep following prior wars, proved inadequate in the context of a lost war and a gravely wounded body politic.

While these practical concerns are undeniably important, the figuring of memorialization as healing evokes epistemological and ethical issues as well. For example, the state's articulation of itself in corporeal terms implicitly presupposes that the body politic has a gender, which in turn implicates a relationship between the repatriation of missing soldiers and the gender of the body politic allegedly healed thereby. As will become clear in what follows, this relationship is not merely incidental to the effort to account for missing soldiers but central: it conditions the very meaning of Vietnam War memorials and of our thinking about the body politic in the aftermath of that war. Further, when wounds to the body politic are articulated in the idiom of recovery and healing, various insights that might serve as cautionary tales are elided. Specifically, the permanence of the loss of those killed during the war is denied, which in some sense, paradoxically, belittles their service to the nation.[2] In addition, metaphors of recovery and healing produce "a set of stories that pacify death, sanitize war, and enable future wars to be thought" (Ferguson and Turnbull, 1999: 109). Because national memorials tend to represent warfare as (at the very least) not inimical but incidental to the survival of the body politic, warrior codes such as national duty, martial honor, and heroic self-sacrifice not only remain intact but are enhanced in that it must be their instantiation in the bodies of individual soldiers that enables the continued existence of the nation.

Ethically speaking, the healing metaphor that helps condition the intelligibility of both the Vietnam Veterans Memorial and the repatriation effort bears two important consequences. First, it contributes to a politics of enmity between the United States and the Vietnamese, who are said to possess the bodies whose absence has proven so detrimental to the healing of the American body politic in the years since the Vietnam War. I will treat this matter in detail in chapter 6, but here the ethical dilemma can be briefly articulated as a foregrounding of the American self at the expense of the Vietnamese, who are, through a curious inversion, transformed into an agent responsible for the continued wounding of the American body politic. Of more immediate relevance to the argument of this chapter is the second ethical consequence of the healing metaphor, one which can be expressed as a clash between memorialization and repatriation. That clash finds material expression in the POW/MIA flag and arises out of the aforementioned belief among some that memorializing the missing on the wall is premature in virtue of their continued absence. The flag is thus a response, and although it can be seen as an instance of memorialization in the vein of cultural memory discussed here, it is also a demand that the body politic never forget the still-missing bodies of the Vietnam War. However, because this demand presents as fact a set of claims whose evidentiary basis is exceedingly thin, the flag ends up doing much to poison the interpretive well from which understandings of the issue of missing Americans are drawn. This, in turn, does much to further the politics of enmity,

These factors strongly imply that in addition to engaging the ethical issues, one must establish a critical perspective on the idea of healing itself and its deployments in the context of Vietnam War memorialization. Such a perspective can be achieved by situating Vietnam War memorials among other practices of memorialization, for example, Holocaust memorials. One might expect that, following an event which ended in millions of dead and absent bodies, memorials to those killed might be explicitly articulated in the idiom of healing. Yet any number of Holocaust memorials do not underscore healing nearly to the extent the Vietnam Veterans Memorial does. Indeed, remembrance is often made the higher value, a move that not only disallows the idea that we might somehow "recover" from the Holocaust, but also asks viewers to reflect upon and engage the interpretive commitments that produced the Holocaust. Against this background, the healing metaphor associated with Vietnam War memorialization represents a uniquely American reaction to loss and the absent body, a reaction that returns one's attention to the political work performed by war memorials generally and by Vietnam War memorials specifically. In addition to allowing future wars to be thought, the idea of healing positions the United States as the wounded victim of the Vietnam War. One notices that Americans do not talk about the need to heal the wounds of World War II, and this despite the deaths of hundreds of thousands more soldiers and the continued absence of tens of thousands more than are currently unaccounted for in Southeast Asia. The fashioning of the many into one thus grows out of an impulse to displace reflection on the causes of the Vietnam War in favor of an interpretation in which the United States is the primary sufferer as a result of the war. The ethos of victimization fuels the demand for the recovery of lost bodies and renders interminable the issue of the missing, thus deferring the closure so actively sought by those who link the accounting effort to finally ending the Vietnam War. Accordingly, Holocaust memorials are instructive counterpoints with respect to the political work that accompanies the linking of cultural memory with the healing of the body politic.

These observations are not meant to imply that Americans either do not or should not feel pain and anguish as a result of the Vietnam War. Certainly (in some cases at least), they do, and certainly it is not difficult to imagine that this pain and anguish is accentuated for families whose loved ones not only failed to return from Southeast Asia alive but failed to return at all. They are meant, however, to draw attention to what is affirmed when a postwar period is articulated in terms of bodies and the healing/memorialization process that must take place as a result of that war. What is needed is a more precise rendering of the links between cultural memory, the body, and the American body politic in the aftermath of the Vietnam War.

THE VIETNAM VETERANS MEMORIAL

Though remarkable in many respects, the Vietnam Veterans Memorial belongs to a long tradition of the memorializing of wars and their participants. It is noteworthy not simply for the uniqueness of its design but for the particularities of its contribution to a practice that has long had a hand in bringing about the intelligible emergence of such concepts as the nation and its people. George Mosse (1990) argues that war memorials make this emergence possible by connecting both the life and the death of the soldier to the nation. In its earliest phases, during the French Revolution and the German Wars of Liberation against

Napoleon, this connection was articulated via the "Myth of the War Experience, which fulfilled a need that had not existed in previous wars —wars which had been fought by mercenary armies with little stake in the cause for which they fought" (Mosse, 1990: 9). Hence the need in question was for practices that more firmly entrenched a sense of membership in and belonging to the nascent nation-state among individuals who were to fight and die in its name. The Myth of the War Experience thus evolved simultaneously with the nation-state. As nation-states came into existence so too did new ways of constituting the individuals comprised in it, namely, as members of a collectivity.

Complementing the Myth of the War Experience was the advent of the citizen army and the professionalization of the military, phenomena that conferred new legitimacy on soldiering and allowed militaries to become national organizations and to be accepted as such in ways they had not before. By reinforcing the connection between the nation-state and the individual soldier, the Myth of the War Experience helped materialize both. Soldiers were now constituted not as so many discrete individuals but as part of the nation-state. Soldiers fought and died qua German and qua French. Simultaneously, the French and German bodies politic materialized as the aggregate of so many individual bodies who were as much *of* those particular nations as they were from them.

Mosse goes on to argue that the death of the soldier in warfare likewise offered an opportunity for strengthening the bonds between the individual body and the body of the nation. Of particular importance were war memorials, national cemeteries, and tombs dedicated to unknown soldiers. Mosse writes, "The burial and commemoration of the war dead were analogous to the construction of a church for the nation, and the planning of such sacred spaces received much the same kind of attention as that given to the architecture of churches" (1990: 32-33). One sees in postrevolutionary France "the nationalization of death" in the form of massive collective tombs that become national places of worship (1990: 37). More noteworthy still was the use of the body of the dead soldier in the construction of monuments:

> The pillars in the arcades were to be made of glass which would be manufactured from the bones of the dead. But the dead were to be commemorated individually as well; medallions with their portraits—also to be constructed from substances of their own bodies—were planned which could

be kept at home. Thus the ancestors might inspire present-day men and women, while the design of the burial place symbolized a collectivity in which the individual had no place: all the pillars were exactly alike. (Mosse, 1990: 37)

Monuments and memorials were the tangible symbols of the Myth of the War Experience. Both in life and in death, the body of the soldier was connected to the body of the nation. Such connections were at one and the same time a further formation of the national body and the individual bodies of which it was composed because these were increasingly understood as members of a discrete, embodied whole.

The Myth of the War Experience "developed, above all, though not exclusively, in the defeated nations, where it was so urgently needed . . . having its greatest impact in nations like Germany which had lost the war and had been brought to the edge of chaos by the transition from war to peace" (Mosse, 1990: 7). Now that war was a national event, a major defeat like that experienced by Germany in World War I was a challenge to the coherence of the national body, one that required compensation through the legitimization of the sacrifice of those killed in a lost cause and the restoration of a sense of unity. Again, war memorials played a leading role. Though war memorials themselves were not new, they had previously focused on generals, kings, princes, and other heroes from a given battle, a circumstance that changed after World War I. In particular, the change meant that "modern war memorials did not so much focus upon one man, as upon figures symbolic of the nation—upon the sacrifice of all its men" (Mosse, 1990: 47). The effect was to connote the enduring presence and legitimacy of the nation-state in spite of the defeat recently suffered in war. By underscoring the connection between the individual and the nation, the war memorial established the nation-state as more enduring and in some ways more important than the individuals who had died in vain for its cause. This sense of permanence reinforced the impression that national memorials could inaugurate a healing process after a lost war. Despite defeat, war memorials preserved and strengthened the terms in which the nation-state was articulated.

One of the ways memorials enhanced these terms was through the listing of the names of those who died in war and those whose bodies could not be located and thus memorialized with an individual grave. As noted, naming marks one of the ways the collective body retains its sense in democratic republics. Absent the king, whose body formerly expressed the substantive unity of the collectivity, the named individual assumes importance as that which both constitutes the body politic and validates its claim to enduring relevance and significance—functions which are fundamentally, if only partially, called into question by the death of the individuals upon whom that body politic has now come to rely for its very existence. Such reliance puts pressure in new places, especially in the context of war memorials in which the relationship between death, the individual, and the past is explicit. The listing of names on modern memorials might therefore be said to point to "a powerful anxiety of erasure, a distinctly modern sensibility of the absolute pastness of the past, of its inexorable loss, accompanied by the most intense desire to somehow recover it, to keep it present, or at least to master it" (Laqueur, 1996: 132). Accompanying this impulse is an additional sense directly related to the emphasis on the individual, and that is "the modern notion that everyone has a memorable life to live, or in any case the right to a life story" (Laqueur, 1996: 135). At the war memorial, these themes intersect in ways that, like the Myth of the War Experience, produce the nation. In the context of defeat, a memorialization of names plays a powerful salutary role, since the emphasizing of the fundamental units of the democratic republic intimates that the republic and its individual citizens are ultimately more enduring than the event memorialized.

A similar logic can be witnessed at the Vietnam Veterans Memorial, which lists the names of every American killed in the Vietnam War and does so in the symbolic center that is the nation's capital, thus helping to link those individuals to the body politic. Accordingly, tropes of the nation and of the unity of the collectivity articulated at war memorials and national cemeteries form a backdrop against which the Vietnam Veterans Memorial must be situated. Another important contextual element is the divisiveness caused by the Vietnam War and the continuation of that divisiveness in the months following the public unveiling of the memorial design. Criticism focused on both the memorial and its designer, Maya Lin, who at the time was a twenty-one-year-old undergraduate architecture student at Yale University. The design, which consisted of two polished black granite walls placed at a 125-degree angle and inscribed with the names of some fifty-eight thousand soldiers killed in the war, was variously labeled a "black gash of shame and sorrow," a "degrading ditch," a "tombstone," a "slap in the face," and a "wailing wall for draft dodgers and New Lefters of the Future" (in Sturken, 1997: 51). Others objected to the modernist, abstract features of the memorial, wanting instead the more explicitly representationalist motifs of a traditional war memorial. Perhaps not recognizing the overtly abstract Washington Monument nearby, "most people can scarcely imagine a monument without statues and classical décor; to build one outside this convention [seemed] a provocation. Clearly, plenty of people were looking for a victory monument" (Sorkin, 1983: 121). Equally, in the minds of those opposed to the design of the memorial, "to be a memorial unlike other memorials is to be an anti-memorial. To be an anti-memorial is to be an anti-war memorial. Therefore, the Vietnam memorial is actually a monument to those opposed to the war" (Sorkin, 1983: 122). Still others objected to the absence, first, of any mention on the memorial of the war whose veterans it was designed to commemorate and, second, of an American flag on the site.

In addition, reaction to the proposed memorial implicitly linked the race of its designer to that of the former enemy. Though born and raised in the midwestern United States, Lin's Chinese heritage in combination with the disagreement over the memorial's design meant that her "status as an American disappeared, and she became simply 'Asian'" (Sturken, 1997: 55). For her part, Lin was not oblivious to the racial tinge of the controversy. As she observed at the time, "I think it is, for some, very difficult for them. I mean they sort of lump us all together, for one thing. There is a term used . . . it's called a gook" (in Sturken, 1997: 55). Lin correctly identified the fear implicitly animating opposition to her design, namely, that the memory of the U.S. defeat in a land war in Asia might be entrusted to an Asian proprietress.[3]

While the issue of race helped structure the controversy, the gendered dimensions of memorializing the Vietnam War came more fully into view in the months after the unveiling of the design, as if the ambiguity occasioned by the designer's non-Caucasian, nonmale body had to be policed at the memorial site itself. This policing took its most explicit form in the addition of another Vietnam War commemoration, a statue of three male soldiers placed, along with an American flag, at a distance of 120 feet from the wall. Designed by Frederick Hart, the statue depicts three male soldiers dressed in combat gear and speaking a body language of resolute fatigue. The statue satisfied those who desired a representational and, it should be noted, explicitly masculine depiction of the Vietnam War soldier.[4] With these compromises arrived at, the project proceeded, and the memorial was dedicated on Veterans Day in 1982.

What is one to make of the decision to add a highly traditional expression of the masculine warrior code to the Vietnam Veterans Memorial, especially *after* the memorial—and the gender and racial heritage of its designer—had been publicly revealed? At one level, the decision bespeaks a basic confusion over how to assimilate a woman designer and, more generally, the supposedly feminine aesthetic of the memorial, into the semiotics of warfare and its memorialization. Indeed, "that a woman—the ultimate outsider—should have won the commission was the final affront, absolute confirmation that the war was to be remembered differently, a monument emasculated" (Sorkin, 1983: 122). Lin herself remarked, "The fund has always seen me as female—as a child. I went in there when I first won and their attitude was—okay, you did a good job, but now we're going to hire some big boys—boys—to take care of it" (in Hess, 1987: 271). The big boy in this case was paid roughly twenty times the amount Lin received for her design of the original memorial (Sturken, 1997: 56).

On another level, however, the addition of the Hart statue is a commentary on the relations among gendered bodies, war, and the body politic. It takes the form of an assurance that even though the war was lost, the masculinity of American soldiers—and by extension that of the body politic—has escaped intact. In much the same way as Mosse's Myth of the War Experience in the defeated nations of World War I, the Hart sculpture signals the intensity of the desire in the United States for reassurance that manhood itself had not also been lost in Vietnam. Given the anxiety occasioned by missing soldiers during and after the war, such reassurance was all the more pressing because thousands remained unaccounted for. The Hart sculpture affords this comfort through the presence of the male. Still, the new statue begs a further question: Why men? Why did the Vietnam veterans who insisted on the Hart sculpture regard the male soldier to be the appropriate symbol, the authentic signifier of the body politic in the aftermath of a lost war?[5] To answer these questions, one must bear in mind the earlier insistence that there is no stable ontological or cultural core that might serve as the basis for fashioning individual bodies into a coherent body politic. Likewise, masculinity itself is never sufficiently stable to serve as the basis for its own legitimation. Hence both the body politic and masculinity require constant rearticulation in order to maintain the fiction of their standing in the world as independent existents. Linking the two in an explicit manner enables the body politic to be narrated in the traditionally masculine terms of a warring body, a protector, an executor of acts of legitimate violence, and so forth, while masculinity in turn is sustained by and derives much of its sense from linkages to the body politic provided by honor, duty, and the organized bellicosity known as interstate warfare.

This logic need not be taken to the extreme in order to reveal that, "the female must by necessity be excluded from the enactment and maintenance of this masculine community. Representing the body, the appetitive, necessity, the domestic, and the mundane, the female stands in direct contradistinction to that which the masculine represents itself as being: the abstract, the immortal, the unchanging, the public" (Jeffords, 1989: 61). If masculinity is forever faced with its own insufficiency, then that which either further dilutes it or fails to render it in terms recognizable by men represents a threat by definition. That the design of the Vietnam Veterans Memorial failed to represent men and masculinity in the heroic terms of the traditional warrior code was therefore not simply a problem of adequately memorializing the war, but an outright provocation because men and masculinity could not recognize themselves in the memorial's highly reflective surface. The explicit masculinity of the Hart sculpture thus makes its appearance at the Vietnam Veterans Memorial site as a means not only of policing the ambiguity of loss and absence but of ensuring the persistence of masculinity as an organizing principle of the body politic. In other words, it matters what Hart's men are portrayed as doing, a portrayal that draws interpretive strength from the idea that soldiers are employed to defend. Hart's soldiers may be defending, but it seems that what they are defending is not the republic but the masculinity of the Vietnam War soldiers so fundamentally called into question by the defeat in Southeast Asia.

Yet this interpretive possibility is complicated by still another statue added to the site, the Vietnam Women's Memorial designed by Glenna Goodacre and dedicated in 1993. Like the Hart sculpture, the Women's Memorial partakes of an explicitly realist motif, portraying three uniformed women surrounding a pile of sandbags, one of whom is holding a wounded male soldier. The message, of course, is clear: even as nurses

—indeed, because they were nurses—women were in some highly significant sense on the frontlines in Vietnam. Still more, they were subjected to the death and dismemberment of the body more continually and more immediately than anyone. As then-Chairman of the Joint Chiefs of Staff Colin Powell remarked at the memorial's groundbreaking ceremony, "I realized for the first time that for male soldiers, the war came in intermittent flashes of terror, occasional death, moments of pain; but for the women who were there . . . and for the nurses in particular, the terror, the death and the pain were unrelenting, a constant terrible weight that had to be stoically carried" (in Sturken, 1997: 69-70).

If, in the context of warfare at least, the body politic is gendered male, then how are we to interpret the decision to add an explicit representation of women to the Vietnam Veterans Memorial site? One answer to this question comes from those who initiated the women's memorial: it is a response to Hart's statue of men. In their words, "The wall in itself was enough, but when they added the men it became necessary to add women to complete the memorial" (in Sturken, 1997: 68). This explanation evokes egalitarian aims in memorializing the role of men and women in the Vietnam War, but it reveals little about the factors which rendered the inclusion of women intelligible in this context, especially since warfare has long been coded as something boys do and girls don't. To identify these factors, one must again address the conceptual predicates that enable the emergence of the body politic and the role of gender therein. Although the body politic is often gendered male, it is also figured as a caretaker of the disparate individual bodies of which it is comprised. And while that role is at times assumed by men (especially when they go off to war), it is more than a little redundant to point out that women have historically been constituted as caregivers, especially in the context of war, in which they have, as Goodacre's sculpture demonstrates, cared for men wounded in battle. In other words, while the presence of women at a national war memorial is certainly merited, what they're depicted as *doing* (read: women's work) is important, just as it is for the men in Hart's sculpture. At the same time, that work is performed stoically, which is to say with the sort of cool detachment typically ascribed to heroic masculinity. Hence, what renders the Goodacre memorial conceptually possible at the site of a national war memorial is the twinning of women's traditional role as caretakers with the masculine warrior ethic of courage under fire.

Such factors imply that the process of fashioning many bodies into one at sites like national memorials neither starts nor ends at a single conception of the body politic. Rather, that fashioning is relational and subject to numerous demands and tensions, one of which is gender. That demand is compounded in the context of warfare and in the ordering and representation of gender implied by its prosecution and memorialization. Rather than assign the body politic a definite gender, one should inquire instead how and when the body politic is (en)gendered. In the two sculptures added to the Vietnam Veterans Memorial site, masculinity and femininity alike are enlisted to shore up elements of the body politic's gendered identity following an event during which that identity was imagined to have been defiled. At the (national) Vietnam Veterans Memorial, both its masculine role as heroic warrior and its feminine role as caretaker are hitched to the larger project of honoring those who fought and died. Not surprisingly, the gender rehabilitations performed by the memorial site are all the more immediate in the context of missing soldiers whose absence has long been represented not as an unavoidable result of mechanized warfare but as a failing on the part of the state. To return to the argument of this chapter, then, if and when the body politic emerges as a coherent entity it is not because it has achieved or discovered a state of unvarnished truth. Rather, coherence is an effect of the representational strategies (in this case, memorials) that permit the manifestation of the body politic as such.

Another dimension of the political work performed by the Vietnam Veterans Memorial site is the essential conservatism of its tone.[6] In particular, the gender rehabilitations performed at the site imply that the United States is the victim of the Vietnam War. The Hart and Goodacre sculptures are especially revelatory. The need to signify the enduring relevance of masculinity and femininity through realist portrayals of them would be quite unintelligible absent some sense that these categories of embodied personhood had been either damaged or destroyed outright. If, then, the sculptures added to the Vietnam Veterans Memorial site tend to read like bedtime stories for adults, it is because they project a fundamentally conservative orientation to the politics, the memory, and the future of the Vietnam War. They partake of an ethic of reassurance: everything will be all right because the war can be, and ultimately will be, assimilated into the project of national coherence and corporeal integrity that allegedly characterized the pre–Vietnam War era.

Practices of Memorialization   175

While the rehabilitation of traditional gender configurations is clearly at work at the Vietnam Veterans Memorial site, the discourse of healing has been an even more prominent means of situating the memorial in the post-Vietnam War era. Indeed, Lin herself has said that she wanted the memorial "to bring out in people the realization of loss and a cathartic healing process" (in Griswold, 1986: 717, n. 17). Presumably, such metaphorics played a key role in the memorial's becoming, in the months following its dedication, the most popular site on the Washington Mall. Again, however, one would do well to avoid simply granting the memorial the power to heal and ask how the discourse of healing achieves intelligibility, and what political work is performed thereby. To begin with, how does the Vietnam Veterans Memorial articulate with the other national symbols on the Mall to produce the sorts of links between the individual and the collectivity that Mosse describes? If the unity and coherence of the nation are conceived in terms of the relations that enable the many to think of themselves as one, then the divisiveness caused by an event like the Vietnam War can be read as inimical to those relations. That in turn authorizes responses articulated in the vernacular of repairing, restoring, and healing. National monuments, one way of staging this response, are a metaphor of healing in a national context. The political work carried out by the healing metaphor is brought into focus by the contextual indications of Holocaust memorials. Because Holocaust memorials seek less to heal than to strive for remembrance and commemoration, they suggest much about the specifically American interpretive commitments materialized by the Vietnam Veterans Memorial site.

With respect to the first of these issues, one of the most frequently heard explanations of the Vietnam Veterans Memorial's popularity cites the memorial's refusal to valorize any one narrative of the Vietnam War and thus offer a space of reconciliation in which virtually everybody can find a place. As Mosse would be quick to point out, much of the capacity of the Vietnam Veterans Memorial to effect this sort of wholeness derives from the iconography of its surroundings, the Washington Mall and the capital city, that is, tropes of the nation that connect the individual viewer to the collectivity. So situated, the memorial emphasizes unity over the divisiveness of the Vietnam War and explicitly suggests that this unity is of national concern. The very possibility of the healing metaphor, in other words, derives in some measure from the location of the memorial within the semiotic horizon of the nation and the attendant suggestion that the nation is ultimately larger and more enduring than the parochial issues associated with this or that memorialized event. This semiotic horizon of the Mall is implied by the two structures to which the Vietnam Veterans Memorial points, the Washington Monument and the Lincoln Memorial. The Washington Monument is both the center of the Mall and an explicitly heliocentric structure. By pointing to it, the Vietnam Veterans Memorial is linked both spatially to the center of the Mall (and, by extension, to the nation) and symbolically to the person of George Washington, signaling that the values for which he lived remain valid even in the context of the Vietnam War.

The Lincoln Memorial, on the other hand, "is a monument to national unity achieved by the martyrdom of Lincoln himself" (Griswold, 1986: 697). The unifying thematics of the Lincoln Memorial and Lincoln's role in reunifying the Union after the Civil War make it all the more meaningful that the Vietnam Veterans Memorial also points to it. Equally noteworthy is the Arlington Memorial Bridge, which "extends from the Lincoln Memorial southwest across the Potomac to General Lee's house. So situated, it symbolizes Lincoln's effort to save the union by reuniting North and South. That Lincoln should, as it were, extend a bridge to his former enemy shows his 'malice toward none' and 'charity for all'" (Griswold, 1986: 698). The deep symbolic reservoir of the Mall generally and of the Washington Monument and Lincoln Memorial specifically lets the Vietnam Veterans Memorial materialize with greater force the unity and wholeness characteristic of national memorials. In drawing upon both Washington and Lincoln, the wall situates the Vietnam War (and, importantly, the bodies of the missing) in a context that brings the nation, in the bodies of the Mall's many visitors, together—and this regardless of divergent political viewpoints on the war itself.

Of note as well is the memorial's listing of names chronologically by date of death and the way in which the listing enables the Vietnam Veterans Memorial to articulate with the symbolism of the Washington Mall. A central component of this articulation is the list's origin where the two walls meet. As described by Charles Griswold (1986: 707),

> the list both ends and begins at the center of the monument. When one has read halfway through the list all the way to the eastern tip, one's eyes are naturally drawn to the Washington Monument. The visitor who con-

tinued to read the names in the proper sequence would be forced to turn and walk to the other end of the Memorial and so to see the Lincoln Memorial. One's reading of the VVM, in other words, is interrupted halfway through by the sight of the two other symbols. The monument thus invites one to pause midway and consider the significance of the names in the light of our memories of Washington and Lincoln.

This subtle symbolic gesture is, of course, entirely deliberate: it contextualizes the Vietnam War within the founding of the nation, its momentary split, and its eventual reunification. The manner of listing underscores the absolute import of the Washington Mall to the Vietnam Veterans Memorial's symbolic efficacy. Placed virtually anywhere else in the country, the memorial would have much greater difficulty making good on the promise of healing and reconciliation that inspired its design. The memorial's presence on the Mall 'bespeaks national recognition of and respect for the veterans' service, and to that extent articulates a certain settling of accounts" (Griswold, 1986: 708).

Other commentators have viewed the memorial's refusal to take an explicit stand on the Vietnam War as an element of its curative attributes. In this view, the memorial is "fundamentally interrogative; it does *not* take a position as to the answers" (Griswold 1986: 711). This feature was explicitly written into the design competition by the Vietnam Veterans Memorial Fund, whose instructions stipulated that "the memorial will make no political statement regarding the war or its conduct. It will transcend those issues. The hope is that the creation of the memorial will begin a healing process" (in Sturken, 1997: 50). According to Griswold, "Veterans and nonveterans alike are encouraged by the VVM to contemplate the difficult questions raised by America's involvement in the Vietnam War, and that too is a salutary effect of the monument" (1986: 712). Further, it is precisely because the Vietnam Veterans Memorial refuses to take an explicit stand on the issues of the Vietnam War that the intricate symbolism of both the memorial and the Mall can come to the fore. This occurs because "the architecture of the VVM encourages us to question America's involvement in the Vietnam War *on the basis of* a firm sense of both the value of human life and the still higher value of the American principles so eloquently articulated by Washington and Lincoln, among others" (Griswold, 1986: 713). The healing induced by the memorial thus lies simultaneously in what it enables—namely, the imbrication of the bodies of the living and the dead—and in what it constrains, a rendering of the Vietnam War that obviates the reconciliation the memorial was designed to achieve.

The names listed on the memorial also further the discourse of healing. In addition to their chronological listing, which leads the viewer to discern a connection with the Washington Monument and the Lincoln Memorial, the names have led some of the memorial's visitors to "imagine that the bodies of the dead lie behind the wall, where Lin envisioned them" (Sturken, 1997: 72). The effect, especially in light of the memorial's minimalist design, is to bring together more than just those soldiers who fought and died in Southeast Asia. Unlike some memorials which keep visitors at a distance, the Vietnam Veterans Memorial makes the names physically accessible; one can approach the wall and touch the names, or, as many visitors do, make a rubbing of a name. The highly reflective surface of the memorial's polished black granite allows visitors to see themselves not simply *before* the memorial but also *within* it: they are physically implicated in the listing of names, the remembrance of the dead, and the project of national reconciliation undertaken by the memorial. Within the symbolically charged surroundings of the body politic's most important national shrine, the body of the viewer is superimposed over the bodies named on the wall.

But what of the bodies of the missing? How is one to assess the Vietnam Veterans Memorial's treatment of the unaccounted-for soldier, above all in view of its explicit commitment to the healing of the body politic rather than to that of any individual body? After all, the memorial itself does not go to great lengths to differentiate the names of unaccounted-for soldiers from those whose bodies were recovered and identified. The names of the missing "are preceded by a small cross, which, in the event that the remains of that person are identified, is changed to a diamond" (Sturken, 1997: 46). In a sense, then, the memorial treats the absent body as more or less equal to the bodies already accounted for, not surprising given the extent to which national memorials seek to foreground a sense of unity and, in this case, healing. Despite the lengthy and often extremely contentious debates in the United States over the fate of missing Vietnam War soldiers, national memorials are not ideally suited to the continuation of such disputes. To say otherwise would imply that particular bodies transcend the body politic which national memorials foreground, an implication that is largely foreign to the sort of collective project which national memorials manifestly are. Hence, by treating the bodies of unaccounted-for soldiers as no different from those whose bodies were recovered at the time of their deaths, the memorial fosters that aspect of its salutary role in which the body politic receives greater emphasis than the individual bodies comprised in it. From this perspective, all bodies are (re)joined to the body politic at the Vietnam Veterans Memorial, a rejoining that brings about a healing of that body politic by reinscribing the wholeness and unity of the nation in the aftermath of the divisive event that was the Vietnam War.

At the same time, the dead named on the wall are themselves missing, or at least absent, just like those whose bodies have yet to return from Southeast Asia. However, the vast interpretive distance separating "missing and accounted for" from "missing and unaccounted for" means that these two absent bodies cannot be so readily conjoined. The confusion is demonstrated by those who claim on behalf of all those listed on the wall that "the absence of these bodies—obliterated, interred—is both eclipsed and invoked by the names on the memorial's walls" (Sturken, 1997: 73). This characterization clearly equates the two: both the missing and the accounted for are listed, hence memorialized, hence rejoined to the body politic at the wall. Yet as is demonstrated by the nation's extensive, ongoing search for its missing Vietnam War soldiers, the matter has not worked out nearly so neatly as this. The equation disregards just how loaded the term *absent* has become in the post-Vietnam War era when used to describe some of its bodies. Moreover, the subsumption of all bodies named on the wall under the rubric "missing" memorializes those still unaccounted for in a manner that tacitly suggests the continued absence of the body of the missing soldier is forgotten at the Vietnam Veterans Memorial.[7] Such circumstances trouble the discourse of healing associated with the memorial because "when that healing process is ascribed to a nation . . . the effect is to erase the individual bodies involved; the wounds of individuals become subsumed into the nation's healing" (Sturken, 1997: 73).

This situation provokes two closely related observations concerning the political work performed by the Vietnam Veterans Memorial. The first recalls the co-constitutive relationship between remembering and forgetting noted earlier. At the Vietnam Veterans Memorial, the absence of the missing is forgotten in the sense that it is not presented as something which might forestall the healing of the body politic. Simply put, the healing will go on just fine in the presence of the names and in the absence of the bodies. Like that of the sculptures by Hart and

Goodacre, then, the political message of the memorial is essentially conservative. Forgetting the missing enables the dominant narrative of the healing of the body politic to proceed untroubled by so many lost and absent bodies (whether accounted for or not). This, in turn, allows the nation to retain its standing as ultimately superior to and more important than the individual bodies which compose it—a representation which, incidentally, is essential to the war-making capacity of the body politic. Moreover, the body of the unaccounted-for soldier is not the only body to go missing at the Vietnam Veterans Memorial, a circumstance that has much to do not only with the focus of the national memorial on the body of the nation, but also with the relationship between remembering and forgetting that such focus necessarily entails. Indeed, "it is rarely noted that the discussion surrounding the memorial never mentions the Vietnamese people. This is not a memorial to their loss; they cannot even be mentioned in the context of the Mall" (Sturken, 1997: 82). The same might be said of the antiwar movement, whose glaring absence is nonetheless imperative if the body politic is to retain its ability to represent war making as an act it undertakes thanks to the willing participation of so many individual bodies.

While absences such as these may be objectionable on some grounds, they are not especially remarkable if we recall the extent to which forgetting is memory's enabling condition. Forgetting is the instantiation of a boundary beyond which the memory in question shall not go, thus helping to constitute it as such. The Vietnamese must remain missing at the Vietnam Veterans Memorial if its narrative of healing is to function comprehensibly. To include them would be to telescope the narrative of the Vietnam War to an unacceptable degree. The act of forgetting is especially important in the context of the Vietnam War because virtually every narrative of the war encompasses something the nation seeks to forget: the My Lai massacre, civilian children scorched by napalm, Agent Orange, the Christmas bombings of 1972, and the Gulf of Tonkin, to name but a few elements of the Vietnam War narrative that are also missing from the Vietnam Veterans Memorial. The deployment of healing metaphors at the wall is therefore registered not just in what to remember but also in how and what to forget.

A discussion of the second point raised above, the political work performed specifically by the discourse of healing, can be rendered more thorough by the contextual counterpoint provided by Holocaust memorials. As James Young (1993: 12) argues, "Public Holocaust monuments are produced specifically to be historically referential, to lead viewers beyond themselves to an understanding or evocation of events." Further, Holocaust memorials "suggest themselves as the basis for political and communal action" (13). In other words, these memorials, by placing less emphasis on the therapeutic dimension of memorializing and more on remembrance itself, are political acts that draw at least as much attention to the event they memorialize as they do to the victims of that event. In many cases at least, the memorial space is thus less immediately committed to reconciliation and the healing of wounds than devoted to keeping alive the memory of the Holocaust in all its horror. The memorial functions as a caution against precisely the kind of national unity that permitted such large-scale extermination in the first place. The viewer of these memorials is presented with effects—death, absence, gas chambers, hair—rather than with a project in which those effects might be somehow redeemed. Consequently, the reflection thereby inspired is less immediately personal and self-referential and calls attention not so much to the overlapping of the individual with an essentially wounded collectivity as to the violent possibilities lying within conventional understandings of the collectivity in the first place.

A striking example of this phenomenon is the Monument Against War and Fascism at Albertinaplatz in central Vienna. Designed in 1978 by the Austrian sculptor Alfred Hrdlicka, the monument was, like the Vietnam Veterans Memorial four years later, instantly controversial. In this case, however, the controversy stemmed not from the race and gender of the designer but from the means by which the memorial proposed to remember those killed in the Holocaust. Of importance in this respect was the proposed location. Albertinaplatz held special historical significance for Viennese: it was the site of two horrific events, a mass murder of Jews in 1421 and an American bombing raid on March 12, 1945, in which two hundred Viennese taking refuge in a bomb shelter were buried alive. Authorities at the time declined to attempt a rescue of the survivors of the bombing, whose attempts at communication could be heard by passersby; they also refused to exhume the bodies for a proper burial. The site was subsequently covered over with sod and shrubs. In light of this history, many believed the central space of Vienna already bore a sufficiently heavy load of death and cultural memory and couldn't support a Holocaust monument. Further symbolic pressure was added to the location by a feature of the memorial's design, a sculpted figure that has come to be known as the street-washing Jew. On hands and knees, brushes in hand and wearing a yarmulke, the figure recalls the days when the Nazis marched Jews through the streets of Vienna and ordered them to clean the streets with their bare hands, shirts, coats, and toothbrushes. This provocative gesture was intended by Hrdlicka as an accusation, something that would recall to viewers photographs of earlier generations of Viennese who stood by laughing at the condition of their Jewish fellow citizens (Young, 1993: 104–10).

The representational audacity of the Hrdlicka monument was a lodestone of controversy. Yet the more important issue here is the political work performed by the various elements of cultural memory employed at the Monument Against War and Fascism. Surely the most arresting of those elements is the prostrate Jew. While it is a realist depiction in the manner of the Hart and Goodacre sculptures, it nonetheless refuses to transform the suffering of the Jews into a monument to their heroism. Rather, the street-cleaning Jew preserves the humiliation of the Jews with stark clarity as a reminder of what happened during the time of the Nazis and in connection with the history of other mass killings of Jews at the same site. One is at pains to imagine what an equivalent representational approach might be at the Vietnam Veterans Memorial. A Vietnamese child scorched by napalm? An American soldier with both legs blown off? The point, of course, is that in this example of Holocaust memorials, remembering the event takes precedence over the effort to overcome it. Keeping the suffering of the Jews very much in the center—both spatially and conceptually—means that the viewer is forced to encounter the memory of six million people exterminated on the mere basis of who they were. This message is even stronger for Viennese and Austrians, who are directly confronted with their collaboration in the atrocity. One might suggest on this basis that the monument not only refuses to foreground healing as an interpretive trope but actually denies the possibility of healing altogether. Just like warfare, the degradation of Jews is an enduring problem, one that is physically emblazoned in the center of Viennese social space. Yet in that space, no effort is made to intimate that this problem is susceptible to the recuperations implied by the discourse of healing. It remains an issue, one that must be dealt with on its own terms or else risk being repeated.

A similar representational strategy can be seen at the site of the My Lai massacre, where Vietnam has built a memorial that deliberately highlights the events of that day. The foundations of the homes burned by American GIs have been left intact, as have the bullet-pocked trees and the ditch in which many of the dead were left lying. Equally prominent are several sculptures whose role seems partly to reprise and therefore to preserve the horror of that day and partly to convey an attitude of defiance toward an ally whose policies included the destruction of Vietnamese villages as a means of saving them. Equally moving are photographs in the site's interpretive center. Like Hrdlicka's street-washing Jew, the photographs deliberately take the viewer back to that day. For an American, at least, the effect of viewing these images at the site of the massacre itself is extreme and, despite the center's liberal use of photos that appeared in *Life* magazine, not at all like seeing them there. Here, the struggle to heal and overcome appears to be absurd and naïve, a strongly willed effort to forget the unforgettable. Thanks to its preservation of the earthly remnants of the site as well as to the addition of the sculptures and photos, the memorial deliberately scars the Vietnamese countryside. The continued visibility of that scar and the quite literal impossibility of healing such a wound is a deliberate feature of its politics.[8]

By invoking the Monument Against War and Fascism and the My Lai memorial and comparing them to the Vietnam Veterans Memorial I do not mean to suggest that the political work performed by all such memorials is similar or accomplished in precisely these ways. But such juxtaposition does indicate that events involving trauma, mass death, and the absence of bodies do not necessarily require recourse to the metaphor of healing. Cultural memory is perfectly free to preserve or even enhance the memorialized event in terms that evoke its most unsettling aspects. Indeed, this appears to be precisely Young's point when he says the goal of Holocaust memorials is "to lead viewers beyond themselves to an understanding or evocation of events." Movement beyond the self—understood either individually or collectively—lets the event stand as a challenge rather than as something over which the self might achieve mastery. This in turn makes it impossible to forget that the event occurred for a reason, in this case because of the hatred toward Jews and the incorporation of that hatred in National Socialism. Young remarks of Hrdlicka's monument that his "real achievement was merely the unveiling of these sore feelings, repressed memories, anger and controversy. Painfully and self-consciously wrought, his monument belongs wholly to those who want to remember without drawing too much attention to their memory-art. Instead of relieving past trauma, memory becomes its own trauma, perpetually deferred" (1993: 112).

In identifying the political work performed by the Monument Against War and Fascism and the My Lai memorial, I do not propose that the Vietnam Veterans Memorial somehow fails to lead viewers beyond themselves in important and provocative ways. The memorial's interaction with other national symbols on the Mall performs this function, as does the chronological listing of those killed. Nonetheless, the political work inspired by the discourse of healing at the Vietnam Veterans Memorial is substantially different and hints at what may be a specifically American way of remembering a divisive, painful event such as the Vietnam War. The political quietism that accompanies the discourse of healing as presented at the Vietnam Veterans Memorial signals this difference. Healing "gives a great deal of comfort to the state, whose hand in causing war and sending men to fight it is thoroughly mystified" (Ferguson and Turnbull, 1999: 131). By obscuring the scar tissue which remains on the body politic after an event like the Vietnam War, healing forestalls dialogue on the interpretive commitments that authorize war in the first place. Instead, that dialogue has been displaced by a preoccupation with overcoming the event, getting beyond the loss, and returning to the status quo ante. This in turn denies the political value of leaving the body politic *unhealed* in the aftermath of war, that is, of leaving certain wounds open as a cautionary tale about the reliance of the body politic upon violence as a mode of existence. Thus depoliticized, warfare is transformed into one among many events for which the body politic must be prepared rather than something that might eventually threaten the existence of that body altogether.

A second way to access the difference in the political work performed by the memorials at Vienna and My Lai is through the issue of missing Vietnam War bodies. In suggesting that the absence of these bodies can be overcome by the body politic, healing is offered as an unqualified good, one of many unremarkable processes that occur following war. But many families of the missing view this process as a tacit forgetting of the absence of these bodies and thus not nearly so unremarkable after all. At the same time, the preoccupation with absent bodies which the discourse of healing simultaneously and necessarily entails is emblematic of the ways in which that discourse disables the effort to politicize and problematize war. In other words, the Vietnam Veterans Memorial may point the viewer beyond herself in certain ways but the effort to heal prevents her from remembering the Vietnam War in all its prolix and painful detail. Rather, she is asked to remember other things, one of which is the continued absence of just under two thousand American soldiers. Paradoxically, the discourse of healing both enables a forgetting of the absent body and allows the collectivity to treat that body as if it were the most substantial of the many problems revealed by the debacle in Southeast Asia. Seen from the perspective of the political work performed by the Monument Against Fascism and War the Vietnam Veterans Memorial appears to be ultimately self-referential (indeed, the viewer is clearly reflected in the memorial's polished granite) since neither the event which inspired the memorial nor warfare itself is ever directly broached. The memorial represents Americans as preoccupied with themselves to the exclusion of the more strenuous interpretive efforts that might prevent such an event from occurring again.

At the Vietnam Veterans Memorial, then, the tension between remembering and forgetting that is present at all memorials has to do with the absent body. At one level, that tension finds practical expression in the confusion over precisely how to think of the absent body in the context of a national memorial. This confusion has resulted in a demand that healing be achieved through the recovery of unaccounted-for bodies. However, the sheer impossibility of recovering every missing body raises the specter of a healing forever deferred. Rather than suggest there are limits to the recovery effort, however, this situation impels the desire for more bodies and inaugurates a never-ending cycle in which the recovery of one body only increases the importance of recovering more by simultaneously validating the discourse of healing and yet exposing that healing as still incomplete. At another level, then, the tension between remembering and forgetting revealed by the absent body finds ethical expression since that body positions the United States as the victim of the Vietnam War. This positioning begins when the absent body is taken as evidence of the continued wounding of the body politic It continues when the discourse of healing presents that absence as something that can be overcome but then fails to make good on that promise, a failing which leads to accusations of cover-up and deceit and bolsters the claim that the missing have been forsaken. Such claims fuel the cycle mentioned above and deflect attention from the political forces that produced absent bodies in the first place. As a result, the status quo is preserved, and the Vietnam War becomes something which pertains solely to Americans, an event during which they were not the producers of trauma but recipients of it.

In view of these factors, it seems unlikely that the Vietnam Veterans Memorial can resolve this tension on its own terms, still less through deployment of a healing metaphor whose efficacy and desirability in the context of missing soldiers are problematic, to say the least. Perhaps it is better, therefore, to suggest that if we can grant the Vietnam Veterans Memorial the healing properties conventionally ascribed to it, we can do so only in the terms noted above, which is to say, by virtue of its location on the Washington Mall, the forgettings it authorizes, and the political and ethical passivity it engenders. If that is the case, then the unidentified body remains in limbo at the Vietnam Veterans Memorial. It is, in some important sense, out of place there, unable to repose among the prominently displayed symbols of the nation. There are, of course, other means of memorializing unidentified bodies, namely, tombs dedicated to unknown soldiers.

THE TOMB OF THE VIETNAM WAR UNKNOWN SOLDIER

Tombs dedicated to unknown soldiers originated almost simultaneously in England and France immediately after World War I, and the practice of returning an unknown soldier from the battlefield and entombing him in a central, public space thus has a long history in Western nations. Like the national cemetery and the national memorial, the Tomb of the Unknown Soldier has served as a site for the generation and celebration of the nation and "as a place for national worship" (Mosse, 1990: 93). Beginning with the selecting of the body and continuing with ceremonies commemorating its return and burial, the unknown soldier has been, like the modern war memorial, explicitly emblematic of the nation rather than the celebration of a particular individual. Upon selection of their World War I unknown soldier, for example, the French stated unequivocally that "the *poilu* [unknown] whom we are going to glorify is not a great man. He is the symbol of the immense number of soldiers who sacrificed themselves for their country" (in Inglis, 1993: 13). The modern practice of naming dead soldiers at war memorials is relevant here, though in a manner whose significance is derived from the *absence* of a name. Because of this absence, the British could say of their World War I unknown that "his is the *only* repatriated body and serves literally as *the* generic body. It makes the attribute of being forever unnamed—not lost or disappeared or simply forgotten, but so anonymous as to become universal—sacred. These are the bones that stand for all bones, the body that could be any body. ... 'The Unknown Warrior'" (Laqueur, 1996: 126). Finally, the ability to link the unknown directly to the nation was also related to the Myth of the War Experience, which, as noted, contributed to an understanding of the body not as a discrete particularity but as something nationally defined. Such definition is central to the symbolic efficacy of the Tomb of the Unknown and "becomes even clearer if one tries to imagine, say, a Tomb of the Unknown Marxist or a cenotaph for fallen Liberals. Is a sense of absurdity avoidable?" (Anderson, 1983: 17–18).

The United States dedicated its Tomb of the Unknown from World War I on November 21, 1921, making deliberate use of features from the European precedent of the previous year in the design of the tomb and in the planning of ceremonies to commemorate the interment ("Our Soldier Unknown," 1937). Yet these European features were present in an American context: "The return and burial of the Unknown Soldier was accompanied by a riot of symbolism, for all the symbols present in the design of military cemeteries, and in the mythology which surrounded the fallen, were compressed into one ceremony—indeed, into one symbol" (Mosse, 1990: 94). The return of the American unknown from the battlefields of World War I occasioned a massive public display in the nation's capital. A description from the time reveals the significance that was attached to this anonymous body:

> Following the gun carriage which bore the precious burden came such a company as never that historic Avenue had seen. The President of the United States, on foot, marching alone—then the Vice President; the Chief Justice of the Supreme Court, the Associate Justices marching four abreast; the members of the Cabinet with the Secretary of State at their head; the Governors of the States and their staffs; the Senators, the members of the House Medal of Honor, men of many wars, representatives of the Army, Navy, Marine Corps and Coast Guard, veterans and many patriotic organizations. General Pershing, who had led the American host to victory three short years before, headed the representatives of the Army. ("Our Soldier Unknown," 1937)

The ceremony was attended by nearly a hundred thousand people. They filed past "a catafalque which had borne the bodies of Lincoln and later the other murdered presidents Garfield and McKinley when *their* bodies had lain here in state" (Inglis, 1993: 12). The World War I unknown provided an opportunity to celebrate both victory in World War I and the nation. The presence of virtually every eminent personage of the time formed part of the symbolism that consecrated the sacrifice of the unknown to the collectivity of which he was a vital, if anonymous, part.

Because the symbolic efficacy of the unknown derived from this anonymous subsumption beneath tropes of unity and nationalism, elaborate procedures were designed not only to ensure anonymity at the time of selection, but also to prevent future speculation as to the identity. Accordingly, in October 1921, four unidentified American bodies were exhumed from military cemeteries in Europe. All records pertaining to each of the four bodies were gathered together and burned. The four sets of remains were laid in separate caskets, taken to city hall in a nearby French town, and placed under overnight guard. The following morning, French and American soldiers rearranged the order of the caskets. In a ceremony later that morning, an American sergeant twice wounded in the war made the final selection of the unknown, who after much ceremony in France was transported back to the United States for final interment. The three unselected remains were later reburied in military cemeteries in Europe ("Our Soldier Unknown," 1937). Similar procedures were observed in the selection of the unknown from both World War II and the Korean War ("Tomb of the Unknown Soldiers," 1964).

Ensuring of the anonymity of the unknown soldier was an acknowledgment of the logic animating the tomb, but also a provision that spoke directly to the symbolic function of the unknown in the production of the nation. The ability of the unknown to symbolize "the immense number of soldiers who sacrificed themselves for their country" was in the first instance dependent on a conception of dead soldiers as "citizens meriting civic honor" (Inglis, 1993: 9). In other words, "as the age of popular democracy and mass movements dawns, the service and death of ordinary soldiers begins to be recognized, on monuments which mourn them as well as celebrating their cause" (Inglis, 1993: 9). Hence, it is no coincidence that the United States, "the most democratic of the nineteenth-century nation-states," was the first to honor publicly an unknown soldier when in 1896 commemoration was made of an unknown from the Civil War (Inglis, 1993: 9). Mass democracy changed the meaning and the means of honoring the individual, who could now be honored not just for singular greatness but because the democratic collectivity was articulated precisely in terms of the individuals comprised in it. Preserving the anonymity of the unknown thus speaks directly to the civic honor of the democratic nation-state because the individual body does not surpass but instead constitutes the body politic. The anonymity of the unknown, by erasing considerations of rank, status, and class, mirrors the commitment to formal equality enshrined in democratic societies.

Anonymity also allows the symbolic functions of the tomb, including its design, location, inscription, and the ceremonies employed to commemorate the soldier within, to be underlined. As in the case of the Vietnam Veterans Memorial, these symbolic functions are frequently achieved by situating the tomb within a semiotic milieu that highlights the nation and various overarching themes and values. France is an instructive example: its unknown soldier from World War I is interred beneath the Arc de Triomphe, symbol of the victories of the nation during the reign of Napoléon I. Hence the unknown formed a symbolic liaison between the victories of Napoléon, the recent victories of World War I, and the defeat suffered at the hands of the Germans in 1870. As Inglis writes, "Burying the *Inconnu* beneath the Arc erased defeat by connecting the outcome of the Great War with the victories celebrated overhead" (1993: 24). The unknown also "erased defeat" partly because his anonymity mirrored emerging presumptions of democratic equality that in turn signified the overarching importance of the nation.

Like France, the United States honors its unknown soldiers in a place of national importance. Nevertheless, certain difficulties accompanied selection of a site for the unknown from World War I. The army's Graves Registration Service worried that the United States lacked a burial place equivalent to London's Westminster Abbey and the Arc de Triomphe in Paris. Such ambivalence was not unfounded, particularly in view of the ceremony that was to surround the unknown's return from Europe and the symbolic function the unknown had assumed in European countries. In Inglis's words, "To say that there was no suitable place for an Unknown American comparable to the sites in London and Paris was to imply that the project did not warrant, as it were, prime sacred space in the capital, within sight of the Washington Monument or the Memorials under construction to Lincoln and Grant" (1993: 25). Eventually, a site was chosen at Arlington National Cemetery, just across the Potomac River from the Washington Mall and connected to the Mall by the Arlington Memorial Bridge. But "Arlington had two disadvantages as a sacred site for the American nation: it was out of the way, and it signaled the hegemony of the Union over the Confederacy. That it was deemed suitable for a Tomb was covert acknowledgement that the experience of what Europeans called the Great War meant less to Americans than to them" (Inglis, 1993: 26).[9] Though adjacent to the Washington Mall, Arlington National Cemetery is not the symbolic center of the nation, and thus the Tomb of the Unknowns is not *on* the Mall in the way other major national monuments are. Given the importance of setting to the symbolic function of national memorials, the location of the U.S. Tomb of the Unknowns, above all that of the Vietnam War, is cardinal. It is in this context, therefore, that the unusual history of the Tomb of the Vietnam War Unknown must be understood.

That history is, at the very least, indicative of the anxiety occasioned not only by unaccounted-for soldiers but also by the unidentified body within the Vietnam War's contentious legacy. The Tomb of the Vietnam War Unknown was conceived in 1973 just prior to the signing of the Paris Peace Accords. In proposing a resolution for a tomb dedicated to Vietnam War unknowns, Representative Hamilton Fish Jr. of New York said that the need for such commemoration lay within the U.S. loss in Southeast Asia and that the tomb, like other monuments to the unknowns, was to be representative of the sacrifice made by all. Fish stressed that "we cannot permit the political controversy to obscure the tremendous contributions made by the 2.5 million young men who have served in Southeast Asia. Through the adoption of this legislation, Congress can demonstrate that, despite diverging opinions on the wisdom of this conflict, that [sic] these boys and their families will not be forgotten" (in Ehrenhaus, 1989: 101). Congress agreed and passed the resolution without dissent, apparently unconcerned about the differential import of Arlington National Cemetery to the project of honoring American soldiers from the Vietnam War. Work on the tomb was completed on October 4, 1974, and on March 28, 1975, the crypt was covered with a five-thousand-pound white marble slab. Curiously, the slab carried no inscription. Then, in an equally inexplicable move less than a month later, the white marble slab covering the tomb was replaced with red granite flooring identical to that used around all of the tombs. The effect was to conceal the tomb and remove any marking or indication of its location. The tomb retained its anonymity for seven years and remained undedicated for nine years (Ehrenhaus, 1989:

102).[10] Naturally the existence of the Tomb of the Vietnam War Unknown was widely unknown from the spring of 1975 until the summer of 1980 (Ehrenhaus, 1989: 105).

In the interim, both President Jimmy Carter and Veterans Administration chief Max Cleland, himself a Vietnam veteran who had lost three limbs to a hand grenade and now uses a wheelchair, were shown in newspaper photographs "situated directly over the hidden crypt while laying wreaths at the other Tombs of the Unknown" (Ehrenhaus, 1989: 105). In 1980, an article in the *Washington Post* detailed the activities surrounding the concealment of the tomb. In response to inquiries, the U. S. Army, which has jurisdiction over Arlington National Cemetery, claimed that the white marble slab had been removed in order "to avoid misleading the public that remains were interred in the crypt" (Ehrenhaus, 1989: 105). The army explained that "due to the sophistication of forensic techniques, all recovered remains could be identified. The crypt was not being concealed, rather public misconstrual of the truth was being averted" (Ehrenhaus, 1989: 105). The explanation was suspect at best. As the *Washington Post* pointed out, the army had announced that it was in possession of unidentifiable remains. At the same time, the Department of Defense was under pressure from families of unaccounted-for soldiers not to declare any remains unidentifiable for fear of the consequences of such a declaration on efforts to fully account for the missing. Finally, although the army claimed it had not attempted to conceal the site it is difficult to believe that the president and top officials in the Carter administration would openly walk upon and wheel across the tomb had they known of its existence (Ehrenhaus, 1989: 105).

In 1982, seven years after the tomb was concealed, the army reversed itself by installing a plaque that read, "This crypt lies empty as the nation continues to identify those American dead who have been recovered from Southeast Asia. In the meantime, there is nothing more important to the soul of our nation than that Americans never forget the sacrifice of those who died for freedom in the Vietnam War" (in Ehrenhaus, 1989: 105). Finally, on Memorial Day 1984, the remains of an unidentified American killed in action in Vietnam were interred in the Tomb of the Unknown at Arlington National Cemetery. Noteworthy about the selection of these remains, however, was the departure from the custom that sought deliberately to ensure that all unknowns would forever remain that way. As it happened, the remains of the Vietnam War unknown had always carried with them a speculative claim to identity. The reasons for this have partly to do with advanced search and rescue techniques employed during the Vietnam War: soldiers both living and dead were recovered much more quickly than in prior wars. Improvements in record keeping and identification techniques also meant that identification of remains was generally much more efficient and accurate. Speculation about the identity of the Vietnam War unknown thus began at the moment his remains and various personal effects, including an ID card and a wallet, were recovered. At some point, however, the remains were separated from the other materials, resulting in a recategorization of the remains as unknown (Spanfelner, 1999). Nonetheless, Tadao Furue, the CIL's lead anthropologist at the time, was convinced the remains could eventually be identified and refused to recommend that they be interred in the Tomb of the Unknown. In a prescient observation from the time, a former CIL sergeant remarked,

> Putting X-26 [the candidate remains] in the Tomb of the Unknowns was politically expedient. At best it was premature. I'll bet Doc considered him unidentified but not unidentifiable. Perhaps it was appropriate to the Vietnam War. So much else about it was political. Everything connected with X-26 has been ordered shredded, but you can't shred what's in men's minds. If we ever get into South Vietnam, the way we got into Laos, and find additional remains that match those in Arlington, there could be a problem. (in Sheehan, 1986: 96–97)

In view of these considerations, the records pertaining to the Vietnam War unknown were not destroyed upon interment of the remains in 1984 as the records of previous unknowns had been, and speculation continued to swirl, albeit behind the scenes, about the identity of the Vietnam War unknown. As described in chapter 1, the unknown was determined to be First Lieutenant Michael J. Blassie, a discovery made in part because of DNA analysis techniques that had not been available in the mid-1980s. Later, the decision was made not to inter any other remains in the Tomb of the Unknown in view of the possibility that improved identification techniques would permit all as-yet-unidentified remains from the Vietnam War eventually to be identified. An inscription placed on the crypt reads, "Honoring and Keeping Faith with America's Missing Servicemen" (Williams, 1999b).

How are we to understand the need to identify the Vietnam War unknown when the unknown warrior had previously given the nation such tremendous symbolic capital? A partial answer lies in the Vietnam

Veterans Memorial, where the metaphorics of unification and healing are explicitly foregrounded. At the memorial, the need to be certain of the identity of those listed on the wall is sublated to the project of healing the body politic. Its function, in other words, is to stress concepts of the nation and to honor those both living and dead who participated in the Vietnam War. Furthermore, much of the memorial's capacity to make good on these claims is derived from its location on the Mall. That siting authorizes a forgetting of elements of the Vietnam War that destabilize its already fragile interpretive frame and reinforce the comforting fiction of a nation restored in the aftermath of a divisive event. In contrast, Arlington National Cemetery, site of the Tomb of the Unknowns, lacks an equally direct connection to metaphors of the nation, and serves rather, by virtue of its many thousands of headstones, as a stark reminder of the death and loss that accompany warfare. Arlington is situated on the periphery of the nation's center, one might say, and is less fluent in the language of forgetting and reassurance that characterizes the Vietnam Veterans Memorial. While it may be sacred space, Arlington National Cemetery is not as sacred as the Washington Mall.

It appears the Tomb of the Unknown "lacks the symbolic power attributed to it. Who now, wanting to meditate on the individual deaths and national wounds inflicted by the war in Vietnam, thinks of doing so beside the Unknown Soldier from that and earlier wars out at Arlington, rather than beside the wall of 60,000 names at the sacred center?" (Inglis, 1993: 26). Not only has Arlington National Cemetery been displaced by the Washington Mall, the Tomb of the Unknowns has been displaced by the Vietnam Veterans Memorial as the site for the healing and reconciliation of the nation in the aftermath of the Vietnam War. This, by extension, explains the exhumation and identification of the Vietnam unknown. If the symbolism of a national memorial's surroundings participates in the consecration of that memorial to the nation, then being located on the edge of those surroundings, as the Tomb of the Unknowns is, perhaps signifies a correlative decline in the symbolic importance of that memorial. In addition, growing speculation about the unknown's identity was occasioned by the research of POW/MIA activists, the news media, and the suspected unknown's family and ultimately rendered the remains eligible for identification. For some, this speculation constituted a violation of the sanctity of the tomb. As the National League of POW/MIA Families stated in a press release at the time, "The ultimate purpose of the Tomb of the Unknowns is to honor all unknowns and represent [sic] for the families of those missing, symbolizing the possibility that he could be their own. This sanctity relies on total anonymity concerning service, location of recovery, forensic information, etc." Because the sanctity of the tomb had been destroyed by media speculation as to the identity of the remains interred therein and because "the purpose of the Tomb had been destroyed," the league's board of directors unanimously voted to support exhumation and identification of the remains within ("Vietnam War Tomb of the Unknowns: Fact Sheet").

Still, such explanations address only the confluence of circumstances that led to the identification of the unknown without suggesting much about the terms in which those circumstances were articulated. Specifically, how did it become possible to remove the unknown from the tomb for purposes of identification? and what enabled that removal to be regarded less as a violation of the sanctity of the tomb than as an incremental step toward the resolution of so much post–Vietnam War anxiety? Perhaps not surprisingly, that decision was justified at an official level through reference to the alleged suffering of the family of the soldier interred therein. As then–Secretary of Defense William Cohen remarked, "We disturbed the hallowed ground of the Tomb of the Unknowns in an effort to identify the Vietnam Unknown and ease the lingering anguish of one American family" (Office of the Assistant Secretary of Defense, 1998). While Cohen's characterization of the tomb as "hallowed" sounds more than a little hollow given its contorted history, the more important point lies in what this statement reveals about the extraordinary power of the families of missing servicemen to manipulate both the interpretive possibilities from which understandings of the unaccounted-for body are drawn and the government policy decisions that flow therefrom. At this level, the decision to exhume and identify the unknown ultimately had little to do with the sanctity of the tomb or lack thereof but rather with a brand of post–Vietnam War politics in which any official accounting effort that falls short of a positive identification is tantamount to deceit, a forsaking of the missing, and a continuation of the Vietnam War.

A more nuanced response to these questions would account for the ambiguous status of the missing body and its relationship to the body politic as portrayed at the Vietnam Veterans Memorial. There, as conventionally rendered at least, the absent body is either rejoined to the body politic through its inclusion in the memorial's list of names and thereby aids the recovery of the afflicted body politic or, via that same listing, is actually forgotten in that inclusion on the wall disregards its continued absence, thereby constituting a further wounding of the body politic. When considering the Tomb of the Unknown from the Vietnam War, it seems clear that the latter side of this interpretive equation has won out. On this reading, the unaccounted-for body remains a problem, one which the Vietnam Veterans Memorial fails to solve despite its much ballyhooed salving faculties. Accordingly, some solution more immediately aimed at solving the problem of absence is required; thus the decision not only to remove the unknown and subject his remains to identification, but also to refrain from interring any more unidentified remains in the tomb for fear of the message this might send concerning efforts to identify others still unaccounted for from the Vietnam War.

Any inquiry into how it became possible to disinter and identify the unknown also requires that one locate the unidentified Vietnam War body within the legacy of the only war the United States has ever lost. Within the interpretations that guide the U.S. martial experience—where victory in World War II reigns supreme while moments of colonial violence like the overthrow of the Hawaiian monarchy in 1893 are subsumed—defeat in Vietnam could not be assimilated. Nothing even remotely approaching either the military loss or the internal dissension of the war years had occurred in the previous one hundred years. In the meantime, practices of memorializing the nation and its warriors had taken on distinctly heroic overtones. The Tomb of the Unknown had, ever since its inception in 1921, partaken of heroic codes that explicitly focused on victory. Following such victories, the anonymous body could be honored as the ultimate symbol of democratic egalitarianism and as the sacrifice of one for the greater good of an essentially unified collectivity. The Vietnam War altered if not outright obliterated the understanding of sacrifice and unity upon which the symbolism of the unknown had formerly relied and, furthermore, placed the body in conspicuous relation to the U.S. defeat. In a war of attrition for uncertain ends, the American body politic was outlasted by that of the enemy and ultimately unable to absorb the many wounds caused by dead and mutilated soldiers. As a result, the post–Vietnam War era has seen efforts not simply to commemorate the nation but to reconstitute it through the deployment of metaphors of healing and redemption. To the degree that such practices exist outside of the effort to repatriate and identify remains, they exist not at the Tomb of the Unknowns but at the Vietnam Veterans Memorial.

Each of these circumstances seems to confirm—though in quite different ways—the earlier suspicion that the salutary effects of the Vietnam Veterans Memorial are indeed limited. The high anxiety over the fate of the missing and the identity of the body KIA in Vietnam has proven insurmountable; insurmountable not only by practices of memorialization that echo those of previous wars, but also by the Vietnam Veterans Memorial and even, it should be said, by the Tomb of the Unknown Soldier, no matter its original meaning as the place where precisely this sort of postwar difficulty was to be contemplated and overcome. Extant commemorative practices have come to be considered insufficient and have therefore given way to alternative ways of mitigating the extreme disorientation and ambiguity of the Vietnam War. To pinpoint what is now obvious, the body has become the site of these practices. It has assumed prominence in the effort to resolve the loss in Southeast Asia, a development due not solely to its amenability to identification, but also to the measure of certainty its materiality allegedly denotes in an otherwise ambiguous situation. Despite the significance previously attached to the unknown, in the context of profound defeat it left unaddressed one of the most pressing problems of the post–Vietnam War era, that of the identity and fate of unaccounted-for soldiers. Consequently, the issue is not so much whether the Tomb of the Unknown is adequate as a memorial. Rather, memorializing itself has been displaced by a quest for certainty to be gained solely through positive identification of the body. To identify the anonymous remains in the Tomb of the Unknown is to replace ambiguity with certainty and thus partially to erase the defeat in Southeast Asia. This process cannot be accomplished in the United States through simple context alone, as is it is in France, for example, through the Arc de Triomphe. Equally impossible is capitalizing on the symbolic power of the unknown warrior because the anonymity of the remains is no longer part of the solution but part of the problem. While the inscription on the now-empty tomb encourages "Honoring and Keeping Faith with America's Missing Servicemen," it is not believed that such commemoration might replace the certainty that comes with the identified body.

Yet the claim that certainty can be achieved through the materiality of the identified body itself makes sense only in a certain kind of world, one in which the body is invested with vastly more worth than its existence as a member of an essentially embodied collectivity might suggest. Were the metaphor still as relevant as it once was, the rejoining of the individual body to the body politic performed by the Vietnam Veterans Memorial might indeed be perfectly adequate for purposes of achieving the kind of closure now sought via the identification of remains. As we have seen, however, in the difficult aftermath of the Vietnam War, the body has assumed much more than a simple in-kind relationship to the collectivity. To the degree it remains unaccounted for, for example, the body signals repeated failures by—and, for some, the outright refusal of—the body politic to retrieve the remains of its military dead. When identified following repatriation, that body then signifies not just a sort of corporeal restoration but reinvigorated national honor, the replacement of deceit with truth, and, perhaps most important, an incremental step toward the true end of the Vietnam War. When that body appears as a Vietnam veteran, it becomes so much debased materiality that fails to redress the loss in Vietnam and, in addition, signifies the continued presence of that loss in the contemporary body politic.

What is more, the body of the post-Vietnam era continues to be signified as a bearer of abstract rights, though in this case the rights are no longer simply those enumerated in the Constitution but apparently the right to be identified following death. Is this why the practice of memorializing Vietnam War bodies seems vaguely anachronistic? Could this be why the sculptures by Hart and Goodacre and to a certain extent the Vietnam Veterans Memorial itself seem so hollow, so disingenuous, so transparently an effort to reanimate a body that has long since passed into obsolescence? Has the conversation perhaps completely bypassed these memorials?

If we answer yes, we can only do so at the expense of upholding, first, an orientation to the issue of missing soldiers supplied primarily by the families of the missing and POW/MIA activists and, second, an attitude toward certainty as a postwar heuristic that relies almost exclusively on the epistemological commitments of modern forensic science. After all, viewpoints such as those under discussion here are quite muted in wartime contexts other than that of the Vietnam War. Elsewhere, memorials appear to function more or less as they always have, irrespective of whether the identity of those being memorialized is definitively known. Indeed, as revealed by the lengthy history of the Tomb of the Unknown Soldier *prior* to the Vietnam War, the issue of anonymous remains was formerly an occasion for celebration of the nation and has only recently become a problem to be solved. Consequently, before deciding that Vietnam War memorials have lost their value (however construed), we must bear in mind the political wrangling that has done so much to ensure that memorializing of the Vietnam War will be seen, at least by some anyway, as inadequate no matter what.

In view of that wrangling, it is no coincidence that the decision to exhume and identify the Vietnam War unknown came at the end of the decade in which the U.S. search for its Vietnam War missing had become much more active and successful. Further, the wartime reliance on bodies rather than territory as a means of gauging success or, as it happened, failure, should again be noted. To the degree that healing in the aftermath of that failure is possible, it requires a remedy in kind. Identification of remains, then, emerges as a corporeal remedy to a corporeal problem, one that materializes the body of the accounted-for soldier by providing the epistemic terms under which highly fragmentary remains can function as a body. Despite the metaphorics of healing for which the Vietnam Veterans Memorial has become so famous, identification of remains has become the default means of healing the wounds inflicted on the body politic during the Vietnam War. The symbolic reservoir of the Tomb of the Unknown, as it turned out, was simply not deep enough to counter the pervasive disorientation and anxiety of the war. The result was both a literal and figurative grave robbing in the service of a body/knowledge interface imagined to be the ultimate certainty.

While certainty through identification of remains has assumed the clearest priority among the many priorities that structure the effort to account for American soldiers missing in Vietnam, it is also true that exhuming and identifying the Vietnam War unknown resolved the identity of only one body out of the many unaccounted for. Once its anonymity was articulated as a problem, the solution was clear. Securing the identity of the unknown, however, gave rise to an additional, somewhat paradoxical, problem in that it forced the nation to return to the Vietnam Veterans Memorial as the only place it could go to honor and remember its warriors from the Vietnam War. This, in turn, meant revisiting the tension at that memorial between remembering and forgetting the absent body and perhaps acquiescing to the memorial's narrative of healing even in the face of the continued absence of so many

Vietnam War soldiers. And so still another means of memorializing the Vietnam War—the POW/MIA Flag—has entered the fray, one that foregrounds the particularity of the missing in a manner that would be impossible at a national memorial. As we will see, the flag deliberately seeks the return of the missing and, what is more, actively bedevils the practice of fashioning so many individual bodies into a coherent body politic.

THE POW/MIA FLAG

The metaphorics of national unity and healing of the body politic at the Vietnam Veterans Memorial and the Tomb of the Unknown subsume the body of the missing within the terms of the nation. However, in the view of family organizations and others active in the effort to account for missing American servicemen, the healing this represents is in actuality incomplete because it neglects the continued absence of the missing and does nothing to secure the return and identification of their remains. By extension, the failure to secure the return of the missing means that the memorial and the tomb tacitly forget them. Forgetting is not an act of healing; quite the opposite, it inflicts a further wound on the body politic. Consequently, the POW/MIA Flag has become a further means of commemorating Vietnam War missing. It does so in a way that not only contests the forgetting inherent in the memorial and the tomb, but also firmly links the act of remembering the missing with the obligation to ensure their return. Before considering the details of the flag, however, it is helpful to contextualize this means of memorializing absent Vietnam War soldiers through brief consideration of two examples of commemorization from other American wars.

The first comes from the *Arizona* Memorial at Pearl Harbor. The victims of the bombing of the *Arizona*, 1,177 soldiers, were left undisturbed within the destroyed vessel because of the impossibility of retrieving even a single body. Those buried there are not thought by anyone to be forgotten simply because their bodies have never been retrieved; on the contrary, they are elaborately and, in the view of many, quite adequately memorialized where they fell. Indeed, Park Service guides at the *Arizona* Memorial explicitly note the absence of these soldiers and portray it as further evidence of their heroism. Although they are technically unaccounted for, those entombed in the sunken ship are joined to the body politic via commemorative practices that consecrate their sacrifice to the nation and also situate their deaths within a narrative of World War II in which that conflict's place in history is secure. In particular, the commemorative practices of the *Arizona* Memorial emphasize that these soldiers died because of the perfidy of the Japanese "sneak attack" on Pearl Harbor, an attack later avenged through victory in the Pacific. Hence, the deaths of these sailors form part of the moral hierarchy in which U.S. actions in the war were not only righteous, but also limited to rectifying the wrongs perpetrated by imperial Japan. The clarity of this narrative has implications for the bodies of the dead. Failure to recover those killed on the *Arizona* indicates little more than an inescapable fact of modern warfare, a largely unavoidable circumstance that does not hinder the process of postwar healing, reconciliation, and memorialization.

The second example, also from World War II, is memorials dedicated to soldiers killed in the war whose bodies were not recovered. "Possibly the most significant innovation introduced in World War II overseas memorials was the wall of the missing. As a design concept, the wall of the missing enabled memorial architects to make a visual connection between the soldiers buried in the cemetery and their missing comrades" (Mayo, 1988: 105). At least two American examples of this commemorative practice can be cited, the Manila American Memorial and Cemetery in the Philippines and the National Memorial Cemetery of the Pacific in Honolulu, Hawai'i, commonly known as Punchbowl. At the latter, "the courts of the missing are used as hierarchical elements along an axis of steps leading to the Memorial Chapel. The metaphorical statement is: Our deaths were steps to victory for God and country" (Mayo, 1988: 106). The link that the walls create between the missing and their comrades reunites the bodies of the missing to the body politic in much the same way as at the Vietnam Veterans Memorial. Their loss, both existential and corporeal, is consecrated above all to the nation.

That said, there is clearly a big difference between the practices of memorializing the absent World War II soldier and the soldier unaccounted for in Vietnam. First, those still missing from World War II have at the very least been granted separate national memorials that specifically cite not only their sacrifice but the fact that their bodies were never recovered. Second, and perhaps more important, the nation to which their sacrifice is consecrated is conventionally narrated as a victorious one, a nation less in need of the sort of healing that has allegedly become necessary in the aftermath of the Vietnam War. Punchbowl is a monument to victory as much as it is a memorial to those who perished in war. Like the *Arizona* Memorial, it both sanctifies and partakes of the World War II story, helping to solidify its place in history. Further, Punchbowl celebrates the deaths of all soldiers in the conventional terms of heroic warfare and "shows the state at work producing the comforting fictions of necessity and freedom: the men freely chose what had to be done (rather than, say, being forced or constrained to do what might be questionable or unnecessary)" (Ferguson and Turnbull, 1999: 131).

The nation from which Vietnam War soldiers are missing, by contrast, has been narrated differently. That difference can be traced in large measure to the ambiguity generated by the issue of missing soldiers in the aftermath of the Vietnam War. In particular, as we saw in chapter 2, the body of the missing soldier has come to symbolize deceit and dishonesty on the part of the U.S. government regarding the issue of missing Americans and its unwillingness to work in good faith toward the fullest possible accounting. So construed, the missing are the evidence that proves the government knowingly left men behind at the end of the war and has since been engaged in a systematic campaign to obscure this fact. Efforts to memorialize the Vietnam War, by extension, are not only premature, given the uncertain fate of the missing, but an organized attempt to *forget* the missing by failing to remain vigilant as regards their return. Because there are men still missing, the Vietnam War is not yet over and therefore cannot yet be memorialized. This view dovetails with assumptions about the nature of the Vietnamese, who, it is alleged, held or continue to hold American prisoners in Southeast Asia as a form of ransom or slave labor. Accordingly, the U.S. government is to be blamed for indolence and the Vietnamese for failing to provide the full accounting of the missing the United States deserves on humanitarian grounds. That censure authorizes an inversion which retroactively justifies the U.S. war effort in Southeast Asia since the missing are definitive proof that the enemy was, and still is, evil, amoral, and malevolent.

The ethical dimension of these interpretive gestures will be taken up in detail in the following chapter. It suffices for the moment to note what is by now clear: on these terms, the body of the missing Vietnam War soldier disturbs the project of national memorialization, reconciliation, and healing sought by the Vietnam Veterans Memorial. Unity is the dominant motif at the memorial, while the absent soldier materializes the absence of such unity. Healing through collective remembering of the Vietnam War and its participants is foregrounded at the wall, but healing without first repatriating the absent body means that the missing are being forgotten. The Vietnam Veterans Memorial offers a narrative in which the bodies of particular soldiers, whether repatriated or not, are subsumed within the terms of a newly unified body politic; the families of missing soldiers, however, often strive to emphasize the particularity of that absence.

These observations form the contextual backdrop against which the flag must be situated. Designed in 1971 at the instigation of the wife of a missing soldier and later commissioned by the National League of Families of Prisoners and Missing in Southeast Asia, the POW/MIA Flag has become a symbol of both the POW/MIA issue and the league itself, long one of the most influential activist groups on issues of Vietnam War missing. In the intervening years, the flag has acquired a rather impressive biography. In 1982, it became the only flag other than the U.S. flag to fly over the White House. In 1989, it was installed in the U.S. Capitol Rotunda at the behest of legislation passed overwhelmingly by the 100th Congress. On August 10, 1990, Congress recognized the POW/MIA Flag and designated it "as the symbol of our Nation's concern and commitment to resolving as fully as possible the fates of Americans still prisoner, missing and unaccounted-for in Southeast Asia, thus ending the uncertainty for their families and the Nation" ("History of the League's POW/MIA Flag"). Legislation passed in 1998 required that the POW/MIA Flag be flown on major holidays in the United States at such public places as post offices, major military bases, all national cemeteries, and the White House, to name but a few ("Display of POW/MIA Flag"). Finally, the buildup to the second Persian Gulf War saw still more legislation related to the POW/MIA Flag, this time in December 2002, when passage of Senate Bill 1226 required flying of the flag at all U.S. war memorials, including the not-yet-constructed World War II memorial (*POW/MIA Memorial Flag Act*, 2002).

From the perspective of cultural memory, then, the POW/MIA Flag provides a counternarrative to the Vietnam Veterans Memorial and the Tomb of the Unknown Soldier, above all in the degree to which it challenges the idea that the wounds to the body politic produced by unaccounted-for soldiers can be healed through acts of memorialization. As one activist has argued, "The Wall is not a shrine and has no mystical power to heal. It is its seemingly endless lines of chiseled names representing lives lost and hopes extinguished that stirs emotions and evokes tears and reflection. Nothing more, nothing less" (Sampley, 1997). Bearing the words "You Are Not Forgotten," the flag explicitly underscores the message that the absent warrior will not be forsaken and enjoins the viewer to remain vigilant in the effort to secure the return of the missing. The words function to bring memory and forgetting into close proximity, again suggesting the degree to which the two are mutually constitutive. The potential paradox of forgetting the missing as we remember the war at the Vietnam Veterans Memorial is here resolved into a statement whose finality refuses to countenance any such possibility. The missing are thus rejoined to the body politic not through their contribution to the unifying project of the wall but through a practice of memorialization that seeks to transform their absence into a presence. This presence, it goes without saying, is to be achieved only through the repatriation and positive identification of soldiers still unaccounted for in Southeast Asia.

In the meantime, the flag is a constant reminder of the absence of missing servicemen. They are presented there as a means of ensuring they will never be forgotten but also as an injunction that everything possible be done to ensure their eventual return. By virtue of its design, its message, and its metaphorics, the flag is less conciliatory than the Vietnam Veterans Memorial, and deliberately so. It implies that whatever rejoining of the missing body to the body politic it might be able to effect is provisional and ultimately unsatisfactory, something that must not permit the rest of the body politic to forget the continued absence of the missing. This is not to say, however, that the flag is necessarily revolutionary since, like the other commemorative efforts considered here, it derives much of its symbolic efficacy from proximity to symbols of the nation. In addition to being flown at the White House, the Capitol, and national memorials and cemeteries, the POW/MIA Flag is increasingly visible at professional sports stadiums, where it nearly always flies in conspicuous proximity to the American flag. Such juxtaposition connects the POW/MIA Flag to other symbols of the nation, though it does so in a manner that harbors a certain suspicion of that nation and its ultimate ability and willingness to ensure the return of absent servicemen.

The particulars of the flag's suspicion offer an entry point into the various political labors it undertakes. The flag takes a much more militant approach to the war's contentious legacy and especially to that of missing service personnel, an approach that finds expression in an interpretive belligerence in which the continued existence of live prisoners is presented as fact and the repatriation and identification of remains the only possible means of adjudicating this fact. This, in turn, leads to conclusions in which absent soldiers always signal something beyond themselves, namely, government deceit, dishonesty on the part of the Vietnamese, and a sustained effort to obscure both of these facts. From here, of course, it is but a short road to the claim that the missing have been forsaken. At first glance, the flag's effort to connect the missing to the collectivity through proximity to symbols of the nation seems designed to ensure that the issue of missing soldiers is not regarded as the exclusive province of a small minority of Americans, but instead as something of national concern. The irony here is that missing soldiers have always been important to the nation, as evidenced by memorials to them in Honolulu and in the Philippines and by the massive effort to recover their remains. The flag, however, lends credibility to the belief that the missing have been forsaken, a state of affairs which becomes something to be rectified by the small minority of Americans in possession of the truth. At the same time, by enmeshing the missing within the symbols of the nation, the POW/MIA Flag effaces the specific features of this inversion and, perhaps most important, the centrality of activist groups to the story of Vietnam War missing and the very possibility of interpreting the absent body as a problem to be solved in the first place.

The politics of the flag are enhanced by the details of its representational agenda. The flag's inscription, "You Are Not Forgotten," is complemented by the image emblazoned above it. The circular image shows the silhouette of a captive soldier with head bowed behind a string of barbed wire with an enemy watchtower in the background manned by an armed guard. Above the image are the letters "POW-MIA" on either side of a five-point star. Despite its highly tenuous evidentiary basis, this image draws much from the belief that the U.S. government knowingly left soldiers behind after the war and that the Vietnamese have since been holding them against their will. In presenting the continued captivity of live Americans as fact, the flag reinforces the narrative of governmental betrayal. The viewer is presented not with an invitation to reflect on the sacrifice of those who gave their lives for their country, but with a rallying cry, one that commingles the permutations of the POW/MIA issue with the war's recalcitrant legacy. At the same time, in a manner not dissimilar to Hrdlicka's Monument Against War and Fascism, the flag insinuates the viewer's complicity in the fate of missing soldiers. Here, though, the relationship of the absent body to the body politic is not so much that of a wound in need of healing but a violation of the code under which an American serviceman is never left behind on the field of battle. Rather than remind viewers of the need to remain vigilant about those being commemorated, the accusation leveled by the flag serves to deflect attention from the interpretive straitjacket into which the issue of the missing has been forced in the years since the end of the war. Such depoliticizing gestures receive a further boost in the league's own literature, in which they argue that "the importance of the League's POW/MIA flag lies in its continual visibility, a constant reminder of the plight of America's POW/MIAS" ("History of the League's POW/MIA Flag"). That the missing are in a "plight" conveniently muddles the way in which imprisoned soldiers got that way in the first place. No longer the consequence of years of military intervention in a foreign country, the absence of Americans becomes the responsibility of the Vietnamese or the effect of dishonesty on the part of the U.S. government.

The message of the flag is enhanced by the letters "POW-MIA" above the image, acronyms that invoke wartime categorizations officially irrelevant to the issue at hand. As discussed in chapter 2, during the Vietnam War, the term *missing in action* meant that no reliable information existed for the soldier in question—his fate was truly unknown. *Prisoner of war*, on the other hand, was a status given only when the government knew the soldier was being held by the enemy, meaning that his fate was known. The POW/MIA Flag represents the two categories as if they were distinct, yet resolves them in favor of prisoner status via the unambiguous image of a detained soldier. The missing, in other words, are probably being held prisoner as well. Again the effect is not thoughtful reflection but acquiescence to narratives that leave little room for alternative interpretation. The abjection of the prisoner portrayed on the flag is overt, his fate is (almost) sealed. The tacit forgetting that occurs upon memorialization of the body politic must be countered by the starkness of the words, "You Are Not Forgotten." The austerity of this message is reinforced by the colors of the flag, black and white. This black, however, is not the polished black of the Vietnam Veterans Memorial, which invites personal reflection as it reflects the image of the viewer. Rather, it is the austere, dull black of the conditions of the forgotten soldier, reflecting the severity of his life and the weight of the responsibility before the nation if the return of the missing is to be ensured. Indeed, reflection is not only discouraged but rendered impossible, subverted by the flag's simple message in black and white.

Another feature of the image of the (clearly male) detained soldier is the extent to which it evokes stereotypical configurations of femininity. He is passive, helpless, a victim unable to defend himself. Accordingly, to be missing or imprisoned is in some very real sense an emasculation. The image encapsulates the gendered dimension of the memorializing of the Vietnam War generally as well as the more specific effort to account for missing soldiers either through liberation from imprisonment or recovery of remains. As seen at the Vietnam Veterans Memorial site and particularly at the Hart and Goodacre sculptures, that effort is not limited to commemorating those who fought in the Vietnam War, but includes a rehabilitation of the gendered terms through which the body politic secures intelligibility. At the flag, the effort is not so much a rehabilitation as yet another accusation, this time one in which femininity is called to task for the difficulties that have accompanied efforts to account for American servicemen. As we saw in chapter 4, this tactic derives much of its sense from long-standing representations of the Vietnam War in which blame for defeat is attributed to the feminine and the consequent weakness and passivity of the U.S. government and the failed masculinity of the soldiers who went to fight (Jeffords, 1989). In like manner, the flag's image of the detained soldier displaces loss of the war, and the apparently permanent loss of some of America's soldiers, onto the terrain of the feminine.

One can certainly suggest, then, that the POW/MIA Flag illuminates the narrative rather than factual dimensions of cultural memory. Specifically, it appropriates a particular understanding of those still unaccounted for in Vietnam that seeks not to memorialize their absence but to bring about action that might ensure their return. That action requires that the body politic delay the reconciliation and healing presented by the Vietnam Veterans Memorial in favor of vigilance, investigation, and active searching. However, to ascribe this limited role to the flag fails to address its contribution to the contentious politics of the POW/MIA issue. At one level, that contribution has to do with its one-sided conception of justice and the correlative statement it makes about Vietnam's responsibility to account for missing Americans. By presenting the continued absence of American bodies as a fact for which the Vietnamese are to be held accountable, the POW/MIA Flag implicitly invokes a legalistic stance in which the obligation to produce the body falls to those in whose custody it presumably remains. The United States left Vietnam in 1973, the Vietnamese were in possession of a certain number of American bodies not seen since, and therefore the Vietnamese must assume the burden for their return. Although the United States willingly assists Vietnam in the repatriation effort, the standard in question locates ultimate responsibility with the Vietnamese and becomes the measure by which their honesty and integrity are assessed.

The question of Vietnam's responsibility will be discussed in detail in the following chapter, but additional features of the politics of the POW/MIA Flag arise in the current context. Those features again have to do, first, with the discourse of healing that has long animated practices of memorializing the Vietnam War and, second, with the interpretive possibilities either valorized or denied when the issue is articulated in this way. As seen at the Vietnam Veterans Memorial, the project of healing the body politic is marked by a tension between remembering the absent body and forgetting it as a way of moving beyond the injurious event in question. With the POW/MIA Flag, that tension takes the form of an overt clash between memorialization and repatriation. Although the flag does not engage overtly in the discourse of healing, it insists that repatriation, not memorialization, is the way to rehabilitate the American body politic and the various modes of embodied personhood —masculinity, for example—sullied by the Vietnam War. Moreover, in its own logical way, this insistence is fueled by the circumstances of the Vietnam War unknown soldier, whose exhumation and identification satisfied precisely the demands set forth by the National League of Families and symbolized by the POW/MIA Flag. However, the version of healing embraced by the flag is not only more strident, but also more pernicious in that it rejects outright the possibility that healing could be achieved in any manner other than repatriation of remains. Put differently, one can be wary of the discourse of healing as presented by the Vietnam Veterans Memorial and still allow the possibility that its many viewers in fact do find it salutary. Interpretively contestable and politically dubious though its manner of achieving that result may be, it is nonetheless an alternative that does not *require* recourse to the absent body. Call it a forgetting if you must but acknowledge that the wall's orientation to the absent soldier is much less parochial than that of the flag and therefore more inclusive and representative of the nation in whose name it purports to speak.

The POW/MIA Flag, on the contrary, endorses a view in which the missing are always an indication of cover-up and conspiracy. That view positions the United States as the victim of the Vietnam War; furthermore, it ensures that the much-sought closure to the Vietnam War will never be achieved because each and every repatriated and identified body only proves further that Americans were left behind in Vietnam. In itself, of course, that proof is not especially remarkable given that bodies have always been left behind following American wars. The difference in this case is that the flag refuses to recognize the distinction between the live body for which we lack definitive evidence and the dead ones everyone acknowledges are there. Instead, the flag offers an interpretation under which every unaccounted-for soldier is alive and being held prisoner, a possibility that can be put to rest only by the repatriation and identification of remains. It simply doesn't matter that the United States has done more than any nation in history to account for the fate and whereabouts of its dead soldiers. It doesn't matter that the Vietnamese have gone to commendable lengths to cooperate with the U.S. accounting effort, especially over the past fifteen years. It doesn't matter that there are limits to any accounting effort, however construed, given the slaughter produced by mechanical warfare. Finally, it doesn't matter that there would be no missing soldier issue had the United States not waged war in Vietnam in the first place. Nothing matters but the cause and the truth its adherents believe they possess.[11]

It does not matter either that the United States has enjoyed considerable success in its effort to account for missing Vietnam War soldiers. In this light, one begins to wonder whether the extremity of the flag's approach to the issue of missing Americans points to something not immediately observable in its symbolism but nevertheless immanent within the interpretive commitments it embraces. Perhaps one might characterize the politics of the flag as an example of the resentment occasioned by Vietnam's victory in the war and the correlative feelings of doubt and anxiety produced by that loss and by the absent bodies that are its most material reminders. The endeavor to make sense of these sentiments and ultimately to subdue them generates a search for some responsible agent (of which the search for missing bodies is the most prominent surrogate). Every absent body and every moment of suffering must find its place in the ledger of torment and victimization assiduously kept by the United States in the years since the Vietnam War. In this context, the POW/MIA Flag becomes a fertile site for the production of agency. At the same time, those agents must ideally be located outside the self, that is, beyond the body politic long conceived as one that never leaves a soldier on the field of battle (Connolly, 1991). To the degree that the responsibility for absent soldiers does lie with the collectivity, it must be the result of a "mindset to debunk" or a willful forsaking of the missing or both. The contingency of mechanical warfare and the attendant possibility that there may be nothing left of the body to retrieve from the battlefield is, on this reading, denied as an effect of political cowardice and as a failure of national resolve, that is, as a failure of responsibility.

With this possibility in place, one might then suggest that what enables the politics of the POW/MIA Flag is less the alleged inadequacy of American attempts to account for missing servicemen than the continued resentment by a certain (perhaps substantial) portion of Americans over the loss of the Vietnam War. We lost, but the war really isn't over because a certain number of soldiers haven't come back yet. Accordingly, the possibility of victory remains so long as we can repatriate and identify the remains of missing soldiers. In the meantime, any intimation of victory that may reside in the repatriation effort must be contested, since that will necessarily leave certain soldiers unaccounted for and hence will keep intact the country's loser status. The POW/MIA Flag therefore emerges as a material expression of the generalized resentment produced by the war in Vietnam and the inability to say for sure what happened to a certain number of American soldiers both during and since.

If this interpretation has any merit, it quickly becomes necessary to find a way to disable the representational economy by which the contingency of the absent body in the age of mechanical warfare is automatically transformed into a quest for a responsible agent. The reasons have already been suggested. Such transformation only fuels the desire for more bodies and thus forever defers the healing and closure imagined to be achieved thereby. Furthermore, such transformation positions the United States as the Vietnam War's primary victim, thus deflecting attention from the enmities and affiliations that produce warfare in the first place. Of equal importance, however, is the effect of such transformation on the range of interpretive possibilities available to Americans when thinking about the issue of missing soldiers. To state the obvious, that range has been greatly reduced by the many memorializations of the Vietnam War, most particularly the Tomb of the Unknown Soldier and the POW/MIA Flag but also the Vietnam Veterans Memorial and its ultimately conservative approach to the memory of U.S. involvement in the war. Perhaps most important, however, the quest for an agent and the corollary pursuit of an agent outside the body politic has had significant, largely deleterious consequences for the Vietnamese, who have, not surprisingly, become the agent most responsible for determining the whereabouts and ensuring the return of America's missing soldiers. To resist this impulse, one must refigure the concept of responsibility and its correlative quest for an external agent and then use that refiguration to foreground the other as the basis for reflection.

chapter six

The Ethics of Accounting

There is also the question of whether it is not bizarre, perhaps even morally obscene—and an insult to the bravery of the dead—to spend so much money searching for bones in a country where children die for want of antibiotics, and thousands of amputees from the war, many of them former Saigon-government soldiers who fought on the American side, hobble on crutches or go armless, because they cannot afford prosthetic devices.
—Sheehan, 1993: 45

Right from the beginning the U.S. side did not consider the MIA issue a humanitarian one It has linked this issue with the normalization of U.S.-Vietnamese relations, making it one of many other political conditions. It is indeed the U.S. side that has caused setbacks in the settlement of this issue.
—Quoted in Stern, 1995: 68

The above epigraphs reflect positions on the U.S. search for its soldiers unaccounted for in Southeast Asia that have been decidedly marginalized in the past thirty years. The quotations question the ethical legitimacy of an accounting effort whose primary motivations are not only blatantly ethnocentric (and therefore fail to redress the war's many lingering effects on the Vietnamese), but also fueled by sordid political and economic considerations that belie the invocations of humanitarianism so often used to justify the search. That criticisms such as these have failed to gain much traction since the conclusion of the Vietnam War is not a great surprise. As my analysis has sought to demonstrate, the search is more correctly viewed as an effort to account for the U.S. defeat in Vietnam, whose lingering presence is most immediately indicated by the materiality of the absent body. Accordingly, both official and unofficial American sources validate the repatriation effort through recourse to interpretive strategies in which recovery of the absent body is a victory of certainty over ambiguity, one that enables some of the many vexing issues of the Vietnam War to be put to rest. Some of these strategies emphasize the needs of the families whose loved ones remain missing; others rehearse the military code of honor under which no American soldier is left on the battlefield; but all see in the materiality of the body an unrivaled means of allaying the ambiguities of a lost war. These explanatory gestures, however, obscure a variety of contextual specifics that structure the issue of missing Americans in the post–Vietnam War era. In particular, they ignore the tens of thousands of American families with relatives still missing from other wars as well as the equally large number of American military dead whose burial overseas occasions no distress. In addition, they do not address the significance of having lost the Vietnam War to a foe who has long occupied troubled space within the American racial imaginary. Finally, such explanations obscure the role of domestic family organizations and the U.S. government in the continuing salience of Vietnam War missing.

Still more important for my purposes, the interpretive commitments that legitimize the effort to account for American soldiers in Southeast Asia lean heavily on notions of responsibility, humanitarianism, and the body which function, on the one hand, as normalizing discourses and, on the other, as justifications of the search on distinctively American terms. These justifications have assumed such potency that virtually any consideration of the moral implications of the search is construed as an attempt to subvert the legitimacy of its goals. That the accounting effort enjoys broad bipartisan support, has been pursued by the administrations of seven American presidents, and has never been subjected to even the most tentative official intimation that it be terminated indicates the hegemony of this understanding of the repatriation effort and helps explain why sentiments such as those expressed in the epigraphs have not gained a great deal of currency.

Following on these observations, I articulate an ethical relation toward the U.S. search for its soldiers missing in Southeast Asia by engaging with the interpretive structure upon which that search is predicated. As such, this analysis is not a quest for unalloyed judgments but an attempt to gain critical and ethical purchase on the understandings of responsibility, humanitarianism, and the body that fund the accounting effort as well as on their reformulation in a way that opens up a more conciliatory relationship to the Vietnamese. At a minimum, such an inquiry offers the possibility of escaping from what has become a tautological, self-generating set of justifications not simply for the accounting effort itself but also for the vilification of the Vietnamese which frequently ensues. It also helps to illuminate the representational economy in which the absent body functions as a metaphor for the continued fragmentation of the American body politic and the continuation of the Vietnam War through the alleged persistence of government conspiracy, cover-up, and dishonesty.

The term *ethical relation* seeks to displace a fixed conception of ethics as a unitary body of thought in favor of a context-sensitive orientation in which the self's debts to the other serve as the basis of reflection (Campbell and Shapiro, 1999: x). This is not an effort to reify the other but to demonstrate that, like the body, the self is derivative, dependent, and relational. Accordingly, any conception of the self as a singular, independent essence must be regarded as favorable to the politics of ethnocentrism that characterizes the American approach to the issue of unaccounted-for soldiers. This, in turn, requires undermining the conceptual basis upon which a unitary understanding of the self is predicated, a move enabled by the distinction between the Said and the Saying articulated by Emmanuel Levinas (1981) in *Otherwise Than Being or Beyond Essence*. Among other things, this distinction seeks to bridge the gap between the American view of missing soldiers as an unproblematic fact, an ontological given which governs its relation with Vietnam, and a more political performative understanding of that relation in which American responsibility to the Vietnamese reconfigures the relationship to those missing soldiers. In introducing the distinction between the ontological Said and the performative Saying, Levinas (1981: 5, 4), asks, "Is not the inescapable fate in which being immediately includes the statement of being's other not due to the hold the *said* has over the *saying*, to the *oracle* in which the said is immobilized? . . . [This immobilization allows being] an invincible persistence in essence, filling up every interval of nothingness which would interrupt its exercise." The Said is thus a function of ontology itself, a striving for conceptual mastery and the production of comprehension that seeks to contain ambiguity and instantiate one version of truth, subjectivity, and ethicality.

In this, it disables the effort to pass over "to being's *other*, otherwise than being. Not *to be otherwise*, but *otherwise than being*" (1981: 3). To provoke this transcendence, Levinas (1981: 5) turns to the Saying, "the proximity of one to the other, the commitment of an approach, the one for the other, the very signifyingness of signification." This establishment of proximity via the Saying requires that the other be allowed to remain other and that the self refuse the impulse to expunge the other on the basis of its difference. Indeed, "the responsibility for the other is the locus in which is situated the null-site of subjectivity, where the privilege of the question 'Where?' no longer holds" (1981: 10). The Saying denies the Said's quest for truth and comprehension by refusing to domesticate alterity; it valorizes the ambiguity of the encounter with the other rather than seeking to assimilate the other in the production of coherence.

In the context of the effort to account for American soldiers, the Said resides in the insistence on the materiality of the body, first, as an expression of antecedent truth about it and, second, by extension, as the sole means of resolving questions concerning the fate and whereabouts of the missing. The Said takes the form of an unrelenting quest for an agent who can be held responsible for lost bodies and, more broadly, for the corporeal and ontological fragmentation occasioned by the defeat in Vietnam. It thus functions ontologically, as a "proposition concerning which the truth or falsity can be ascertained" (Critchley, 1999: 7). That truth, as we have seen throughout, has historically maintained that the full recovery of bodies will unproblematically resolve the ambiguities of the post–Vietnam War era and bring the war to a close. Falsity, on the other hand, consists in the departure from any number of truth claims that have come to constitute the Said, for example, the claim that "the war won't really be over until they're all accounted for" (Dillow, 1995: A5).

An ethics of accounting must therefore refuse the propositional Said in favor of a performative Saying, one that acknowledges the Vietnamese as the interlocutor and understands an "expressive position of myself facing the Other" as an injunction to engage with the interpretive commitments on which the search for the missing is predicated (Critchley, 1999: 7). Such engagement would no longer be construed as a challenge to the legitimacy of the search but would instead become part of how that legitimacy comes to be in the first place. Further, the focus on the Saying resists the positing of a fixed ethics (whereby the accounting effort might be subjected to either wholesale condemnation or valorization) and recognizes the validity of the interlocutor as prior to any interpretive gesture. Questions like those raised in the epigraphs would be placed in meaningful relation to the search for the missing and no longer expunged as a matter of course. This would in turn help enact the shift from the constative Said to the performative Saying. The Saying would become part of any given interpretive gesture, thus unsettling the received understandings that legitimate some practices while marginalizing others. Portrayals of the accounting effort that regard departures from its truth claims as threats to the project of resolving the ambiguities occasioned by the absent body would no longer remain unchallenged. Perhaps most important, acknowledging "an expressive position of myself facing the other" would entail foregrounding the Vietnamese, upon whom the United States relies almost entirely for the success of the search. While this reliance is routinely acknowledged (and well remunerated), such compensation often obscures a deeper moment of misrecognition in which the Vietnamese are figured as radically other, an alterity that plays a prominent part in the American desire to repatriate bodies in the first place.

The argument begins by interrogating the assertions of Vietnamese responsibility to account for missing Americans made by the families of missing servicemen and the U.S. government. The ways in which race motivates the claim of Vietnamese responsibility for the resolution of unaccounted-for cases are examined, as is the absent body's role in structuring a self/other hierarchy in which the United States assumes the dominant position. An important example of this hierarchy was the twenty-two-year diplomatic and economic embargo imposed by the United States against Vietnam following the withdrawal of American forces in 1973—an embargo maintained solely over the issue of missing service personnel. Also crucial here is the way in which responsibility functions performatively to produce the subject positions and underwrite the claims that justify the search in the first place. In the encounter with a peculiarly American Said, Vietnamese alterity has been conceived not as a relation of proximity but as a threat both to the unity imagined by the fullest possible accounting and to an American self articulated as the primary victim of the Vietnam War.

The performative dimension of responsibility motivates a larger critique of the concept and its deployments in the context of missing American soldiers. The importance of such a critique is underscored by the links between attributions of responsibility, the drive to identity, and existential resentment—links which fuel the accounting effort in the first place and impel the production of agents who can be held responsible for the return of absent bodies. Such connections are also related to the defeat in Vietnam and to the suffering allegedly produced by the absent body. As one commentator observed, "The longing for recovery, retrieval, and reconciliation is so pervasive that it cannot be due merely to the claims of some people, especially family members, that Vietnam is still holding MIAs in prison. It can only signify some deeper sense of loss associated with the war. We hated losing, and still hate the Vietnamese for it" (in Isaacs, 1997: 103). From this perspective, the link between American resentment over the defeat and the quest for agents who can be held responsible for the resulting suffering is manifest. Again, the unaccounted-for soldier plays a central role. Like the quest for certainty in the form of identifiable remains, the production of missing bodies serves as the gauge by which Vietnamese responsibility for alleviating American suffering is measured and the means by which further resentment will be produced should that production come to a halt.[1] Equally visible is the sense of exceptionalism that links suffering, resentment, and the fullest possible accounting in American attributions of responsibility. Americans should not have to put up with the ambiguity of absent soldiers, and they should not be denied what is rightfully theirs. Emanating from an aggrieved sense of self achieved at the expense of denying that self's debts to alterity, responsibility is put forth by the United States as a universal truth capable of separating right from wrong and good from bad.

Following the critique of responsibility, I examine the U.S. claim that the work of accounting for missing Vietnam War soldiers is a humanitarian mission dedicated to absent soldiers themselves and to their families and the nation. In a manner not unlike the U.S. characterization of responsibility, humanitarianism is here conceptualized as a pure and independent entity detachable from other issues shared by the two countries. Thus articulated, however, this justification is but a further example of a nonreciprocal assertion of the American self at the expense of the Vietnamese that has come to characterize relations between the two countries in the matter of the accounting effort. Accordingly, humanitarianism must itself be subjected to critical scrutiny: how does it keep the United States mired in the ontology of the Said? and how does it obviate the ethical relation's emphasis on the other as the basis of reflection? Finally, as are the many other events discussed in this book, the complex of responsibility, identity, resentment, and humanitarianism is again staged on the body. Hence the chapter concludes with a look at the role of the body within the interpretive structure of the search for the missing and the attendant refusal to entertain alternative means of resolving individual cases; one such alternative is that proposed by the Vietnamese in which closure would be achieved in the absence of remains as long as a determination of the soldier's fate had been made. Of vital importance here is the extent to which the body becomes a universal of its own, affording upon identification material evidence of the return of missing Americans and, through its absence, an opportunity to blame the Vietnamese for perpetuating the issue. As a way of suggesting how the interpretive commitments of the accounting effort might be transformed, I speculate on how the ethical relation might bring the accounting and interpretive practices of the United States and Vietnam into closer proximity. This allows for contemplation of a conclusion to the accounting work not via the mathematical calculus currently animating it, but through a more conciliatory relationship to alterity, ambiguity, and the Vietnamese.

RESPONSIBILITY, HUMANITARIANISM,
AND THE ETHICAL RELATION

The trajectory of the interpretive commitments that guide the search for absent Vietnam War soldiers leads directly to the families of missing servicemen. Particularly through the organizing efforts of the National League of Families of Prisoners and Missing in Southeast Asia, family members have breathed a great deal of life into the discourse of responsibility that drives the endeavor to resolve the fate and repatriate the remains of missing soldiers. As noted in chapter 2, the league initially came together as an ad hoc support group for the wives of missing servicemen. It eventually incorporated and assumed a more overtly political character when members came to recognize that relatively few direct measures were being taken by the U.S. government to secure the release of POWs. The league's publicity efforts dovetailed with the Nixon administration's Go Public campaign, which was designed explicitly to rally public support for the Vietnam War in the late 1960s and early 1970s. Not until after the American withdrawal from Vietnam in 1973, however, and the repatriation of 591 American POWs during Operation

Homecoming did the National League of Families take on the form and function for which it is known today, namely, the largest private organization in the United States dedicated to the fullest possible accounting of Americans still missing in Southeast Asia.

A series of apparently minor yet nevertheless pivotal circumstances contributed to the evolution in the political orientation of the National League of Families, circumstances that continue to affect the manner in which the league approaches the issue of missing soldiers and therefore the ethical dimension of the quest for the fullest possible accounting. Among these was the power of the military service branches, operating under the provisions of the Missing Persons Act, to change the status of a missing soldier through a "presumptive finding of death" if one year had elapsed since the incident of loss with no new information on the soldier in question. Given the intense publicity surrounding missing servicemen in the years before the end of the war and the expectation that more soldiers would be returning home than actually did, it was not surprising that certain families took exception when the U.S. government began initiating status changes for soldiers who failed to return during Operation Homecoming. These families, no matter the extremely slim chance that any soldier still listed as MIA one year after the cessation of hostilities could still be alive, thought their relatives were being forsaken. Families feared that as a result of status changes, further efforts to account for their loved one through conclusive determination of fate and the recovery of remains would be suspended. At the fifth annual convention of the league in June 1974, this perception galvanized an especially vocal minority. Composed primarily of parents of missing servicemen, this minority succeeded in forcing the league to adopt an official position strongly opposing status changes unless new information specifically warranting the change was forthcoming (Clarke, 1979: 39–40).

The league's new position had immediate repercussions as to both status changes and the evolving issue of missing soldiers. First, certain families in the league were willing and able to back up their position with legal action, which they undertook in 1973 in an effort to prohibit the service branches from issuing presumptive findings of death.[2] The court battles that followed would halt the status review process for the next four years.[3] When President Carter eventually authorized the resumption of unsolicited status reviews, he was roundly castigated by the league, who saw the decision as "deceitful and disgraceful," an attempt "to administratively 'kill off' the remaining POW/MIA's by declaring them all legally dead," and "the final blow in what has become a long list of broken promises" (in Clarke, 1979: 109). Second, apart from these somewhat apocalyptic charges, the legal wrangling instigated by the families marked the gradual transformation of the issue of missing soldiers into a legally justiciable question, a phenomenon that complemented the already strong compulsion to produce subjects who could be held responsible for the fate and whereabouts of missing soldiers.

An additional factor in the evolution of the National League of Families' position on missing soldiers was an effect of the Go Public campaign. Because that campaign included strident publicizing of the issue of missing servicemen, a close working relationship had been forged between the league and the government. Despite occasional setbacks over issues like status changes, the league enjoyed leverage and influence on policy relating to missing servicemen and their families. By the late 1970s the closeness of this relationship prompted one observer to remark, "There is a direct correlation between the actions of the Government and the pronouncements of the League" (Clarke, 1979: 114). The leverage exercised by the league increased in later years, especially after President Ronald Reagan characterized unaccounted-for soldiers as a matter of "the highest national priority'" (U.S. President, 1983: 131). In particular, the executive director of the league, Ann Mills Griffiths, was granted a seat on the Interagency Group on POW/MIA Affairs, which at the time served as the government's principal policy-making organ for the handling of unaccounted-for cases. Along with representatives from the State and Defense Departments, the National Security Council, and the Joint Chiefs of Staff, Griffiths attended meetings, received limited access to classified intelligence, and participated in overseas delegations, all without the formal accountability to national policy she might have been held to as an actual government employee (Isaacs, 1997: 130). Not surprisingly, a close correspondence developed between the views of the league and government policy on Americans unaccounted-for in Southeast Asia.[4]

On one level, the importance of calling attention to the National League of Families derives from their influence on policy concerning the missing. On a second level, the significance of the league lies in the relationship between the desire to repatriate the body and the Vietnamese who are held responsible for its return. The league's position paper entitled "Vietnam's Ability to Account for Missing Americans,

April 9, 2004," notes that it continues to oppose the 1995 normalization of relations with Vietnam, arguing that the United States should have waited "until Hanoi made the decision to cooperate fully to resolve the POW/MIA issue." The league proposes instead a policy of reciprocity in which the United States would respond only after Vietnam carried out specific acts of cooperation. The paper continues by underscoring "U.S. expectations that hundreds of Americans could readily be accounted for by unilateral Vietnamese actions to locate and return remains."

These claims are predicated upon modes of apprehension conditioned by the ontological and are thus at odds with the ethical relation's emphasis on the performative, the political negotiation of truth and responsibility, and the attempt to assume responsibility for the other as the ground for understanding the self. Context is ignored, replaced by a drive to impose an interpretive framework in which subject positions are clearly fixed; the understanding is that it's the Vietnamese who must act, while Americans will react only when convinced of the sincerity of Vietnam's efforts. Equally noteworthy are claims made between the lines, namely, the league's indictment of the Vietnamese on the basis of presumptions about what they could have done but did not do. The absence of the body, rather than prompting reflection on the nature and consequences of war and the major material sacrifices it demands, is transformed into an accusation in relation to which the league assumes the role of judge and jury. The absence of the body requires a guilty subject, an insistence that enables the production of an agent who shall then be responsible for resolving the suffering produced by that absence.

The one-way attribution of responsibility contained in the league's position paper is notable, too, for its portrayal of the United States as being somehow immune from postwar miseries, of which unaccounted-for soldiers are fundamentally a part. In yet another version of the captivity narrative, it is the Vietnamese who hold the key, and were they simply to turn it over the United States could just pack up and go home. No mention is made of the U.S. contribution to this quagmire of existential resentment or, for that matter, of why *any* country should expect a full accounting of its service personnel under any circumstances. Still more, the league disregards the obligation that an external belligerent might have to a country devastated by that belligerence, in particular the estimated three hundred thousand unaccounted-for Vietnamese soldiers (to say nothing of the $3.25 billion in aid promised by President

Nixon in 1973). Finally, by presenting as fact Vietnam's inability to "act in good faith," the league's position invokes long-standing American stereotypes in which the Asian character is figured as devious, treacherous, and deceitful.[5] Although Vietnam's motives in the issue of missing Americans have not always been beyond reproach, the language of the league's position draws from a uniquely Western understanding of "good faith" and then imposes that understanding on the Vietnamese. Responsibility, to put it differently, is put forth as a universally applicable criterion that can be attributed to the Vietnamese as if it were free of the political and ontological constraints that enable its existence. Seen from the relational perspective endorsed here, however, responsibility in the context of the accounting effort is a resentment-fueled discourse that fixes subject positions and creates structures of meaning in which certain beliefs and actions become valuable while others are denigrated as untruthful.

The league goes on to argue that "at the end of the war, U.S. intelligence and other data confirm that over 200 unaccounted for Americans were last known alive or reported alive and in close proximity to capture." As we saw in chapter 2, however, such unambiguous claims are exceedingly difficult to prove, a circumstance not mitigated by reference to "U.S. intelligence and other data," which were themselves subject to much disagreement even during the war. The wording of this claim also takes certain liberties with the question of live prisoners by conflating "last known alive" and "reported alive and in close proximity to capture." For the league to argue that such data "confirm" the existence of more than two hundred living Americans at the end of the Vietnam War is, like the POW/MIA Flag discussed in chapter 5, an instance of presenting the radically contingent as unambiguous truth. American foreign policy toward Vietnam was for twenty years plus staked to the resolution of the issue of missing soldiers and to the question of live prisoners, so this is not just a semantic debate: it cuts straight to the heart of the matter. Such unambiguous claims underscore the by-now-familiar politics of imposition that characterizes the U.S. relationship to Vietnam in the aftermath of the war. The result is a uniquely American conception of the truth of the missing, one forcibly immunized against all data that do not confirm the story it wishes to tell and fortified against Vietnamese thinking on the matter.

The racial hierarchy implicit in statements by members of the league and other family members is patent. As Carol Hrdlicka, the wife of an

Air Force pilot missing since 1965, claimed in testimony before the U.S. Senate, "The Vietnamese are slowly and methodically out-negotiating our negotiators and once again are ignoring that my husband is one of these forsaken. They know where my husband is. I know this. It is embarrassing as an American citizen to see my country manipulated again and again by this tiny country" (in Sammon, 1992f: 3764). Griffiths, always among the most strident critics of Vietnamese cooperation in the resolution of unaccounted-for cases, states, "They lift their skirt a little to show you what they've got, and then don't give it to you. But our government knows what they've got" (in Schwarz, 1995: 24).

The overtly racial/sexual subtext of these statements is shorthand for an overall dismissal of the Vietnamese as subjects worthy of moral solicitude and calls attention to the racialized vocabulary in which assertions of Vietnamese responsibility get made. The United States is once again being manipulated by the wily Asian, the childlike, "tiny country" of Vietnamese who, because they have yet to advance to a full stage of moral or humanitarian maturity, must resort to trickery and deception to keep American negotiators at bay. Carol Hrdlicka knows that the Vietnamese know where her husband is, not through reference to verifiable evidence or to admissions by the Vietnamese that he is in fact still in their custody but through reference to a racial hierarchy that reinscribes white superiority as it discards the possibility that the Vietnamese truly do not know her husband's fate (after all, David Hrdlicka was shot down over Laos). Griffiths's deliberate feminization and sexualization of the Vietnamese draws heavily on the idea of the Asian seductress, a tease who tempts the white man only to renege at the last moment by failing to give herself up as promised. "Our government" knows what she's got, however, the implication being that this feminized caricature of the Vietnamese will be forced to "give it up" eventually whether she wants to or not. Among the many effects of these appalling assertions is the consolidation of a "we" figured as superior to, and therefore more worthy than, the interlocutor. The specifically racial figurations of the Vietnamese in these statements partake of the idea that "we" would never do such a thing as hold a POW after cessation of hostilities or fail to account satisfactorily to the families of missing servicemen through repatriation of remains.

I do not mean to suggest that family organizations like the league are necessarily and always racist in their approach. I do say, however, that race consciousness frequently structures the field of interpretive possibilities when the issue of Americans missing in Southeast Asia is broached. That consciousness is descended from the Vietnam War itself; race clearly configured the enmities and affiliations through which self and other were constructed—configurations which themselves have a history within the American approach to warfare. In his impressive study of racialization in World War II, John Dower (1986: 11) has reflected on how race functions within the wartime representational economy: "In countless ways, war words and race words came together in a manner which did not just reflect the savagery of the war, but contributed to it by reinforcing the impression of a truly Manichaean struggle between completely incompatible antagonists. The natural response to such a vision was an obsession with extermination on both sides—a war without mercy.' While the specifics differed, the importance of race in the waging of the Vietnam War cannot be denied. A remark made by an American soldier about the "gook syndrome" is symptomatic: "The Americans don't want to be there and don't know why in hell they are there. The result is, the Vietnamese become their only visible enemy, and according to the syndrome, all Vietnamese are equally bad. You looked around and all the Vietnamese you saw were whores, black marketers, VC, ARVNs not worth a damn, dirty old men and women" (in Polner, 1971: 71). Sentiments as strong as these are no doubt rare in the present-day effort to account for missing Americans, but the point is that the effort is justified via an assertion of the American self determined against the Vietnamese other based at least partially on racialized conceptions of self and other descended from the Vietnam War.

From here, it is but a short step to the insistent attributions of Vietnam's responsibility to account for missing American soldiers. Such imputations derive from the marked tendency among the families of Vietnam War missing to adhere to the possibility that a missing serviceman survived his incident of loss in spite of either long odds or even evidence to the contrary. Holding out hope for a more comprehensive accounting is understandable, as is the reluctance to force what may be a false sense of closure in the absence of identifiable remains; but the task of the ethical relation is to engage with the interpretive structure wherein the outlook of families of the missing who choose to continue to hope comes to constitute U.S. government policy on the missing. As we have seen, that outlook reveals not simply the quest for an identifiable agent, but also the presence of a racial animus that demarcates the range of interpretive possibilities. The strength of the National League of Families and its close rapport with the government make this all the more central, above all in light of the league's emphasis on remains repatriation and its lingering suspicion that the Vietnamese continue to hold American prisoners.

Largely owing to this rapport, views like those promulgated by the families of the missing are often evident in the government's position on the role Vietnam must play in the accounting agenda. Here, conceptions of the Vietnamese as racially inferior are less strident, but responsibility nonetheless retains its standing as a universal through which unilateral Vietnamese action can be compelled. As we saw in chapter 2, the country's determination to hold Vietnam responsible for an accounting found some of its most concise articulation in the Paris Peace Accords, which, among other things, required North Vietnam to provide the United States with lists of all personnel held captive in Southeast Asia at the end of the war. Although nearly six hundred Americans were eventually repatriated during Operation Homecoming, American skepticism about the comprehensiveness of the lists persisted after the signing of the accords, expressly vis-á-vis those who had been held captive in Laos. Combined with the rapid deterioration of the military and political situation in South Vietnam in the months following the withdrawal of American forces—which inhibited initial accounting efforts—such uncertainty made some in the United States highly suspicious of the honesty and intentions of the Vietnamese. Suspicion was exacerbated by a number of discrepancy cases in which an American soldier about whom the Vietnamese refused to supply information was known to have been alive in Vietnamese custody but failed to return at Operation Homecoming.

From the very beginning of the postwar period such suspicion loomed large in the formation of American policy toward Vietnam. In addition to blocking the admission of Vietnam to the United Nations in 1976, the United States maintained that a full accounting of all missing Americans was the "absolute precondition" for any progress toward normalization of relations between the two countries (Stern, 1995: 21). In spring 1976, the U.S. State Department reiterated that "the humanitarian concern for a full accounting of our missing men will be one of the primary issues of the United States in such discussions. Until this issue is substantially resolved, there can be no real progress toward normalization of relations" (in Stern, 1995: 21). Vietnam responded to such claims by referring to two of the more important articles of the Paris Peace Accords: Article 8(b), under which both sides were obliged to help the other obtain information about missing servicemen, and Article 21, which committed the United States to providing postwar reconstruction assistance to Vietnam. Vietnam argued that while it was fully prepared to carry out its obligations under Article 8(b), "the American side must also assume its obligations regarding the contribution to healing the wounds of war and to post-war reconstruction in Vietnam" (in Stern, 1995: 22). The United States, however, claimed that "a full accounting of those Americans missing in action and the return of the remains of those killed in action is a matter of primary concern to the United States. . . . [The] United States does not consider that it has an obligation to provide reconstruction assistance to Vietnam" (in Stern, 1995: 22). Effectively, then, U.S. skepticism about the adequacy of the prisoner lists became the basis for an almost wholesale disregard of its obligations under the Paris Peace Accords.

As might be expected, the Vietnamese have not failed to draw attention to the rather lopsided attribution of responsibility inherent in the U.S. position. On repeated occasions in the immediate postwar period, for example, Vietnam argued that its responsibility to account for missing Americans under Article 8(b) of the peace agreement needed to be articulated in relation to the U.S. obligations under Article 21. An article in a Hanoi newspaper pointed out in 1985, "It is quite preposterous that while Mr. Reagan is imposing on Vietnam the responsibility of seeking American MIAS in Vietnam, that is, those who had come to Vietnam and committed crimes, he is washing his hands of all responsibility of the United States for having caused suffering and death to millions of Vietnamese and its duty to help heal the wounds of war in Vietnam" (in Stern, 1995: 33). Although Vietnam has on many occasions stated its position on the search for missing Americans and has requested that various of their non-search-related needs be addressed in concert with the accounting effort, such utterances have gone largely unheeded by the United States because of its conviction that such action first required more progress and greater levels of cooperation from Vietnam. Simply put, it has been the responsibility of the Vietnamese not only to account for missing Americans but also to qualify for American reciprocity through increased cooperation and "tangible progress." In an attempt to so qualify, Vietnam has over the years made a range of concessions to American demands, beginning especially in the 1980s as economic backing from the Soviet Union became increasingly tenuous and normalization with the United States increasingly attractive. Such concessions commenced with Vietnam's decision to back away from its insistence on the reconstruction assistance mandated by Article 21 of the Paris Peace Accords. The Vietnamese then gradually began allowing American search teams into the country for joint field searches of graves and aircraft crash sites, facilitated access to Vietnam's wartime archives, decreased the response time on live-sighting investigations, and expedited research on discrepancy cases. Finally, Vietnam also agreed for the first time to assist the United States in resolving MIA cases that occurred in areas of Laos that had been under Vietnamese control during the war (Stern, 1995: 48).

Despite these concessions, the perceived culpability and responsibility of the Vietnamese remained constant even after the lifting of the economic embargo in 1995 and the restoration of diplomatic relations. Indeed, the debate occasioned by the normalization decision revealed a continuing compulsion to lay blame for the responsibility of missing Americans at the doorstep of the Vietnamese and, in some cases, the deliberate portrayal of the Vietnamese as a people who must be coerced into upholding their end of a bargain. In excoriating the decision to normalize relations, Senator Robert Dole argued before the U.S. Senate that "Vietnam . . . has made a conscious decision to keep the POW/MIA issue alive by not resolving it" and that therefore, "now is not the time to normalize relations with Vietnam. The historical record shows that Vietnam cooperates on POW/MIA issues only when pressured by the United States; in the absence of sustained pressure, there is little progress on POW/MIA concerns, or on any other issue" (in Lesinski, 1998: 131).

The continuing distrust of the Vietnamese contained in these statements is exemplary of the U.S. relationship to the ambiguity of the absent body and to the alterity of the Vietnamese believed to be in possession of that body. While some skepticism has over the years not been unfounded, as many of the discrepancy cases trenchantly reveal, the primary relevance of such doubt lies in the way it functions to produce the concept of responsibility and the Vietnamese as responsible agents. Such production is especially noteworthy given that not a single living, unaccounted-for American has been returned to the United States from Southeast Asia since the conclusion of Operation Homecoming in 1973. Mired within the ontology of the Said, the United States fails to place itself in an expressive position with Vietnamese alterity. Hence, the Vietnamese are seen as a people who have information and could assist the United States in the accounting were it not for their deviance and maliciousness. Otherness figured in adversarial terms thus remains a hallmark of the American conception of Vietnamese subjectivity and a principle of their intelligibility, a constant threat to the ontological unity imagined to be achieved by the repatriation of remains. In turn, the means by which facts come to be constituted as such proceed from a relationship to the Vietnamese which finds in their racial inferiority a justification for the continued insistence on their responsibility to provide "the fullest possible accounting." Finally, projecting upon the Vietnamese responsibility for absent soldiers consolidates an American body politic whose materialization as a warring body escapes implication in the production of such absences. That body politic once again becomes but an innocent victim of circumstances for which it bears no responsibility.

In addition to restricting Vietnamese subjectivity, the emphasis on their responsibility to account for missing Americans recalls the language of resentment contained in the POW/MIA Flag. The flag's message, "You Are Not Forgotten," was seen to be motivated by a politics of "generalized resentment" in which suffering must always be redeemed by a proportional amount of responsibility (Connolly, 1991: 22). Such resentment can also be detected in American presumptions about the burden Vietnam ought to bear in the accounting work, resentment which derives much of its sense from the defeat in Vietnam and the well-developed tendency of Americans to see themselves as victims (Engelhardt, 1995). Indeed, attributions of Vietnamese responsibility find one of their conditions of possibility in the logic of identity in which the United States is the primary victim of the Vietnam War and continues to suffer as a result of the absence of some number of soldiers. The problems that ensue are not difficult to identify, since identity itself is predicated on the capacity to make distinctions that serve as the basis for recognition of the self. Although by definition this relational constitution of selfhood offers the possibility of acknowledging the self's debts to others, it is also susceptible to interpellations of the other designed to maximize difference by positing the self as the superior term in a hierarchy whose opposites include evil, irrationality, abnormality, danger, etc. Especially when motivated by resentment over some as-yet-unredeemed moment of suffering, the identity in question turns its attention toward warding off those iterations of alterity imagined responsible for that suffering and whose very existence it finds threatening by definition (Connolly, 1991: 65–66). The sheer volume of political work undertaken by identity articulated in this manner is impressive. In the present context, it not only enables the production of Vietnamese agents who can be held responsible for the return of missing American bodies, but also preserves the unaccounted-for body as a way the United States might unburden itself of so much postwar existential angst. Like the opposition between the absent body and the Vietnam veteran discussed in chapter 4, the encounter between the United States and Vietnam is a functional requirement of the search for the missing not simply on a practical level but because it shores up the identity configurations upon which the United States relies for the very legitimacy of that search.

In this light, the value of the ethical relation to an understanding of the effort to account for missing American soldiers becomes clearer. If, as we have seen throughout this analysis, the search is not merely one among many normal postwar events but is rooted in—if not constitutive of—American identity, then a critical engagement with the specifics of how that identity is produced and sustained becomes at least as important as the absent bodies that are represented as self-evident expressions of a wounded body politic. Consequently, responsibility loses its status as a universal and becomes more nuanced, first, as pernicious attributions of it are seen to be located in American existential resentment and, second, as the United States assumes responsibility for the Vietnamese as the other who might positively disrupt ossified notions of the self. At the very least, the ethical relation begins to offer a reordering of priorities in which the absent body is no longer an instrument by which unilateral Vietnamese behavior is compelled by the United States.

One of the ways to effect this reordering of priorities can be accessed through the work of Daniel Warner (1999: 12–13), who argues for "imputation" as a means of circumventing the agent/act schism whereby guilty subjects and innocent victims are unambiguously constituted:

> The process of imputing responsibility is a backward process. It does not begin with a fixed subject and then analyze its actions and their consequences. On the contrary, the process of imputation begins with conse-

quences in order to define the subject. Thus, imputation is issue-specific and contextual. . . . [Through imputation,] it may be possible for the person judging to hold people responsible who were not directly involved in an action. Collective, indirect responsibility can arise beyond the immediate cause-and-effect actors. . . . Both those imputing and those being held responsible are not limited by the legal system.

Because it is issue-specific and contextual, imputation enables the Vietnamese to be unlinked from the unidirectional understanding of responsibility enforced by the interpretive structure of the search for the missing. Imputation thereby performs the ethical relation by reinstating the political and disabling the drive to produce overarching values, revealing in the process the dependence of unilateral responsibility on an apolitical ontological unity in which self and other are irremediably antagonistic. The attempt to bring self and other into closer proximity is thereby enhanced by a valorization of the encounter, one that disables the quest for absolute judgments. Through an appeal to context, imputation disables the insistent attributions of Vietnamese responsibility to account for missing servicemen.

One of the elements of that context is consideration of how missing soldiers got that way in the first place, which is to say, primarily through an intensive bombing campaign carried out over many years and through the presence of several hundred thousand American combat personnel in Southeast Asia. Clearly, any military engagement of such magnitude will result in a certain number of missing soldiers, and some among them may simply never be recovered. That such an obvious point requires belaboring suggests the value of imputation to the ethical relation in the context of the accounting effort. In other words, failure to begin with consequences separates the issue of missing Americans from contextual variables and abets the compulsion to transform the Vietnamese into a responsible agent. Imputation thus broadens the horizon of responsibility by locating the issue of missing servicemen within the purview of the lengthy U.S. military intervention in Southeast Asia. This both negates the effort to foist responsibility for missing servicemen unilaterally upon the Vietnamese and permits the United States to assume responsibility for the alterity of the Vietnamese as that which cannot be subsumed into the Same. That such factors are not part of the U.S. approach to missing servicemen generally and do not mitigate assertions of Vietnam's responsibility to account for the missing specifically, betrays the dependence of American interpretive commitments upon a Said in which alterity is transmuted into an agent who can then be deemed culpable for the unknowable.

In addition to exploring the ways in which the emphasis on Vietnamese responsibility inhibits the ethical relation, one must pay attention to the production of positive principles that justify that effort beyond the somewhat publicity-unfriendly disparagement of the Vietnamese that occurs through continued insistence on responsibility. Noteworthy in this regard is the hoary, oft-repeated claim that the search for Americans missing in Southeast Asia is a humanitarian mission. As one official long associated with the search once described it, "By far the most satisfying feature [of the search] was the knowledge that ours was simply a mission of great humanitarian importance, that of helping determine the fate of our comrades-in-arms. No one who has served in the military could possibly wish for a more fulfilling assignment" (Mather, 1994: xiii). At one level, humanitarianism is not entirely divorced from the concept of responsibility since Vietnam's claim to being a humanitarian people is often staked to their cooperation in the accounting effort. More significant, however, the U.S. emphasis on the humanitarian nature of the search justifies its insistence that accounting for missing Americans is to be pursued in isolation from other issues affecting the two countries. Humanitarianism becomes a claim that privileges and naturalizes the search from the perspective of the United States and furthers the transformation of responsibility from a reciprocal into a one-sided obligation. The result is a strengthening of the Said within the interpretive commitments of the search and increased compulsion to subsume the other within the same. This circumstance calls to mind a critique advanced by David Campbell (1998: 498), who argues that humanitarianism, "conceived as an unchallenged good characterised by impartial charity for a common humanity, and something which transgresses the confines of state sovereignty," all too frequently denies the "condition of possibility for the concept itself, which renders humanitarianism as inherently and necessarily political." Thus, when the United States invokes humanitarianism in its articulation of Vietnam's responsibility to account for missing Americans, it appeals to a set of presumed-yet-unspoken principles whose universality is imagined to be unfettered by the very conditions which make them possible. The task, in Campbell's view, is to reinstate the political within humanitarianism by dispensing with overarching codes and frameworks altogether.

The close correspondence of this project to the ethical relation should be noted. In particular, the "anti-humanism" which Campbell valorizes corresponds to Levinas's view that "humanism has to be denounced only because it is not sufficiently human"—because, in other words, it too often fails to recognize the other as prior to the ontological aim of producing overarching values (in Campbell, 1998: 507). Recall as well the specifically political value of the ethical relation's displacement of the ontological through movement into closer proximity with the other. For Levinas (1981: 15) that movement is achieved not by attributing responsibility *to* an other (via the Said) but by assuming responsibility *for* an other (via the Saying):

> Responsibility for the other, in its antecedence to my freedom, its antecedence to the present and representation, is a passivity more passive than all passivity, an exposure to the other without this exposure being assumed, an exposure without holding back, exposure of exposedness, expression, saying. This exposure is the frankness, sincerity, veracity of saying. Not saying dissimulating itself and protecting itself in the said, just giving out words in the face of the other, but saying uncovering itself, that is, denuding itself of its skin, sensibility on the surface of the skin, at the edge of the nerves, offering itself even in suffering—and thus wholly sign, signifying itself.

As an explicit refusal of the dictates of the Said, the Saying transforms responsibility and humanitarianism into vehicles that bring the self into closer proximity with the other, thereby performing the ethical relation.

Following Campbell, then, the effort to gain critical purchase on the U.S. assertion that the search for the missing is a humanitarian issue divorced from all others between the United States and Vietnam is not simply about including Vietnam in extant codes of humanitarianism. Rather, the objective is to refigure humanitarianism itself through a context-sensitive discourse like that achieved through imputation, one that not only reinstates the political within assertions of the humanitarian, but also rearticulates responsibility in a manner that foregrounds the U.S. obligation to the Vietnamese as prior to the quest for the truth of the missing. Invocations of humanitarianism thus become performative rather than ontological insofar as alterity no longer buttresses a nonreciprocal attribution of responsibility to the Vietnamese but instead constitutes the basis upon which humanitarianism and responsibility are predicated. One way to achieve this refiguration is by devoting attention to the many ways in which an attitude of nonreciprocity has been characteristic of American dealings with the Vietnamese beyond the simple attribution of a unitary conception of responsibility. I've already noted that the humanitarian nature of the search has long been invoked by the United States as a way of decoupling its obligation to provide reconstruction aid from Vietnam's responsibility to assist in the full accounting of missing Americans. Subsequent developments reveal a similar penchant of the United States for articulating the search in a manner that denies its political context.

In particular, Vietnam continues to lack for some of the most basic resources needed to address problems resulting from the lengthy U.S. military intervention. The Vietnamese Foreign Ministry estimated in 1991, for instance, that 842,405 Vietnamese soldiers were killed in action during the "America War" and another 484,324 were wounded (Stern, 1995: 137).[6] Among the many resources needed immediately after the war, adoption and relocation assistance for wartime orphans might be cited. Needs which began with the war and persist to this day include prosthetics and related care for amputees, assistance to victims of chemical weaponry, and aid in dealing with birth defects and other widespread forms of contamination caused by the liberal use of the defoliant Agent Orange. When compared to the approximately $100 million the United States spent on remains recovery in 1995 alone, the cost of recovering and identifying a single unaccounted-for American was about $3 million. Yet in the same time period, U.S. aid to Vietnam for prosthetic devices totaled $1 million, for assistance to displaced and orphaned children $1.5 million, and for disaster relief from typhoon flooding $245,000 (Sheehan, 1993: 46; Sheehan, 1995: 78). Although such issues have been raised by the Vietnamese throughout the three decades since the end of the war, they are often included among the issues the United States insists can be addressed only after it has observed greater Vietnamese cooperation and tangible progress in the search for missing Americans.

An attitude of nonreciprocity also characterized the American side of the debate over normalization of relations and its assessments of Vietnamese cooperation and progress in the accounting program, assessments which served as the baseline for determining when, if ever, relations between the two countries would be normalized. In this case, the United States was in a position to compel various sacrifices from Vietnam precisely because it occupied a position of vast economic, military, and diplomatic superiority. As a result, the demand for cooperation and progress as precursors to the lifting of the economic embargo and the normalization of diplomatic relations can be considered humanitarian only through a suspect process of foregrounding the self at the expense of the other.

Again, it is important to bear in mind that Vietnam has not always been as forthcoming and as responsive as it could have been. On numerous occasions prior agreements and commitments were inexplicably disregarded, and often there were strong indications that Vietnam was in a position to do more than it agreed to do. However, sensitivity to context requires that attention be paid to Vietnam's overall ability and willingness to provide the cooperation and progress required by the United States, particularly in light of ongoing constraints imposed at the time by the economic embargo. Indeed, the Vietnamese often "drew a connection between the pace of progress on accounting for the missing and the scope of U.S. 'attention to humanitarian aid to Vietnam.'" Vietnam argued that "the lifting of the embargo would have an immediate positive impact on the 'atmosphere' in which Vietnam sought to cooperate with Washington on efforts to account for missing service personnel" (Stern, 1995: 77). Still, the United States repeatedly insisted that "any further steps in U.S.-Vietnamese relations will strictly depend on further progress by the Vietnamese on the POW/MIA issue" (U.S. Department of State, 1993a: 500). Quid pro quo was a constant condition even though Vietnam went so far as to establish an office within their government, the Vietnam Office for Seeking Missing Persons (VNOSMP), whose mission involved not the search for missing Vietnamese but for missing Americans.

Reinstating the political within American declarations of the humanitarian nature of the accounting effort directs attention to still another contextual element, namely, the three hundred thousand unaccounted-for Vietnamese soldiers mentioned earlier. Here, too, the United States has consistently refused to assist systematically in accounting for missing Vietnamese servicemen. The United States has on several occasions turned over large stores of wartime documents that may contain information about missing Vietnamese and in 1999 allowed a Vietnamese delegation unfettered access to the National Archives for the same purpose (Office of the Assistant Secretary of Defense, 1999b), but such concessions are quite different from the systematic excavation and identification program undertaken by the United States on behalf of its own unaccounted-for soldiers. The disparity in accounting practices eventually became something of a domestic issue in Vietnam as pressure from families of the missing and the Vietnamese military began to build. As government officials frequently pointed out, "The Vietnamese people were hard pressed to understand why the Vietnamese government was dedicating personnel and resources to look for American MIAs when many Vietnamese were still unaccounted for" (Stern, 1998: 52). This example underscores Campbell's earlier point about the political conditions that enable invocations of humanitarianism. In light of the number of Vietnamese missing and the relative lack of attention they receive, U.S. insistence on the humanitarian nature of the accounting effort looks not like a universal category but like a parochial assertion of the self obtained at the expense of an other.

The limitations of the American claim that the accounting effort is "a mission of great humanitarian importance" are revealed even more starkly by the means of accounting to which the Vietnamese are forced to resort in the absence of sustained governmental funding from either Vietnam or the United States. In the face of such constraints, the families of unaccounted-for soldiers in Vietnam have turned in increasing numbers to psychics as a means of locating and identifying the bodies of their loved ones. The departure from the American means of verifying the retrieval and identity of a missing soldier through forensic science is striking indeed. For a fee equivalent to about $3.50, relatives in Vietnam can consult a psychic, who addresses the spirits to reveal the burial location of the relative (Larimer, 1995: F7). Other families send photographs and documents to a television station that regularly broadcasts information about missing servicemen in the hope that someone might recall something that would aid in the recovery of remains (Mydans, 2000: 14). Behind these efforts, of course, is a desire not unlike that driving the Americans, to give the dead a proper burial. Vietnamese place high value on burial because of the importance of ancestor worship in Vietnamese culture. As one family member who located a relative through a psychic remarked, "The Vietnamese honor the dead and they would like to bring them home to bury in the village cemetery so that later generations can come worship them, rather than leaving them in the jungle" (in Mydans, 2000: 14).

The discourse of certainty discussed in chapter 3 reappears here, though this time in a way that further illustrates the disparities between American and Vietnamese practices of accounting for the missing. As we have seen, American insistence on an absolutely certain determination of the fate and whereabouts of missing Vietnam War soldiers has generated a search effort unlike any in the history of warfare. Yet its priorities and practices are not extended to the missing from the one nation upon whom the United States depends the most for the recovery of its missing; and this despite clear indications that families of Vietnamese missing would very much like to account for their loved ones as well. Hence the certainty provided by the body is neither given in its materiality nor a right to which families are automatically entitled in the aftermath of war. Rather, it is conditional and relational, a feature amply demonstrated by the families of absent Vietnamese soldiers, who manage to get on even though they are denied the level of certainty which American families have claimed as their most material of entitlements. Moreover, even if the families of missing Vietnamese soldiers did expect this same certainty, it would be altogether misplaced given the extreme financial constraints under which accounting efforts proceed in Vietnam. Among other things, the disregard for such concerns at the heart of the U.S. "humanitarian concern for a full accounting of [its] missing men" bears more than a family resemblance to the peculiarly American belief, articulated so infamously by General William Westmoreland during the war, that the Vietnamese do not value human life as much as Americans do. This inequality indicates yet again the force of the Said within the American approach to the search for the missing and therefore the importance of underscoring an attitude of reciprocity as a means of enabling the Saying to confront the interpretive commitments of the accounting effort.

In staging that confrontation, it is important to bear in mind Warner's (1999: 14) admonition that even the backward process of imputation does not necessarily solve the larger problem of the production of guilty subjects. Such admonition is drawn from the acknowledgment that the relationship between identity, existential resentment and responsibility is so tight as to render naïve the attempt simply to dispense with responsibility altogether: "We are not predesigned to be responsible agents, but we cannot dispense with practices of responsibility. This is the gap that must be maintained and honored in a *political* theory of responsibility" (Connolly, 1991: 116). Accordingly, any challenge to extant codes of responsibility must embody the awareness that "responsibility is both indispensable to life and acutely susceptible to inflation through existential resentment, [and that] the best response is to challenge, contest, subvert and abridge theories and practices that create the environment for such inflationary spirals" (Connolly, 1991: 121). That the effort to account for American soldiers missing in Southeast Asia has created an environment in which American existential resentment over the defeat in Vietnam can flourish has by now been amply demonstrated. Such resentment, furthermore, has become a strong contributory force to American identity, an identity sustained largely by the very accounting work that was allegedly intended to pacify the lingering hostilities of the Vietnam War. That this has not occurred can be traced to the demand for the certainty of the identified body in the face of the uncertainty occasioned by its radical fragmentation and the permanent absence of some number of bodies as a result of the extreme violence of mechanized warfare. Resentment and responsibility have become the twinned expressions of this condition, the result of the continuous foregrounding of those absent bodies that have for so long been interpreted as the most material expressions of American suffering.

Combined, these circumstances underscore the value of emphasizing the Vietnamese in the manner proposed by the ethical relation and of drawing the American self closer to the alterity represented by the Vietnamese so as to disable not simply the exclusive focus on the absent body but to get beyond the identity configurations that both enable that body's significance and draw interpretive strength from it. As indicated, this is not an attempt to eliminate responsibility and identity altogether. Rather, it is an effort "to politicize identity and responsibility" by adopting "an ambiguous stance toward indispensable constructions and unavoidable fictions, endorsing identity without capitalization and responsibility within a text of ambiguity, in the interests of exposing and contesting the logic of sacrifice built into established doctrines of identity, responsibility, and otherness" (Connolly, 1991: 118). As in the case of Campbell's reformulation of humanitarianism, responsibility on this reading is forced to relinquish its standing as a universal now that it is resituated onto the terrain of the political. Further, "such a doctrine treats the positions of its competitors as positions it expects to persist on the field of discourse, and construes itself as another possibility to be advanced in competition and contestation with them. It presents itself as a subjugated possibility growing out of the unstable tradition of western discourse about identity and responsibility" (Connolly, 1991: 119).

Of particular importance in these possibilities for identity and responsibility is their compatibility with Levinas's emphasis on the value of the interlocutor as prior to the interpretive gestures of the self. In what might be termed a conversational mode of identity, the self's parochial-but-nonetheless-indispensable fictions emerge as one possibility among several equally valid options. The other options, of course, come from the interlocutor, who is now not only not expelled from the conversation but embraced in the hope that the persistence of her equally indispensable identity claims might disrupt the claims of the self, who has long naturalized them as the only path to truth, identity, and the accountability that we imagine must be available to redeem the suffering and unfairness of life. Within the accounting for missing soldiers, the United States might take something of a lesson from the Vietnamese. Despite their much larger number of absent bodies, they have not succumbed to the impulse so prominent among Americans to invest them with the sole power of determining the truth of war's balance sheet; and they have not used them as a bludgeon to coerce certain behaviors by agents deemed responsible for their absence. Vietnam's sheer inability to endow the absent body with such preeminence because of financial constraints might itself be a "subjugated possibility" that points the way toward the reconciliation of the hostilities which pursuit of that body seems resolutely unable to achieve.

THE BODY AND THE ETHICAL RELATION

A final consideration locates the practices which result in the accounted-for body within an array of interpretive commitments that inhibit the ethical relation. As we saw in chapter 3, these practices require a verifiable correspondence between a body of circumstantial evidence about the absent soldier in question and a body of forensic evidence achieved through remains identification, which produces the body whose name can be removed from the list of the missing. Hence, what counts as a body in this context is that which certifiably materializes within the epistemic field of modern forensic science rather than, say, the phenomenological body of day-to-day life which once left for Vietnam and never returned. This requirement has both its positive and negative consequences. On the plus side, the identified body relieves to a great extent the ambiguity formerly occasioned by its absence, especially for the families of missing servicemen. On the negative side, the often paltry quantity and highly fragmentary nature of the remains recovered occasionally compound the ambiguity for some families, even when positive identification of those remains is made. Rightly or wrongly, they conclude that such a minuscule quantity of the body perhaps indicates that the rest of it is still alive somewhere in Southeast Asia. Beyond this admittedly rare circumstance, the protocol requiring identifiable remains activates modes of discernment in which the body becomes the sole basis for reflection. Like responsibility and humanitarianism, the body assumes the character of a universal principle available for use in making judgments about the adequacy of both American and Vietnamese efforts in the search for the missing.

Among other things, such modes of discernment are complicit in the project of producing an agent who can then be held responsible. This is crucial when it comes to the search for the missing because of the role played by the discourse of responsibility in the effort to account for missing American soldiers. Posited as the primary means of assessing Vietnamese cooperation in the accounting effort, the continued absence of the body is easily interpreted as another instance of Vietnam's disruption of the corporeal and ontological unity of the American self. For their part, the Vietnamese have repeatedly voiced their discomfort with the strict standard of proof imposed by sole reliance on the identified body and have long insisted that determination of the fate of a missing soldier, even when no remains are recovered, should be adequate for purposes of removing that soldier's name from the list of the unaccounted for.[7] That the United States refuses to entertain the possibility of resolving cases in this manner not only underscores the importance of the body within the interpretive structure of the search for the missing, but also implies the continued force of the existential resentment generated by loss of the war which animated the desire to repatriate bodies in the first place. In consequence, the relationship between the body KIA and its (possibly) live counterpart is reinforced, thereby bolstering the uncertainties among some in the United States over the live prisoner question and then, to complete the circle, legitimating an accounting protocol that requires recovery and positive identification of the body. Yet that protocol becomes increasingly difficult to apply as time goes by and the easier cases are resolved—all without the discovery of a single live prisoner. Yet the United States steadfastly rejects adoption of the accounting method proposed by the Vietnamese. The relationship of superiority and inferiority at work here is unmistakable, as are the relations of force which allow a vastly more powerful country to intervene in the domestic affairs of another and compel obedience to a unilaterally dictated set of conditions. Such relations also make possible the deployment of a conception of the other which consolidates the self as the superior term in a moral binary.

Like National League of Families' declarations that the Vietnamese are responsible for accounting for missing Americans, references to the untrustworthiness of the Vietnamese—the characteristic that might lead them to hold back prisoners and that thus requires Americans to demand the body as a means of verification—implicate their nature. The former American POW Laird Gutterson, in surmising why the Vietnamese might have kept some POWs after the war, suggested that someone "with an Eastern mind that has been contaminated by Communism" might indeed look favorably upon keeping American prisoners, perhaps as bargaining chips or as slave labor (in Boettcher and Rehyansky, 1981 960). The authors of the article that contains this observation claim that "in thinking about this issue, then, it is necessary to consider, at least, the possibility that we are dealing with people for whom cruelty is fun, people who, purely for revenge and not for any tangible gain, confine men under conditions so barbaric that we can barely imagine them" (Boettcher and Rehyansky, 1981: 960). In this scenario, the need not simply to repatriate the body but also to ensure its positive identification is beyond dispute. Because of their "Eastern mind[s] . . . contaminated by Communism," the Vietnamese cannot be trusted to resolve cases of the missing or to return these bodies themselves. Left to their own devices, the Vietnamese, seeking revenge or, more prosaically entertainment, would simply continue to hold prisoners under barbaric conditions. As a result, any effort to account for missing Americans will have to cope not only with challenges of climate, terrain, and the passage of time, but also with the nature of the Vietnamese, which, in the view of some, poses perhaps the most daunting obstacle of all.

Here again the body count contributes to the hostilities and antagonisms of the Vietnam War by activating modes of apprehension in which responsibility, resentment, and race play a preponderant role. Not surprisingly, given the commitment to materiality as an unrivaled means of resolving so many postwar ambiguities, all of these factors go undetected within official discourse concerning the accounting effort. To repeat, however, there is an alternative to this discourse, and that is Vietnam's proposal that unaccounted-for cases be resolved in the absence of remains. The ethical relation, by embracing the Vietnamese qua other, might therefore enable the United States to see in Vietnam's accounting method not a manifestation of the "Asian mind" but an epistemological counterpoint that does not require unambiguous truth claims about the body. Such an approach would refuse to assimilate Vietnam's means of accounting for missing Americans into a received script in which those means are understood as an effort to conceal the existence of living American prisoners. It might also draw the Americans closer to the Vietnamese and away from the epistemic framework in which the knowledge claims of forensic science constitute the sole ground for an accounting of the missing. As elements of the self—for one, a desire for the fullest possible accounting of missing servicemen—came to be recognized in the other, proximity would forestall denigration of the Vietnamese on the basis of a racial hierarchy. Thus articulated, the value of the ethical relation lies in the fact that it allows modification of the guiding interpretive commitments of the effort to account for missing American soldiers. Accordingly, the aim here is not necessarily to advocate suspension of the search so much as to rearticulate the ontological compulsions that render the search legitimate in the first place and the hierarchy that governs self-other relations when the goal is the pacification of ambiguity, the reduction of alterity to sameness, and the construction of seamless interpretive horizons as a means of coping with divisive events. As always, however, these compulsions engender material consequences, some of which this book has attempted to identify and explain. What this means is that recovery of the Vietnamese from their exile at the margins of the interpretive practices that guide the accounting effort must also be accompanied by a cessation of the hostilities that have characterized relations between the United States and Vietnam since the termination of armed conflict in 1973. After all, the ultimate effect of the language of responsibility and accountability that inspires the search for the missing has been the continuation, rather than the resolution, of the hostilities occasioned by war. Such language inhibits reconciliation in the act of establishing accountability and prolongs the agonies of war in the attempt to parse out responsibility for its consequences. As a result, the Vietnamese continue to be seen as the enemy, because the violence of the wartime representational economy has failed to change after the laying down of arms. Vietnam, after all, was officially designated an American combat zone until 1996, twenty-three years after the signing of the Paris Peace Accords (Barrett, 1996). Perhaps, then, it is time to ask, How much is too much? how far is too far? and ultimately, ought "the fullest possible accounting" be pursued at all?

epilogue

Same as It Ever Was

We will try all we can, any way we can to bring back our missing. The mission will continue for as long as it takes to find our missing from all wars.
—Redmann, 2003

On April 7, 2001, a helicopter crash claimed the lives of sixteen members of an IE working to recover the remains of Americans killed in action in Vietnam. Part of the 65th Joint Field Activity between the United States and Vietnam, the team was composed of seven Americans and nine Vietnamese. Declining to blame the accident on the aged Soviet-made MI-17 helicopter, the public affairs officer for the JTF-FA acknowledged, "Every mission is a dangerous mission. It's a very difficult area to operate in" (Ishikawa, 2001: A5). Conceding the danger, however, did little to mitigate the impression that the effort to account for American soldiers missing in Southeast Asia had finally exacted an unjustifiably high price and that perhaps the greatest tribute to those killed in the crash would be the admission that the accounting effort could not be validated in terms of further lives lost in Vietnam. Presented with this interpretive possibility, however, the U.S. government took the opposite approach, choosing instead to consecrate the lives of those killed to the continuation of the search. In a public statement directed to the families of servicemen still unaccounted for, Secretary of Defense Donald Rumsfeld was quick to declare, "Our mission will continue, even in the face of this tragedy" (U.S. Department of Defense, 2001b). At a memorial service held on April 25, Deputy Secretary of

Defense Paul Wolfowitz said, "On behalf of those we honor today, on behalf of those still missing, we rededicate ourselves to the fullest possible accounting of every American. We offer our deepest thanks to our Vietnamese colleagues who grieve with us, and who will renew with us the charge of our valiant dead." Wolfowitz went on to praise their efforts "to remove the veil of uncertainty and reveal the light of knowledge" (U.S. Department of Defense, 2001c).

At a minimum, the crash of the helicopter revealed that the effort to account for American soldiers missing in Southeast Asia will be pursued even if it entails additional lives lost and that the quest for certainty at all costs has become so sedimented within the American response to the absent Vietnam War body as to overrule virtually every other possibility. Further, the irony that the search for dead bodies had produced more dead bodies not only went unacknowledged in the aftermath of the crash but was subsumed within familiar narratives in which the recovery of the body enables evidently higher values to be realized, in particular the restoration of certainty. Ultimately, such narratives mean that the postcrash press conference was scripted decades before the ill-fated crew even deployed to Vietnam. These missions are dangerous, as a long line of American officials have not hesitated to remind us (indeed, searchers in Southeast Asia receive hazard pay), and it is therefore surprising that such loss of life had not yet occurred. As important as the state's seemingly effortless ability to enlist virtually any death for its purposes, however, were the implications of the crash for the future of the interpretive parameters that govern the U.S. relationship to unaccounted-for soldiers—a future that appears quite rosy indeed. The reasons stem not so much from the supposed success of the search for Vietnam War missing as from the total absence of any recognition that the quest for certainty might itself be part of the problem. Absent such recognition, overwhelming circumstantial evidence will remain insufficient, failure to produce the positively identified body will continue to indicate a forsaking of the missing, and the production of additional dead bodies will remain justifiable as part of the humanitarian effort to provide "the light of knowledge" (U.S. Department of Defense, 2001c). Along the way, other important factors will remain obscured, in particular the causal relationship between mechanized warfare and absent bodies, the often decisive role played by families of missing soldiers, and the propensity among Americans to see in the materiality of the absent body further proof of their status as victims of deceit and conspiracy. At the very least, then, it seems current and future efforts to recover missing American soldiers are doomed to repeat all of the most sordid elements of the effort to account for American soldiers missing in Southeast Asia.

A series of events arising out of the loss of Navy Lieutenant Commander Michael Scott Speicher during the first Persian Gulf War dramatically underscore this assertion. More than any other, this case reveals the ambiguity that still obtains when the United States fails to repatriate and identify the bodies of military personnel. The details of the Speicher case reveal the degree to which unaccounted-for Vietnam War bodies have conditioned the range of possibilities open to the United States when soldiers go missing. Like those surrounding many missing soldiers, these details initially seemed entirely coincident with, and therefore the unsurprising result of, mechanized warfare: Speicher's aircraft was hit by a missile, a large fireball was observed by other American pilots in the vicinity, no distress signals were received to indicate survival, and Speicher's plane was not located at any of the several auxiliary landing zones designated for pilots in trouble. In the confusion, however, the initial report of Speicher's loss was not filed until twelve hours after he was shot down; in addition, the coordinates of his probable crash site were erroneously reported, errors that substantially hampered search and rescue efforts. Meanwhile, then-Secretary of Defense Dick Cheney reported during a press conference that American forces had suffered a single lost aircraft and that the pilot had not survived. Though Cheney did not mention Speicher by name, the reference was obvious since Speicher was the only American pilot who failed to return from the night's engagements. Almost immediately after being shot down Speicher was officially presumed dead by even the highest ranking officials in the American military (Yarsinske, 2003: 36–41).

At first glance, of course, neither the confusion that accompanied Speicher's loss nor the presumption of his death appears out of line with the circumstances of his loss. Still, if the evidentiary requirements for KIA status are kept in mind, there is no question Cheney's statements were premature—there was no evidence Speicher was dead, only the knowledge that his plane had been shot down and that he had not returned to base. Having said that, of course, it is equally plausible that explosions of the kind experienced by Speicher's F-18 may not leave any evidence of death behind, in particular, the body whose positive identity is now the sole means of making such a determination. The point is that in the post-Vietnam War era, the (possibly) live body and its definitively dead counterpart have assumed very active lives of their own, becoming along the way the basis for claims whose most salient feature is the absence of unambiguous truth. Subsequent events in the Speicher case suggest the point, specifically, the Americans' presentation to the Iraqis of lists of missing and imprisoned Americans, for whom the Iraqis were expected to account as a condition of the cease-fire's continuation. In yet another variation on the Vietnam War theme, these lists have become a point of contention because the U.S. government, in its eagerness to present as bloodless a picture of the war as possible, failed to report *any* ground or air troops falling into Iraqi hands from the opening days of the war. It stuck to this story until the Iraqis made videotapes of the POWs and played them over major news media (Yarsinske, 2003: 92). Later lists, however, made no mention of Scott Speicher, in part because he was presumed dead. A curiosity presents itself here. If he was indeed KIA, there should have been an effort to recover his remains, and so his name should have made it onto the list of the unaccounted for. If, on the other hand, he had survived being shot down, then all the more reason to list him among those whom the United States expected to see again. Familiar winds begin to blow. In the absence of the body we can't be sure Speicher is dead, so we must consider him alive, a situation which can only mean that "Saddam was essentially handed a trophy prisoner because of that prisoner's omission from the list' (Yarsinske, 2003: 92).

Or so it seems. Yet Speicher *was* listed as MIA by the Department of Defense despite Cheney's assumption of his death, largely because his body had not been recovered and because even the site of his crash had yet to be determined. Accordingly, the process of changing his status to KIA/BNR was begun, just as it is for all American soldiers listed as MIA following the cessation of hostilities. The official change occurred on May 22, 1991 (Yarsinske, 2003: 113). Yet in view of the complicated legacy of missing Vietnam War soldiers, perhaps one should not be surprised that questions about Speicher's ultimate fate and whereabouts did not end there. Perhaps one should not be surprised, in other words, that live-sighting reports—always from "credible" yet "anonymous" sources—began trickling back to the United States in the five years following the Gulf War; or that remains alleged to be Speicher's failed to match DNA provided by his parents because, as they admitted afterward, Speicher had been adopted as an infant. Perhaps it is not surprising either that the continuation of his life mandated by the absence of his body meant that the United States would be forced to take seriously the live-sighting reports, the later discovery of Speicher's crash site through satellite imagery that suggested he may have successfully ejected from his aircraft, and the vague symbols on the desert floor that may have been Speicher's search and rescue codes. Though eerily similar to elements from the Vietnam War that have yet to produce a single, living, unaccounted-for soldier, the contentious legacy of absent military bodies ultimately meant the United States had no choice but to send a CILHI investigative team to Iraq in December 1995 to excavate the site where Speicher's plane had gone down.

That CILHI's investigation failed to resolve fully Speicher's fate and whereabouts, can, of course, be interpreted charitably or cynically, depending on your viewpoint. Certain details, however, are more or less beyond dispute. The plane was found right side up inside a ring of debris approximately sixty feet in diameter. Its fuselage, wings, and engines were all in remarkably good shape; it had not been obliterated in midair after all. The canopy was found a substantial distance from the wreckage. No human remains or personal effects belonging to Speicher or any other American were found at the site, clues which indicated the pilot had ejected. In addition, a member of one of Iraq's many nomadic tribes had found a flight suit like those worn by American pilots a few kilometers away from the crash site, though extensive analysis of the suit by both the FBI's crime lab and the AFDIL failed to determine whether the suit belonged to Speicher or what had happened to whoever had been wearing it. Once again, no conclusive evidence of Speicher's death was found. Indeed, it seemed not wholly implausible to suggest that Speicher had survived at least the incident of loss, if not beyond. Nonetheless, DPMO recommended affirming Speicher's status as KIA/BNR, a recommendation accepted by the Navy on October 2, 1996. Yet even as they affirmed Speicher's current KIA/BNR status, the Navy confused matters still more by retroactively changing Speicher's status from KIA/BNR to MIA for the period between May 22, 1991, and October 2, 1996, as if he hadn't been quite so dead during that time after all. This retroactive change meant that whatever promotions and pay he would have received during the five and a half years he had spent as KIA/BNR would accrue to him and his primary next of kin, respectively (Yarsinske, 2003: 217). In the meantime, the pilot's flight suit—

easily the most important piece of forensic evidence recovered by the CILHI investigative team—was lost at the end of 1997 and has not been seen since.

By this point, the storm surrounding Speicher's fate and whereabouts had overtaken the ability of government investigations, classifications, and affirmations to bring the case to any sort of close. Live-sighting reports—unverifiable to the last—continued apace, as did detection of man-made symbols in the area around Speicher's crash site; and many of the usual suspects in the United States, including family organizations like the National Alliance of Families for the Return of America's Missing Servicemen and members of Congress, including Senator Robert Smith (R-NH) and Senator Pat Roberts (R-KS), were on the scent. More inquiries were launched, commissions formed, letters sent, and testimony given. Speicher was making a remarkable comeback, in part through a sustained process of cultural iatrogenesis and in part through legitimate concerns over his fate and whereabouts, many of which did not receive the investigative attention they deserved. Eventually, the possibility of yet again reclassifying Speicher from KIA/BNR back to MIA gained momentum. This time, of course, it would remain that way, at least until positive identity of his remains could be made or until he was liberated from the Iraqi prison in which many now believed he was being held. Sure enough, on January 11, 2001, the U.S. Navy once again changed Speicher's status to MIA (U.S. Department of Defense, 2001a). Following familiar precedent, government officials acknowledged that the evidence of Speicher's continued life was circumstantial but that they could not rule out that possibility since Iraq had failed to account for him through repatriation of his remains. In remarks accompanying the decision, President Clinton said, "We have some information that leads us to believe he might be alive. And we hope and pray that he is. But we have already begun working to try to determine whether, in fact, he's alive, if he is, where he is and how we can get him out" (in Yarsinske, 2003: 245).

The merits of the evidence notwithstanding, the departure from precedent represented by Speicher's reclassification was dramatic and marked the first time an American serviceman had been reclassified from KIA to missing. The import of this development was not lost on POW/MIA activist groups, who were quick to point out what they believed were similarities between Speicher's case and scores of cases from the Vietnam War, Korean War, Cold War, and World War II. While lauding Speicher's change of status, they wondered how the Vietnam War missing could be the "nation's highest priority" in the absence of any similar action on their behalf ("Bits n Pieces," 2001b). Hence, despite acknowledging that this was "the most extraordinary event within the POW/MIA issue, in the last 15–20 years," Speicher's status change produced still more suspicion, distrust, and cynicism ("Bits n Pieces," 2001a). As did the helicopter crash, Speicher's status change revealed just how restricted the field of interpretive possibilities concerning absent bodies had become, bounded on the one side by a deceitful government whose every effort on the issue of missing Americans is to be discounted and, on the other, by the figure of the absent body, whose materiality proves the government has not done enough to ensure its return. In a classic no-win situation, the intelligibility of the absent body now seems derived exclusively from the materiality of a signifier long since detached from any identifiable signified.

This poisoning of the interpretive well, however, was not restricted to more skirmishing between the government and POW/MIA activist groups. As was the case with the families of those missing from the Vietnam War, the families of other soldiers killed in action in the Persian Gulf War were implicated in Speicher's status change. One especially trenchant example was the fourteen-member crew of an Air Force gunship that crashed in the Persian Gulf after being hit by a shoulder-fired rocket on January 31, 1991, and remained undetected for more than a month. Only five bodies were positively identified after recovery operations, and the extreme fragmentation of the remains of the other nine led the military to propose burial in a mass grave, a request rejected by the families in favor of an apportionment plan in which each family received an equal quantity of unidentified remains for individual burial. In the wake of the latest Speicher reclassification, the families of two of the soldiers who had received unidentified remains began to have doubts as to the actual fate of their loved ones. Said one, "If you have some doubt, and your husband wasn't identified, it certainly gives a question mark for your mind. You always have this 'what if.' If I could really know for sure that my husband were dead, or alive, that would bring the final peace to my heart" (in "Bits n Pieces," 2001c). Similar doubts led another family to ask Congress for a new investigation of the crash and to consider petitioning the government for a status change similar to Speicher's. Said the sister of one of the soldiers killed, "If it takes a reclassifying to MIA, we will go that far. If there weren't survivors, fine, then give us the proof" (in "Bits n Pieces," 2001c).

In perhaps the ultimate irony, the body, which in the post–Vietnam War era has become the only means of reclassifying a soldier from missing to killed, now becomes the reason accounted-for Persian Gulf War soldiers should be reclassified from killed to missing. The reasoning behind such statements is entirely circular and self-generating. Because of the extreme fragmentation of the recovered body, one can't be sure the soldier in question is deceased, and since one can't be certain the soldier is deceased one cannot rule out the possibility that he is still alive, and since one cannot rule out the possibility that he is still alive that soldier must be maintained in a missing status until the materiality of the body can verify his fate—verification that because of its extreme fragmentation will then be taken not as proof of the soldier's death but of the possibility of his continued life. In short, because there is no proof of death to give its absence will not only be seen as denying the validity of even the most overwhelming circumstantial evidence but also be taken as proof of life. The quest for certainty exceeds itself on its own terms. Materiality, which formerly provided the certainty required to resolve the ambiguity occasioned by the absence of the body, is now confounded by interpretive commitments in which continued *uncertainty* becomes the higher value.

Yet even Speicher's latest status change did not put an end to the story (one suspects that nothing will). For obvious reasons, the change from killed to missing meant that the United States had no choice but to continue its efforts to determine whether Speicher had, in fact, survived his loss and, if not, to repatriate and identify his remains. Eager to lend a hand, Congress proposed Senate Bill 1339, otherwise known as the Persian Gulf War POW/MIA Accountability Act of 2001. The legislation offered asylum to "any alien who is a national of Iraq or a nation of the Greater Middle East Region who . . . personally delivers into the custody of the United States Government a living American Persian Gulf War POW/MIA" (Persian Gulf War POW/MIA Accountability Act, 2002). All the while, live-sighting reports and photographs of Speicher continued to surface, and still more investigations, committees, and special delegations were formed. It seemed Speicher was not only MIA but perhaps still alive and being held by the Iraqis. In February 2002, Senator Roberts went public with his conviction on this point in a letter to Secretary Rumsfeld and recommended that the more appropriate classification for Speicher would be POW: "I believe the status of POW sends a symbolic message not only to the Iraqis, but to other adversaries, current and future—and most importantly to the men and women of the U.S. armed forces and the American people" (in Yarsinske, 2003: 259). Any deviation from this conclusion was simply further evidence of the "mindset to debunk" that had hampered efforts to free American POWs in Southeast Asia. This mindset "would prevent 'ninety-nine percent of all chances of a successful recovery from being planned or executed' (in the words of one case insider) because their [officials in charge of the accounting process] image or credibility or political position would be negatively affected if a successful mission brought Scott Speicher home" (Yarsinske, 2003: 274).

Not improbably, given the pressure, yet another status change was in the offing, this time one that would place Speicher in the much more definitive category of prisoner. Conveniently, of course, the United States now had at its disposal a new set of categories that enabled an American soldier to be held by a hostile power but in a manner that did not entail the certainty of detention required by POW status. Accordingly, on October 11, 2002, Navy Secretary Gordon England officially changed Speicher's status from MIA to "missing/captured," saying at the time that he had "no evidence to conclude that Captain Speicher is dead." Though he acknowledged that the information at his disposal was circumstantial, England said he was "personally convinced the Iraqis seized him sometime after his plane went down" and therefore "the government of Iraq knows what happened to Captain Speicher" (in Mount, 2002). In another twist still more bizarre than the last, circumstantial evidence—for three decades disparaged as a stand-alone means of accounting for American soldiers missing in Southeast Asia—becomes the sole rationale for placing an American soldier in captured status despite the absence of even a single verifiable clue as to his continued life. The separation between death and the body to which that death pertains inaugurated by Vietnam War missing comes full circle as the absence of the body becomes reason to believe the death never occurred.

Incredibly, the nadir was yet to come. Although the rationale that breathed new life into Speicher's absent body was at odds with both the evidentiary basis previously required for captured status and the limitations formerly placed on circumstantial evidence, Speicher was nonetheless following with almost uncanny precision a path that had been blazed years before. As we have seen, that path began in the late 1960s when the materiality of the body was enlisted to resolve the many ambiguities occasioned by missing Vietnam War soldiers; it continued throughout the ensuing decades as the relationship between the (possibly) live body and the definitively dead one not only became increasingly entangled but assumed ever greater significance within the contentious legacy of the Vietnam War. The decision with which this book opened, to exhume and identify the remains of the Vietnam War unknown soldier, was no doubt a further point along the way, the moment at which the symbolism of anonymity was no longer strong enough to combat the ambiguity of absence. In view of the Speicher case, however, one begins to wonder whether the identification of the unknown perhaps marked the moment at which this conceptual trajectory doubled back on itself or simply came off the rails altogether; one wonders further whether the collateral damage caused by the war on ambiguity might now be revealing itself in the absence of interpretive restraint and a renewal of the institutionalized cynicism that marked the Vietnam War years. That this may be so is suggested by Amy Waters Yarsinske, the author of the book from which many of the above details of the Speicher case are drawn. Yarsinske argues that "the United States needs a permanent fix to written armistice documents to ensure each has a clause inserted authorizing military action into enemy areas postconflict to recover POWs and MIAs" (2003: 286). The tumor metastasizes once again as the production of additional dead and missing bodies is now *advocated* as a policy response to dead and missing bodies whose existence cannot be verified. In its perverse and sickening way, of course, it makes perfect sense: more death, more anguish, more ambiguity, more absence—all redeemed by the "need to know."

Happily for her, of course, Yarsinske got her "military action" in the form of the second Persian Gulf War in the spring of 2003. Perhaps not coincidentally it was during the buildup for the invasion that Scott Speicher definitively made it back from the dead, a circumstance which received scant attention at the time. There wasn't much discussion either as to the rationale that would have led Saddam Hussein to keep an American POW for twelve years despite withering economic sanctions and the continuing presence of UN weapons inspectors inside his country, or as to why he would have failed to use Speicher as a bargaining chip when it became abundantly clear that an American-led invasion of Iraq was imminent. Former executive chairman of the United Nations

Special Commission for Iraq Richard Butler offered his response to this problem in 2001: "The Iraqis would exact a terrible price for him. They have a ten-year investment in keeping him. If he's still alive—and they would keep him going to use him—it means they've kept him against a rainy day, for a tremendous thunderstorm" (in Yarsinske, 2003: 101). While this logic perhaps worked for a time as a rejoinder to the rationale question, it appears to have washed away in the "tremendous thunderstorm" of March 19, 2003, otherwise known as Operation Iraqi Freedom. Like the weapons of mass destruction that have so infamously failed to appear, Speicher appears also to have missed his cue. Tens of thousands of American military and civilian personnel inside Iraq since the invasion have not liberated a single living American POW from the first Gulf War, and no remains of any unaccounted-for Gulf War soldier have been recovered.

And yet the search for Scott Speicher continues. Borrowing a tactic from the Old West, Senator Roberts and Senator Bill Nelson (D-FL) backed a sense of the Senate resolution calling for the distribution of wanted posters with Speicher's picture on them throughout Iraq and a $1 million reward for information that resolves his fate—a reward, curiously enough, that also applies to any American soldier unaccounted for from the Korean War and the Vietnam War (Goldstein, 2003). Just to be on the safe side, the senators stipulated that terrorists and those who may have been responsible for Speicher's imprisonment are not eligible for the money. Despite the willingness of some to sacrifice American lives for the return of unaccounted-for soldiers, it appears Scott Speicher's life is not quite worth the price of dealing with "terrorists." In remarks accompanying the announcement, Roberts seemed baffled that Speicher had yet to be found: "It's a little hard not to be discouraged. We had hoped by this time that we would have had more specific word" (in Goldstein, 2003). In the meantime, House Resolution 103, "Establishing a Select Committee on POW/MIA Affairs," gradually gains momentum in Congress. Its purpose: to "conduct a full investigation of all unresolved matters relating to any United States personnel unaccounted-for from the Vietnam era, the Korean conflict, World War II, Cold War Missions, or Gulf War, including MIA's and POW's" (U.S. Congress, House, 2003). Lured by the Siren song of certainty, propelled by the winds of resentment, and convinced of its own victimization, the United States once again finds itself mired in a quagmire of its own making.

notes

1 BODY TROUBLE

1 Butler is aware of the dangers that come with arguing for the discursive construction of the body. Although various analyses of a postmodern stripe may have called our attention to the role of external forces such as power, discourse, or culture, Butler (9) argues that often "the grammatical and metaphysical place of the subject is retained even as the candidate that occupies that place appears to rotate." As a result, we are left with the idea that "construction is not an activity, but an act, one which happens once and whose effects are firmly fixed" (9). Discourse thus "creates" the things of which it speaks in much the same manner as the all-powerful Enlightenment subject was presumed to do, in the process consigning human agency to the dustbin of discursive history. At the outset, then, Butler's (7) project involves a rethinking of any idea of construction that requires "an 'I' or a 'we' who stands before that construction in any spatial or temporal sense of 'before.'"

2 The first Persian Gulf War also played a noteworthy role in the effort to redeem the Vietnam War's many failures. Supporters of the war waved signs reading "No More Vietnams," while President Bush jubilantly exclaimed in 1991, "We've kicked the Vietnam syndrome once and for all!" (Franklin, 1993b: 22). That Operation Desert Storm would play a role in resolving the ambiguity caused by the Vietnam War served as a reminder of the disorientation and perplexity that still marked the American experience of the war in Southeast Asia. Accordingly, it is no small irony that the efforts of President George W. Bush in Iraq have done so much to revivify the specter of Vietnam.

3 See chapter 3 for an extended discussion of the remains recovered from Pakse, Laos, in which such evidence was discovered by the wife of a missing Air Force pilot.

254 Notes to Chapter 3

2 FROM UNRECOVERABLE TO UNACCOUNTED FOR

1 See Missing Person's Act, ch. 166, 56 Stat. 143 (1942); current version at 37 U.S.C. §552(a) (1988) and 5 U.S.C. §5562(a) (1988).

2 For an extended discussion of the legal dimensions of the effort to account for missing American soldiers, see Stahl (1996) and Hawley (2003).

3 In 1993, the Senate Select Committee on POW/MIA Affairs investigated this incident and concluded that "U.S. Army intelligence did in fact provide a long range camera, polygraph and other equipment and financial support to Mr. Gritz in support of his group. This equipment and financial support, however, was [sic] provided in advance of that intelligence component receiving full approval to provide such support, and in fact the request . . . was ultimately denied. The equipment and money had, however, already been released" (U.S. Congress, Senate, 1993: 221).

4 Several elements of the Gritz story reinforce this claim. First, he was singled out for special praise by General William Westmoreland in his autobiography *A Soldier Reports* (1976). Second, Gritz was explicit in his belief that he was the only man in America capable of rescuing American POWs since, as he commented at one point prior to the raid, "both Teddy Roosevelt and John Wayne are dead" (in Franklin, 1993a: 137). Finally, one of the more influential POW rescue movies, *Rambo: First Blood, Part II* (1985), starring Sylvester Stallone, was closely modeled on Gritz's raid—appropriate modifications to the outcome notwithstanding. In addition to the influence of such forays on the POW/MIA issue, their not-so-tacit effort to reconstitute American manhood supposedly emasculated by defeat in Vietnam must also be noted. See chapter 4 for a more comprehensive discussion of this last point.

3 THE BODY OF THE ACCOUNTED-FOR SOLDIER

1 One way to contextualize the difficulties associated with attempting to recover and identify the remains of soldiers lost during the Vietnam War is through comparison to the attacks on the World Trade Center in 2001. Despite having immediate access to the disaster site, investigators have been able to positively identify only half of the 2,792 people killed ("Mourning a Firefighter at Last," 2003).

2 The U.S.-Russia Joint Commission on POW/MIA Affairs (USRJC) was formed in 1992, primarily in response to allegations that U.S. servicemen may have been transferred to the Soviet Union during the Korean War and the Vietnam War. Its work is also designed to enable both the United States and Russia to account for their respective missing service members. The

commission is divided into four working groups: World War II, the Cold War, the Korean War, and the Vietnam War. It also researches the archives of former Warsaw Pact nations, including Poland, the Czech Republic, and Hungary, to name a few ("Personnel Recovery and Accounting: POW/MIA Accounting," 15–16). The commission's "The Gulag Study" for June 2002 can be viewed at http://www.dtic.mil/dpmo/jcsd/gulag_study_20020622.pdf.

3 The Joint POW/MIA Accounting Command is the product of a reorganization that took effect October 1, 2003, and that combined two formerly separate entities, the JTF-FA and the CILHI. Because this change is comparatively recent, some of the citations in this chapter come from sources obtained when the two were still separate organizations.

4 The investigation of Case 0954 in 1993 illustrates the point. Although an earlier expedition to this remote aircraft crash site in the mountains of Vietnam resulted in a recommendation not to excavate because of the hazards involved, the commander of Detachment Two in Hanoi and another detachment member later returned to the area to determine if an excavation might be feasible. Three aerial reconnaissance missions failed to locate a landing zone near the site owing to the ruggedness of the terrain. As a result, the two searchers were forced to begin from the nearest road by climbing uphill for five hours to a small farm, where they remained overnight. From the farm, the two hiked an additional two hours to reach the site itself, located at an elevation of 4,780 feet on the side of a mountainous rock formation varying in slope from thirty to sixty degrees. The two determined that an excavation could be done if a team of extremely physically fit searchers could be assembled. In the meantime, the Vietnamese managed to cut a helicopter landing zone on the side of the mountain, thereby reducing the climbing required to reach the site and permitting a decision to excavate. Over a two-day period, six helicopter trips transported twelve American and fifteen Vietnamese RE members with water, equipment, and other supplies to the landing zone. From the landing zone, searchers carried equipment for two hours over rugged terrain to a base camp. The crash site itself was a further hour's climb from the base camp, and the terrain so steep as to require hand over hand climbing up rock faces. Over the ensuing sixteen days, the team climbed up from the base camp every day, excavated the crash site, then returned to the base camp. Their efforts were rewarded with the recovery of 718 bone fragments, 16 teeth, life support equipment, and other aircraft wreckage (U.S. Department of State, 1994a: 105).

5 The Southeast Asian villagers and farmers hired to assist in this task are paid wages well in excess of the average daily wage in their country—by some estimates nearly thirty dollars per day, per worker. Like so many other facets of American involvement in Southeast Asia, this issue has also been the subject of controversy: the *San Jose Mercury News* charged in 1996 that

256 Notes to Chapter 4

higher-level bureaucrats in Vietnam skim off much of this money for themselves, leaving workers in the field to take home paltry wages (Huckshorn and Larimer, 1996).

6 Although the United States has never waived standard entry requirements in exchange for human remains, some Vietnamese have gone to extraordinary lengths to procure remains for this purpose, including modifying the remains of Southeast Asian Mongoloids to make them resemble the larger, longer bones of Caucasoids. In one case, a set of remains obtained from Vietnamese boat people contained two human femurs. Analysis at CIL revealed that both bones had been "lengthened" through a process that included cutting them in half, inserting a two-inch-long steel bar lengthwise in the bone, and then reattaching the two ends (Command Briefing, CILHI, 2000).

7 Some extraordinary identifications have been made through dental information. In one case, the identity of a missing soldier was positively established using not a tooth but the hole left in the lower mandible after extraction of the tooth by a dentist. According to the antemortem dental record, the missing soldier in question had had the tooth removed six days before his death. Included in his remains repatriated in 1985 was a portion of the mandible containing the socket of the extracted tooth. Analysis of the healing pattern of the affected socket correlated to an extraction date of six days prior to death, thus confirming the identity of the remains (Dailey, 1991).

8 In yet another of the peculiarities of the Pakse identifications, the court fails to mention how the information concerning the bandages, the parachutes, and the symbol in the grass could have been classified and therefore unavailable to both the status review board in 1978 and to CIL in 1985 yet unclassified and therefore available to the House select committee in 1976.

4 THE BODY OF THE VIETNAM VETERAN

1 Juxtaposing the World War II narrative with that of the Vietnam War in the manner done here does not automatically entail granting to the former its traditional place as the good war whose interpretive boundaries are always seamless and unwavering. Indeed, all narratives, even those whose primary lineaments have taken on the appearance of truth, require constant rearticulation. The publication of Tom Brokaw's *The Greatest Generation* (1998) and *The Greatest Generation Speaks* (1999) is only one of several recent examples of this requirement in the context of the World War II story (the work of Stephen Ambrose might also be cited). What makes Brokaw's species of generational hagiography so repugnant, however, is its refusal to acknowledge anywhere the slaughter in Vietnam as an event conceived in support of the "greatest generation's" most cherished ideals, in particular,

mindless anticommunism, evangelical patriotism, and childlike faith in the superiority of the American Way.

2 In discussing the treatment of American POWs in terms of how it was represented in the United States I do not deny that American prisoners were often tortured; deprived of food, water, and sleep; and subjected to intense propagandizing at the hands of their captors. I simply mean, first of all, that no single account of a given situation ever exhausts its interpretive possibilities, and, second, that the existence of any single representation is not dependent on its "truthfulness." Rather, the issue is one of intelligibility, the assertion here being that the intelligibility of the Vietnam veteran derives in substantial measure from that of the POW. For a comprehensive and often disturbing account of the treatment of American prisoners during the Vietnam War, see Rochester and Kiley (1998).

3 Cynthia Enloe (1983: 32–37) has commented on the explicitly gendered dimension of the American military presence in Vietnam. As she argues, "Rape is obviously not an exclusive preserve of military men. But it may be that there are aspects of the military institution and ideology which greatly increase the pressure on militarised men to 'perform' sexually, whether they have a sexual need' or emotional feelings or not." Perhaps this explains why "'Double veteran' became a common slang phrase among American soldiers in Vietnam: 'Having sex with a woman and then killing her made one a double veteran.'"

4 "Veterans Find Jobs Faster," *New York Times*, May 3, 1968, 35:7.

5 "The Re-Entry Problem of the Vietvets" *New York Times*, May 7, 1967, VI, 23.

6 Jay himself inadvertently reveals the pressure to recuperate American masculinity in the years after the Vietnam War when he responds to his own question with the claim that "the heroic rescue of the *Mayaguez* that demonstrated our virility following our withdrawal from the battlefield supports this hypothesis." The interpretive gymnastics here are revealing, not least because the "heroic rescue" of the crew of the *Mayaguez* was an unmitigated disaster that, if it did anything at all, further impugned American virility. A U.S. merchant ship operating in the Gulf of Siam two weeks after the withdrawal of American forces from Saigon in April 1975, the *Mayaguez* was captured by the Cambodian Khmer Rouge. Acting on his belief that the 40-man crew was being held on nearby Koh Tang Island, President Gerald Ford ordered an American assault based partly on intelligence estimates that no more than 20 or so Cambodians would be there. When the Marines invaded with 175 men they were met by 150 to 200 dug-in Khmer Rouge troops, and the slaughter was on. Worse, the crew of the *Mayaguez* was not on Koh Tang Island but aboard a fishing boat nearby, where they were recovered without incident two hours after the attack had begun. Significantly for present purposes, Jay declines to reveal that this "heroic" ex-

hibition of American "virility" came at the expense of 40 Americans killed and 50 wounded (Tucker, 2000: 251–52). Perhaps he could not have known that the bodies of many of the dead were also unaccounted for, not to be repatriated to the United States until the spring of 2000 (CNN.com, 2000).

7 Cynthia Enloe (1983: 76) has remarked on this circumstance from the often-ignored perspective of women's postwar readjustment issues. As she puts it, "Women, who during wartime were urged to define themselves chiefly as defence workers, will now have to be encouraged to think of themselves once again as mothers. If they do work for wages after the war—and many women who lose their high-paying industrial jobs are still in demand at lower wage rates in service jobs—women will still have to be urged to see mothering, replenishing the nation, as their principal vocation."

8 See Franklin (1993a: 127–63) for an extended discussion of the POW rescue genre and the role of the Vietnam veteran within it.

9 My thanks to an anonymous reviewer for suggesting this point.

5 PRACTICES OF MEMORIALIZATION

1 Figuring the nation as a contingent effect rather than a fact discovered in nature has been a project undertaken to great effect by writers such as James der Derian (1987), William Connolly (1991), and Michael Shapiro (1997), among others.

2 My thanks to Tim Kaufman-Osborn for this insight.

3 Sturken (1997: 55) is right to note that "with the volatile and complex politics between China and Vietnam, this conflation of ethnic identities is a particularly American one."

4 Proponents of these additions had initially wanted the statue placed on the ground at the center of the wall's "V" and the American flag centered at the top of the wall. The sexual connotation of this "penetration" is difficult to miss.

5 I owe much of the language and many of the insights provided here to Kathie Kane (1994), whose reading of memorials, gender, and the nation in post-1945 Germany has substantially enhanced my understanding of these issues in the post–Vietnam War United States.

6 This argument has been advanced in great detail by Daniel Abramson (1996: 702), who argues that "at the Vietnam Veterans Memorial a remarkable ideological conceit is proposed. On the one hand, the sunken, circular chronology of names depicts the war as decisively over and *closed*. At the same time the walls upon which the names are inscribed rise up to point *outward* at the Washington Monument and Lincoln Memorial. . . . Thus the lost war—its uniqueness symbolized by the memorial's unprecedented form—appears connected to American history. Just as significantly, these

two icons of American history are given a new lease on life, revivified as the symbols that equilibrate the vertiginous trauma of the Vietnam War and bracket all attempts at historical understanding."

7 This possibility would seem to be confirmed by the Veterans Vigil of Honor, which 'maintains a twenty-four-hour watch at the memorial for the MIAS" (Sturken, 1997: 64). In this case, the need to re-present the absent body at the wall requires the presence of the living body of the veteran.

8 An additional reading of the My Lai memorial is James Tatum (1996), "Memorials of the America War in Vietnam."

9 James M. Mayo (1988: 189) elaborates on the second of these two difficulties through reference to the Tomb of the Unknown Dead of the War Between the States, which contains the remains of 2,111 unknown soldiers who died at the Battle of Bull Run. In his words, "As a form of national spite, General Montgomery Miegs placed the memorial so near to the Custis-Lee Mansion in order to discourage the Lees, a southern family, from returning home. Another memorial, the Temple of Fame, honors the first Union officer buried in Arlington, and it was located in the Rose Garden for the same purpose."

10 Ehrenhaus (1989: 102) perceptively notes that the construction of the tomb and subsequent removal of the white marble slab coincided with North Vietnam's southward march and the eventual fall of Saigon.

11 My thanks to an anonymous reviewer from Duke University Press for suggesting this last point.

6 THE ETHICS OF ACCOUNTING

1 William Connolly (1991: 121) makes the following comments on the relationship between suffering and responsibility: "People tend to demand, to put it all too briefly, a world in which suffering is ultimately grounded in proportional responsibility. We resent a world in which it appears that this is not so. But resentment must locate an appropriate object if it is to be discharged as resentment. It thereby seeks a *responsible agent* that it can convince itself is worthy of receiving the load of incipient resentment it carries. Otherwise its existential rancor must be stored or translated into something else. So, part of the drive to insistent attributions of responsibility flows from existential resentment."

2 An interim solution to the problem of status changes required a family member to initiate the request for a change. As Douglas Clarke (1979: 44) points out, this put some wives and in-laws in the difficult position of being "the instrument of a husband's 'death,' if only on paper." The issue was to prove very divisive for the league, since the legal action initiated by a small number of families unavoidably affected all MIA relatives. Commented one

wife, "I would hope that no primary next of kin ever has to ask for a review as I did. That was the cruelest blow of all. My children and I had to find peace of mind. When the services were not allowed to proceed because of some people's greed, bitterness or frustration, I had no choice but to ask the Navy to review my husband's case. The agony has to be over" (in Clarke, 1979: 44).

3 See *McDonald v. McLucas* (1974).

4 The closeness of the relationship between the National League of Families and the U.S. government is not without its detractors among families of the missing. Indeed, many families take this rapport as evidence that the league, and especially Ann Mills Griffiths, have sold out to the U.S. government's still-untrustworthy approach to the issue of missing soldiers. For some, "it was hard not to escape the impression of a deal: the government would legitimize the National League and its insistence that there were surviving POWs; Griffiths in return would legitimize the government's record on the MIAs—no small matter, in a climate where conspiracy theories were widely promoted and, it seemed, almost as widely believed" (Isaacs, 1997: 131).

5 Much of the language in Garnett "Bill" Bell's (2004) lengthy memoir of his involvement in the accounting effort is illustrative in this respect. After referring to North Vietnam's negotiators as "inhumane merchants of human bones," Bell continues: "All these years later, Americans need to understand that the Communist POW/MIA strategy was more than a simple clash of political philosophy or a Vietnamese negotiating tactic. It was a deliberate, calculated policy, designed to gain them economic and political concessions in return for answers about American POW/MIAs, and Americans need to remember that the ability to lie effectively to Westerners is considered an asset by the North Vietnamese" (128).

6 For the sake of comparison, just over 58,000 Americans were killed in the Vietnam War, with 153,303 wounded; 74,000 of the wounded survived as quadriplegics or multiple amputees (Tucker, 2000: 64).

7 Regarding a list of discrepancy cases presented by the United States, for example, the Vietnamese pointed out that "in 20 cases, remains had been recovered and identified. In 7 cases, remains that were uncovered required further analysis before they could be positively identified and associated with a particular case. In 33 cases, remains could not be recovered, in 51 cases no further search for remains should be required, and in 7 cases there was not enough information to justify further work. In none of the cases, [they] emphasized, was there any indication that the individual involved was still alive" (Stern, 1995: 74).

bibliography

Abramson, Daniel. (1996). "Maya Lin and the 1960s: Monuments, Time Lines, and Minimalism." *Critical Inquiry* 22 (Summer): 679-709.

Altonn, Helen, and Leila Fujimori. (2001). "Home At Last: Cheering Crowd Welcomes Freed Crew Members to Hawai'i." *Honolulu Star Bulletin*, April 12: A1.

Anders, Steven E. (1988). "With all Due Honors: A History of the Quartermaster Graves Registration Mission." *Quartermaster Professional Bulletin*, September: http://www.qmfound.com/grave.htm.

Anderson, Benedict. (1983). *Imagined Communities: Reflections on the Origin and Spread of Nationalism*. London: Verso.

Anton, Frank, with Tommy Denton. (1997). *Why Didn't You Get Me Out?: A POW's Nightmare in Vietnam*. New York: St. Martin's Press.

"Archival Research: Highlights and Activities." (nd). http://www.dtic.mil/dpmo/archival/highlights/htm.

"Archival Research: Our Role in DPMO." (nd). http://www.dtic.mil/dpmo/archival/role.htm.

Austin, J. L. (1975). *How to Do Things With Words*. Cambridge: Harvard University Press.

Bainham, Andrew, Shelley Day Sclater, and Martin Richards, eds. (2002). *Body Lore and Laws*. Oxford: Hart Publishing.

Baker, Mark. (1981). *Nam: The Vietnam War in the Words of the Soldiers Who Fought There*. New York: Berkley Books.

Barnes, Scott, with Melva Libb. (1987). *BOHICA: A True Account of One Man's Battle to Expose the Most Heinous Cover-up of the Vietnam Saga!* Canton, Ohio: Bohica Corporation.

Barrett, Master Sgt. Stephen. (1996). "Executive order ends Vietnam combat zone." *Armed Forces Information Service*, June 20: http://www.dtic.mil/dpmo/newsre/1996/960620_afis_sea_vn.htm.

Beidler, Philip D. (1998). *The Good War's Greatest Hits: World War II and American Remembering*. Athens: University of Georgia Press.

Bell, Garnett "Bill," with George J. Veith. (2004). *Leave No Man Behind: Bill*

Bell and the Search for American POW/MIAs from the Vietnam War. Madison: Goblin Fern Press.

Berg, Rick, and John Carlos Rowe. (1991). "The Vietnam War and American Memory." In *The Vietnam War and American Culture*, ed. John Carlos Rowe and Rick Berg, 1-17. New York: Columbia University Press.

"Bits n Pieces." (2001a). Newsletter of the National Alliance of Families for the Return of America's Missing Servicemen: January 13.

———. (2001b). Newsletter of the National Alliance of Families for the Return of America's Missing Servicemen: January 27.

———. (2001c). Newsletter of the National Alliance of Families for the Return of America's Missing Servicemen: February 3.

———. (2001d). Newsletter of the National Alliance of Families for the Return of America's Missing Servicemen: May 5.

———. (2002). Newsletter of the National Alliance of Families for the Return of America's Missing Servicemen: August 10.

———. (2003). Newsletter of the National Alliance of Families for the Return of America's Missing Servicemen: August 16.

Blakeman, Karen. (2001). "Copter Crash Kills 16 in MIA Search: Victims Probably on Advance Team." *Honolulu Advertiser*, April 8: A1.

Blumenthal, Sidney. (1992). "The Mission: Ross Perot's Vietnam Syndrome." *The New Republic*, July 6: 16-23.

Bodnar, John. (1992). *Remaking America: Public Memory, Commemoration, and Patriotism in the Twentieth Century.* Princeton: Princeton University Press.

Boettcher, Thomas D., and Joseph A. Rehyansky. (1981). "We Can Keep You . . . Forever." *National Review*, August 21: 958-62.

Boyarin, Jonathan. (1994). "Space, Time, and the Politics of Memory." In *Remapping Memory: The Politics of Timespace*, ed. Jonathan Boyarin, 1-37. Minneapolis: University of Minnesota Press.

Brainard, Gary S. (1991). "Kissing the Boys Goodbye." *The New American*, February 12: 20-21.

Brokaw, Tom. (1998). *The Greatest Generation.* New York: Random House.

———. (1999). *The Greatest Generation Speaks: Letters and Reflections.* New York: Random House.

Brophy, Beth. (1993). "The Search for Truth About POWs Goes On." *U.S. News and World Report*, April 26: 16.

Broyles, William Jr. (1982). "Remembering a War We Want to Forget." *Newsweek*, November 22: 82-83.

Buckley, Jr., William F. (1995). "What To Do About the MIAs?" *National Review*, August 14: 62-63.

Butler, Judith. (1993). *Bodies That Matter: On the Discursive Limits of "Sex."* New York: Routledge.

Butler, Steven. (1995). "MIAs in Vietnam: A Painful Search for the Missing." *U.S. News and World Report*, May 1: 62.

Campbell, David (1992). *Writing Security: United States Foreign Policy and the Politics of Identity*. Minneapolis: University of Minnesota Press.

———. (1998). "Why Fight: Humanitarianism, Principles, and Poststructuralism." *Millennium: Journal of International Studies* 3: 497-521.

———, and Michael J. Shapiro, eds. (1999). *Moral Spaces: Rethinking Ethics and World Politics*. Minneapolis: University of Minnesota Press.

Capra, Frank. (1942). "Why We Fight." Film series produced for the Special Service Division of the Army Service Forces in cooperation with the U.S. Army Signal Corps.

Cary, Peter. (1993). "Troubling Evidence on Vietnam POWs: Are the Numbers Higher Than We Were Told?" *U.S. News and World Report*, November 22: 26-30.

———. (1994a). "Trying to Decipher a Vietnam Mystery: Were Some American Airmen Left Behind?" *U.S. News and World Report*, January 17: 49-51.

———. (1994b). "The Hunt for U.S. Servicemen." *U.S. News and World Report*, February 14: 22.

———. (1995). "A Treasure Trove of Vietnamese Horrors: Does Hanoi Know More About POW/MIAS?" *U.S. News and World Report*, February 20: 59-60.

Chanda, Nayan. (1993). "Research and Destroy: Origins of Vietnam War POW Document Remain Obscure." *Far Eastern Economic Review*, May 6: 20-21.

Clark, Michael. (1991). "Remembering Vietnam." In *The Vietnam War and American Culture*, ed. John Carlos Rowe and Rick Berg, 177-207. New York: Columbia University Press.

Clarke, Alan. (1993). "Habeas Corpus: The Historical Debate." *New York Law School Journal of Human Rights* 14 (Winter): 375-434.

Clarke, Douglas L (1979). *The Missing Man: Politics and the MIA*. Washington: National Defense University Press.

CNN.com. (2000). "Remains of 6 Marines identified from 1975 Mayaguez incident." (May 16): http://cnn.com/2000/US/05/16/marines.maya guez.ap/index.html.

Cole, Paul M. (1994). *POW/MIA Issues*. Santa Monica, Calif.: Rand.

Command Briefing. CILHI. (2000). Official briefing regarding the activities of the Central Identification Laboratory, Hawai'i, Hickam Air Force Base, Hawai'i: May 12 and June 22.

Command Briefing JTF-FA. (2000). Official briefing regarding the activities of the Joint Task Force-Full Accounting, Camp H.M. Smith, Hawai'i: February 29.

Connolly, William. (1991). *Identity/Difference: Democratic Negotiations of Political Paradox*. Ithaca: Cornell University Press.

Cooper, Mary H. (1993). "U.S.-Vietnam Relations." *CQ Researcher*, December 3: 1059–79.

Corn, David, and Jefferson Morley. (1988). "The War on the Wall." *The Nation*, June 4: 780.

Corry, John. (1994). "The MIA Cover-up." *The American Spectator*, February: 26–34.

———. (1995). "A Reporter's Revenge." *National Review*, February 6: 68–70.

Crandell, William F. (1971). "Opening Statement of William Crandell." *Winter Soldier Investigation*: http://lists.village.virginia.edu/sixties/HTML_docs/Resources/ Primary/Winter_Soldier/WS_entry.html.

———. (1994). "What Did America Learn from the Winter Soldier Investigation?": http://lists.village.virginia.edu/sixties/HTML_docs/Texts/ Narrative/Crandell_Winter.html.

Critchley, Simon. (1989). "The Chiasmus: Levinas, Derrida and the Ethical Demand for Deconstruction." *Textual Practice* 3, April: 91–106.

———. (1999). *The Ethics of Deconstruction: Derrida and Levinas*. 2d ed. West Lafayette, Ind.: Purdue University Press.

Dailey, Curtis J. (1991). "The Identification of Fragmented Vietnam War Remains Utilizing a Healing Extraction Site." *Journal of Forensic Sciences*, January: 264–71.

Danto, Arthur C. (1985). "The Vietnam Veterans Memorial." *The Nation*, August 31: 152–55.

Dean, Eric T. (1992). "The Myth of the Troubled and Scorned Vietnam Veteran." *Journal of American Studies* 26.1: 59–74.

der Derian, James. (1987). *On Diplomacy: A Genealogy of Western Estrangement*. Oxford: Oxford University Press.

Dillow, Gordon. (1995). "Vietnam Search Goes on for POWs." *Honolulu Advertiser*, March 5: A5.

"Display of POW/MIA Flag." (nd). From the website Our American Heros [sic]: http://www.gaylasgarden.com/powmia/flyflag.htm.

Dower, John. (1986). *War Without Mercy: Race and Power in the Pacific War*. New York: Pantheon Books.

DPMO Website. (2003). Official website of the United States Department of Defense Prisoner of War/Missing Personnel Office: http://www.dtic.mil/dpmo.

Duffy, Brian. (1992a). "Grand Juries and Dark Conspiracies: The POW Saga Takes Some Startling New Turns." *U.S. News and World Report*, June 29: 40.

———. (1992b). "Anatomy of a Sellout?: After 19 Years, Nixon Aides Will Try to Explain Why U.S. Soldiers Were Left Behind in Vietnam." *U.S. News and World Report*, September 28: 36–38.

Ehrenhaus, Peter. (1989). "Commemorating the Unwon War: On *Not* Remembering Vietnam." *Journal of Communication* 39 (Winter): 96–107.

Engelhardt, Tom. (1995). *The End of Victory Culture: Cold War America and the Disillusioning of a Generation*. Amherst: University of Massachussetts Press.

Enloe, Cynthia. (1983). *Does Khaki Become You?: The Militarization of Women's Lives*. London: South End Press.

———. (1990). *Bananas, Beaches, and Bases: Making Feminist Sense of International Politics*. Berkeley: University of California Press.

"Fact Sheet: Joint Task Force-Full Accounting." (nd). Pamphlet printed by the Joint Task Force-Full Accounting (JTF-FA).

Feldman, Allen. (1991). *Formations of Violence: The Narrative of the Body and Political Terror in Northern Ireland*. Chicago: University of Chicago Press.

Ferguson, Kathy, and Phyllis Turnbull. (1999). *Oh Say Can You See?: The Semiotics of the Military in Hawai'i*. Minneapolis: University of Minnesota Press.

Figley, Charles R., and Seymour Leventman. (1980). *Strangers at Home: Vietnam Veterans Since the War*. New York: Praeger.

Fleming, Robert H. (1985). "Post Vietnam Syndrome: Neurosis or Sociosis?" *Psychiatry* 48, May: 122-39.

Foucault, Michel. (1972). *The Archaeology of Knowledge and the Discourse on Language*. New York: Pantheon Books.

———. (1977). "Nietzsche, Genealogy, History." In *Language, Counter-memory, Practice: Selected Essays and Interviews*, ed. Donald F. Bouchard, 139-64. Ithaca: Cornell University Press.

———. (1979). *Discipline and Punish: The Birth of the Prison*. New York: Vintage.

———. (1980). *The History of Sexuality*. Volume I: *An Introduction*. New York: Vintage.

———. (1997). *The Politics of Truth*, ed. Sylvère Lotringer. New York: Semiotext(e).

Frankel, Fred H. (1994). "The Concept of Flashbacks in Historical Perspective." *International Journal of Clinical and Experimental Hypnosis*, October: 321-36.

Franklin, H. Bruce. (1992). "Mythifying in Action: Who's Behind the M.I.A. Scam—and Why." *The Nation*, December 7: 699-704.

———. (1993a). *M.I.A. or Mythmaking in America: How and Why Belief in Live POWs Has Possessed a Nation*. New Brunswick, N.J.: Rutgers University Press.

———. (1993b). "The Myth of the Missing: The POW/MIAs Keep the Vietnam War Alive." *The Progressive*, January: 22-25.

———. (1993c). "M.I.A.sma." *The Nation*, May 10: 616-17.

———. (1995). "Just a Mythtake." *The Nation*, January 2: 22-24.

Frie, Cpt. Arnd, et al. (1998). "Fallen Comrades Mortuary Affairs in the U.S. Army." *Quartermaster Professional Bulletin* (Winter): 30-35.

"Fullest Possible Accounting, The." (1999). Video produced by the Joint Task Force-Full Accounting (JTF-FA): April.

Galloway, Joseph L. (1994). "Digging Out from Under a Long-Ago War." *U.S. News and World Report*, February 14: 3.

Garamone, Jim. (1999). "Tomb Inscription Dedicated." *American Forces Information Service*, September 17: http://www.dtic.mil/dpmo/newsre/1999/990917_afis_us_unknown_tomb.htm.

Goldstein, David. (2003). "U.S. Will Use Reward, Posters in Effort to Find Downed Navy Pilot." *Kansas City Star*, May 29: http://www.vfwnc.org/articles/030615/Kansas%20City%20Star.pdf.

Greenhouse, Steven. (1995). "Senior Clinton Aides Urging Full Relations with Vietnam." *New York Times*, May 20: A1.

Griswold, Charles L. (1986). "The Vietnam Veterans Memorial and the Washington Mall: Philosophical Thoughts on Political Iconography." *Critical Inquiry* 12 (Summer): 688–719.

Gromer, Cliff. (1994). "A Full Accounting: Our Government Brings High Tech to Bear in the Search for Vietnam War MIAs." *Popular Mechanics*, September: 41–45.

Grosz, Elizabeth. (1994). *Volatile Bodies: Towards a Corporeal Feminism*. Bloomington: Indiana University Press.

———. (1995). *Space, Time and Perversion: Essays on the Politics of Bodies*. New York: Routledge.

Halbwachs, Maurice. ([1950] 1980). *The Collective Memory*. New York: Harper and Row.

Hale, Nathan G. (1995). *The Rise and Crisis of Psychoanalysis in the United States: Freud and the Americans, 1917–1985*. New York: Oxford University Press.

Haraway, Donna. (1991). *Simians, Cyborgs and Women: The Reinvention of Nature*. New York: Routledge.

Hart v. United States. (1990). 894 F.2d 1539.

Hawley, Thomas M. (2002a). "Bodies and Border Practices: The Search for American MIAs in Vietnam." *Body and Society* 8, no. 3: 49–69.

———. (2002b). "The Ethics of Accounting: The Search for American Soldiers Missing in Vietnam." *Millennium: Journal of International Studies* 31, no. 2: 271–95.

———. (2003). "Accounting for Absent Bodies: The Politics and Jurisprudence of the Missing Persons Act." *Studies in Law, Politics, and Society* 28: 75–95.

Herman, Ellen. (1995). *The Romance of American Psychology: Political Culture in the Age of Experts*. Berkeley: University of California Press.

Herr, Michael. (1968). *Dispatches*. New York: Avon Books.

Hess, Elizabeth. (1987). "Vietnam: Memorials of Misfortune." In *Unwinding*

the Vietnam War: From War Into Peace, ed. Reese Williams, 262–80. Seattle: Real Comet Press.
Heussner, Todd, and Dr. Thomas Holland. (1999). "Worldwide CILHI Mission to Bring Home Missing Heroes." Quartermaster Professional Bulletin (Summer): 10–17.
"History of the League's POW/MIA Flag." (2003). From the website of the National League of Families of American Prisoners and Missing in Southeast Asia: http://www.pow-miafamilies.org/flaghistory.html.
Hoar, William P. (1992a). "President Bush to POW/MIA Families: 'Shut Up and Sit Down!'" The New American, August 24: 4–9.
———. (1992b). "The Abandoned." The New American, September 21: 40.
———. (1995). "Final Abandonment of POWs?" The New American, August 21: 15–16.
Hobbes, Thomas. (1968). Leviathan. New York: Penguin Books.
Hogle, Linda F. (1999). Recovering the Nation's Body: Cultural Memory, Medicine, and the Politics of Redemption. New Brunswick, N.J.: Rutgers University Press.
Hornik, Richard. (1992). "My Search for Colonel Scharf." Time, January 13: 13–16.
Howes, Craig. (1993). Voices of the Vietnam POWs: Witnesses to Their Fight. New York: Oxford University Press.
———. (2000). "Talk, Write, Talk: Bobby Garwood, MIAs and Conspiracy." Unpublished manuscript, University of Hawai'i at Manoa.
Huckshorn, Kristin, and Tim Larimer. (1996). "U.S. Fails to Monitor Hanoi's Spending." Honolulu Advertiser, April 28: A1-A2.
Inglis, Ken S. (1993). "Entombing Unknown Soldiers: From London and Paris to Baghdad." Journal of the Australian War Memorial 23, October 1: 7–31.
Isaacs, Arnold R. (1997). Vietnam Shadows: The War, Its Ghosts, and Its Legacy. Baltimore: Johns Hopkins University Press.
Ishikawa, Scott. (2001). "Copter Crash Kills 16 in MIA Search: 7 Americans Among Dead in Vietnam." Honolulu Advertiser, April 8: A1.
Jasper, William F. (1991). "Official Policy: Abandon POWs." The New American, February 12: 16–19.
Jay, Jeffrey A. (1973). "After Vietnam: I. In Pursuit of Scapegoats." Harper's (July): 14–23.
Jeffords, Susan. (1989). The Remasculinization of America: Gender and the Vietnam War. Bloomington: Indiana University Press.
Jensen-Stevenson, Monika. (1997). Spite House: The Last Secret of the War in Vietnam. New York: Avon Books.
Jensen-Stevenson, Monika, and William Stevenson. (1990). Kiss the Boys Goodbye: How the United States Betrayed Its Own P.O.W.s in Vietnam. Toronto: McClelland and Stewart.

"Joint Task Force-Full Accounting: Fiscal Year 1999." (1999). Pamphlet printed by the Joint Task Force-Full Accounting (JTF-FA): November 1.

"Joint Task Force-Full Accounting: The Fullest Possible Accounting." (nd). Pamphlet printed by the Joint Task Force-Full Accounting (JTF-FA).

JPAC Website. (2004). Official website of the United States Joint POW/MIA Accounting Command: http://www.jpac.pacom.mil/index.htm.

Kane, Kathleen O. (1994). "Hidden in Plain Sight: The Metaphysics of Gender and Death." PH.D. diss., University of Hawai'i at Manoa.

Kantorowicz, Ernst H. (1957). *The King's Two Bodies: A Study in Medieval Political Theology*. Princeton: Princeton University Press.

Karner, Tracy. (1996). "Fathers, Sons, and Vietnam: Masculinity and Betrayal in the Life Narratives of Vietnam Veterans with Post-Traumatic Stress Disorder." *Midcontinent American Studies Journal*, 63-94.

Kaufman-Osborn, Timothy. (1997). *Creatures of Prometheus: Gender and the Politics of Technology*. New York: Rowman and Littlefield.

Keating, Susan Katz. (1994). *Prisoners of Hope: Exploiting the POW/MIA Myth in America*. New York: Random House.

Klein, Joe. (1992). "Perot's Jungle Fever." *Newsweek*, June 15: 29.

Kozaryn, Linda D. (2000). "Cohen Reaffirms Full Accounting Promise at Hanoi Dig." *American Forces Information Service*, March 13: http://www.dtic.mil/dpmo/newsre/2000/000313_afis_secdef_hanoi.htm.

Kulka, Richard A., et al. (1990). *Trauma and the Vietnam Generation: Report of Findings from the National Vietnam Veterans Readjustment Study*. New York: Brunner/Mazel.

Lacayo, Richard. (1992). "Bad Dream Factory." *Time*, January 13: 10-12.

Lakoff, George, and Mark Johnson. (1980). *Metaphors We Live By*. Chicago: University of Chicago Press.

Lamb, David. (1997). "Costly Search for MIAs in Vietnam Poses Hard Questions." *Sunday Oregonian*, December 28: A3.

"Laos-MIAs." (1999). Story from National Public Radio: November 22. http://www.npr.org/ramfiles/atc/19991122.atc.12.rmm.

Laqueur, Thomas W. (1996). "Names, Bodies, and the Anxiety of Erasure." In *The Social and Political Body*, ed. Theodore R. Schatzki and Wolfgang Natter, 123-41. New York: Guilford Press.

Larimer, Tim. (1995). "Psychics Search for Missing Soldiers." *New York Times*, December 31: F7.

Lefort, Claude. (1986). *The Political Forms of Modern Society: Bureaucracy, Democracy, Totalitarianism*. Cambridge: MIT Press.

Lembcke, Jerry Lee. (1997). "Myth, Spit, and Vietnam Vets: More on the Politics of Memory." *Tikkun*, March/April: 11-14.

———. (1998a). "The 'Right Stuff' Gone Wrong: Vietnam Veterans and the Social Construction of Post-Traumatic Stress Disorder." *Critical Sociology* 24, 1/2: 37-64.

Lembcke, Jerry Lee. (1998b). *The Spitting Image: Myth, Memory, and the Legacy of Vietnam.* New York: New York University Press.

Lesinski, Jeanne M. (1998). *MIAS: A Reference Handbook.* Santa Barbara, Calif.: ABC-CLIO.

Levinas, Emmanuel. (1981). *Otherwise Than Being or Beyond Essence.* Translated by Alphonso Lingus. The Hague: Martinus Nijhoff.

Lin, Maya. (2000). "Making the Memorial." *New York Review of Books,* November 2: 33–35.

Liu, Melinda. (1992). "'A Conspiracy of Silence': A Guide to the Latest Vietnam MIA Evidence." *Newsweek,* August 24: 50.

Lovering, Daniel. (2000). "Laos: Exploding the Past." *Bulletin of the Atomic Scientists,* September/October: 28–34.

Lowe, Donald M. (1995). *The Body in Late-Capitalist USA.* Durham: Duke University Press.

Lyons, Paul. (1998). "Toward a Revised Story of the Homecoming of Vietnam Veterans." *Peace and Change* 23, April: 193–200.

Mather, Paul. (1994). *M.I.A.: Accounting for the Missing in Southeast Asia.* Washington: National Defense University Press.

Mayo, James M. (1988). *War Memorials as Political Landscape: The American Experience and Beyond.* New York: Praeger.

McConnell, Malcolm, with research by Theodore G. Schweitzer III. (1995). *Inside Hanoi's Secret Archives: Solving the MIA Mystery.* New York: Simon and Schuster.

McDonald v. McLucas. (1974). 371 F. Supp. 831, 836 (S.D. N.Y. 1974). (three-judge court), $aff'd$ *mem.*, 419 U.S. 297.

"Meeting the Challenge." (1999). Annual report of the Defense Prisoner of War/Missing Personnel Office (DPMO). http://www.dtic.mil/dpmo/special/99_annual_report.pdf.

"MIA Hunter in Hanoi Chains Himself to Gate." (1995). *New York Times,* June 15: A5.

Mihesuah, Devon A., ed. (2000). *Repatriation Reader: Who Owns American Indian Remains?* Lincoln: University of Nebraska Press.

Morganthau, Tom. (1982). "Honoring Vietnam Veterans—At Last." *Newsweek,* November 22: 80–86.

———. (1985). "The War That Won't Go Away." *Newsweek,* April 15: 32–37.

Morris, Stephen J. (1993). "The '1205 Document': A Story of American Prisoners, Vietnamese Agents, Soviet Archives, Washington Bureaucrats, and the Media." *The National Interest* (Fall): 28–42.

Mosse, George L. (1990). *Fallen Soldiers: Reshaping the Memory of the World Wars.* New York: Oxford University Press.

Mount, Mike. (2002). "Navy Changes Status of Missing Pilot." *CNN.com,* October 11: http://www.cnn.com/2002/US/South/10/11/missing.pilot/.

"Mourning a Firefighter at Last." (2003). *New York Times.* September 8:

http://www.nytimes.com/aponline/national/AP-Attacks-Firefighter.html.

Mydans, Seth. (2000). "Viet Psychics Kindle Hope to Find Dead." *New York Times*, November 19: 1.

"National POW/MIA Recognition Ceremony: Remarks as Delivered by Secretary of Defense William S. Cohen, Arlington National Cemetery Friday, September 17, 1999." (1999). *Armed Forces Information Service, Defense Viewpoint*. September 17: http://www.dtic.mil/dpmo/newsre/1999/990917_afis_us_secdef_remarks.htm.

Neocleous, Mark. (2001). "The Fate of the Body Politic." *Radical Philosophy* 108 (July/August): 29–38.

Nicosia, Gerald. (2001). *Home to War: A History of the Vietnam Veterans' Movement*. New York: Three Rivers Press.

"Not to be Forgotten: United States Army Central Identification Laboratory Hawai'i." (nd). Pamphlet printed by the Central Identification Laboratory, Hawai'i (CILHI).

O'Daniel, Larry J. (1979). *Missing in Action: Trail of Deceit*. New Rochelle, N.Y.: Arlington House.

Office of the Assistant Secretary of Defense. (1998). "Secretary of Defense William S. Cohen's Statement Concerning the Identification of the Vietnam Unknown." News release, June 30: http://www.dtic.mil/dpmo/newre/1998/980630/_osd_pr332_sea.htm.

———. (1999a). "Secretary of Defense Approves Recommendations Concerning the Vietnam Unknown." News release, June 17: http://www.dtic.mil/dpmo/newsre/1999/990617_osd_pr296_sea.htm.

———. (1999b). "Vietnamese POW/MIA Researchers Visit the U.S." News release, August 27: http://www.dtic.mil/dpmo/newsre/1999/990827_osd_pr395_sea.htm.

"Our Soldier Unknown." (1937). Document from the archives of the U.S. Army Quartermaster Museum, Fort Lee, Va.: http://www.qmfound.com/soldier_unknown.htm.

Paterson, Thomas G., and Dennis Merrill, eds. (1995). *Major Problems in American Foreign Relations*. Volume 2: *Since 1914* (4th ed.). Lexington: D.C. Heath.

Persian Gulf War POW/MIA Accountability Act. (2002). Pub. L. No. 107-258, 116 Stat. 1738.

"Personnel Recovery and Accounting: POW/MIA Accounting." (2000). Pamphlet printed by the Defense Prisoner of War/Missing Personnel Office (DPMO): January 6.

Peters, Katherine McIntire. (1996). "The Endless Search." *Government Executive*, April: 26–31.

Polner, Murray. (1971). *No Victory Parades: The Return of the Vietnam Veteran*. NewYork: Holt, Rinehart and Winston.

POW/MIA Memorial Flag Act. (2002). Pub. L. No. 107-323, 116 Stat. 2787.

Purdum, Todd S. (1995). "Clinton Promises Full Effort to Account for MIAs." *New York Times* May 30: A3.

Rainie, Harrison. (1978). "After Vietnam: II. The Myth of Public Innocence." *Harper's* (July) 23-25.

———. (1992). "New POW Evidence: The 'Clusters' Theory." *U.S. News and World Report*, July 20: 11.

Rather, Dan. (1994). "Guest Editorial." *National Review*, April 4: 16.

"Records Relating to American Prisoners of War and Missing in Action from the Vietnam War Era, 1960-1994." (1995). Reference Information Paper 90, Washington: National Archives and Records Administration.

Redmann, Brigadier General Steven J. (2003). "Remarks as Prepared for Delivery, National League of Families Air Force Luncheon, Hilton Hotel, Washington, D.C." June 27: http://www.pacom.mil/JTFFA/redmannspeech.htm.

Roach, Mary. (2003). *Stiff: The Curious Lives of Human Cadavers*. New York: W.W. Norton.

Robertson, Chimp (1995). *POW/MIA America's Missing Men: The Men We Left Behind*. Lancaster, Penn.: Starburst Publishers.

Rochester, Stuart I., and Frederick Kiley. (1998). *Honor Bound: American Prisoners of War in Southeast Asia, 1961-1973*. Annapolis: Naval Institute Press.

Sammon, Richard. (1992a). "Pentagon Knew Soldiers Held After War, Panel Leaders Say." *CQ*, June 27: 1896.

———. (1992b). "Witnesses Open Old Wounds; Tempers Flare in Hearing." *CQ*, September 26: 2695.

———. (1992c). "Images in Laos Rice Paddy Divide Senate Panel." *CQ*, October 17: 3259.

———. (1992d). "Senate Panel Races Deadline as Nation Honors Veterans." *CQ*, November 14: 3638.

———. (1992e). "Kerry Urges Reward for Vietnam: Republicans Say It's Premature." *CQ*, November 28: 3717.

———. (1992f). "Senate Wraps up POW Probe But Big Question Remains." *CQ*, December 5: 3763.

———. (1993a). "No Proof That Prisoners Remain in Southeast Asia, Panel Finds." *CQ*, January 16: 138.

———. (1993b). "Unearthed Military Document Sparks Publicity, Questions." *CQ*, April 17: 964.

Sampley, Ted. (1997). "America's POW/MIA Flag Is Not Allowed at the Wall ... Have You Ever Wondered Why?" March/April/May: http://www.usvetdsp.com/story49.htm.

Sappol, Michael. (2002). *A Traffic of Dead Bodies: Anatomy and Embodied So-*

cial Identity in Nineteenth-Century America*. Princeton: Princeton University Press.

Scarry, Elaine. (1985). *The Body in Pain: The Making and Unmaking of the World*. New York: Oxford University Press.

Shatzki, Theodore R., and Wolfgang Natter, eds. (1996). *The Social and Political Body*. New York: Guilford Press.

Schuetz, Alfred. (1944-45). "The Homecomer." In *Strangers at Home: Vietnam Veterans Since the War*, ed. Charles R. Figley and Seymour Leventman (1980), 115-22. New York: Praeger.

Schwarz, Adam. (1995). "Unfinished Business: MIA Issue Continues to Bedevil Ties With U.S." *Far Eastern Economic Review*, May 4: 24-25.

Scott, Wilbur J. (1993). *The Politics of Readjustment: Vietnam Veterans Since the War*. New York: Aldine de Gruyter.

Shapiro, Michael J. (1989). "Textualizing Global Politics." In *International/Intertextual Relations: Postmodern Readings of Global Politics*, ed. James der Derian and Michael J. Shapiro, 11-22. Lexington: Lexington Books.

———. (1997). *Violent Cartographies: Mapping Cultures of War*. Minneapolis: University of Minnesota Press.

———. (1998). "The Events of Discourse and the Ethics of Global Hospitality." *Millennium: Journal of International Studies* 27, no. 3: 695-713.

———. (1999a). *Cinematic Political Thought: Narrating Race, Nation and Gender*. New York: New York University Press.

———. (1999b). "The Ethics of Encounter: Unreading, Unmapping the Imperium." In *Moral Spaces: Rethinking Ethics and World Politics*, ed. David Campbell and Michael J. Shapiro, 57-91. Minneapolis: University of Minnesota Press.

Sheehan, Neil. (1993). "Prisoners of the Past." *New Yorker*, May 24: 44-51.

———. (1995). "The Last Battle." *New Yorker*, April 24: 78-87.

Sheehan, Susan. (1986). *A Missing Plane*. New York: G.P. Putnam's Sons.

Showalter, Elaine. (1998). *Hystories: Hysterical Epidemics in Modern Culture*. New York: Columbia University Press.

Silverman, Kaja. (1992). *Male Subjectivity at the Margins*. New York: Routledge.

Smiley, Brenda. (1996). "Excavating MIAs: Archaeologists Probe Vietnam Crash Sites for Remains of U.S. Pilots." *Archaeology*, March/April: 20-22.

Smith, Garry L. (1992). *The Search for MIAs*. Spartanburg, S.C.: Honoribus Press.

Solotaroff, Paul. (1995). *The House of Purple Hearts: Stories of Vietnam Vets Who Find Their Way Back*. New York: Harper Collins.

Sorkin, Michael. (1983). "What Happens When a Woman Designs a War Monument?" *Vogue*, May: 120-22.

Spanfelner, Roxyann. (1999). "Identifying the Unknown Soldier." *Vietnam*, June: 46–51.
Spratt, Steven D. and Lee G. Spratt. (1993). *Scars*. Portland, Ore.: Strawberry Hill Press.
Stahl, Pamela M. (1996). "The New Law on Department of Defense Personnel Missing as a Result of Hostile Action." *Military Law Review* 152 (Spring): 75–177.
Starr, Paul. (1973). *The Discarded Army: Veterans After Vietnam: The Nader Report on Vietnam Veterans and the Veterans Administration*. New York: Charterhouse.
Steele, Scott. (1992). "Yeltsin's Surprise." *Maclean's*, June 29: 36–37.
Stern, Lewis M. (1995). *Imprisoned or Missing in Vietnam: Policies of the Vietnamese Government Concerning Captured and Unaccounted For United States Soldiers, 1969–1994*. Jefferson, N.C.: McFarland.
Stevens, Jacqueline. (1999). *Reproducing the State*. Princeton: Princeton University Press.
Stewart, Ian. (1996). "Viet Pond Sifted for MIAs." *Honolulu Advertiser*, December 9: A3.
"Stop that Monument." (1981). *National Review*, September 18: 1064.
Sturken, Marita. (1997). *Tangled Memories: The Vietnam War, the AIDS Epidemic, and the Politics of Remembering*. Berkeley: University of California Press.
Sutter, Robert G. (1991). *Vietnam–U.S. Relations: The Missing-in-Action (MIAs) and the Problem of Cambodia*. Congressional Research Service, Library of Congress: February.
Sutton, David Lee. (1994). "The Fullest Possible Accounting: The Myth of American PCW/MIAs in Southeast Asia, 1973 to 1993." Ph.D. diss., University of Georgia.
Swiers, George. (1984). "'Demented Vets' and Other Myths: The Moral Obligation of Veterans." In *Vietnam Reconsidered: Lessons from a War*, ed. Harrison Salisbury. New York: Harper and Row.
"Talk of the Town." (1992). *New Yorker*. February 17: 23–24.
Tatum, James. (1996). "Memorials of the America War in Vietnam." *Critical Inquiry* 22 (Summer): 634–78.
Tempest, Rone. (1997). "U.S. Team Reaches B-24 Crash Site." *Honolulu Advertiser*, January 15: A3.
"Tomb of the Unknown Soldier." (1963). *Quartermaster Review*. September/October: http://www.qmfound.com/tomb_of_the_unknown_soldier.htm.
"Tomb of the Unknown Soldiers." (1964). *Quartermaster Review*. January February: http://www.qmfound.com/tomb_of_the_unknown_soldiers_1964.htm.

Tucker, Spencer C., ed. (2000). *The Encyclopedia of the Vietnam War: A Political, Social, and Military History*. New York: Oxford University Press.

Turner, Fred. (1996). *Echoes of Combat: The Vietnam War in American Memory*. New York: Anchor Books.

Turner, Karen Gottschang, with Phan Thanh Hao. (1998). *Even the Women Must Fight: Memories of War from North Vietnam*. New York: John Wiley and Sons.

Uhl, Michael. (1994). "The Missing Story: Searching for Vietnam MIAs." *The Nation*, November 14: 573–76.

U.S. Congress. House. Select Committee on Missing Persons in Southeast Asia. (1976). *Americans Missing in Southeast Asia: Final Report of the House Select Committee on Missing Persons in Southeast Asia*. Washington: GPO.

———. (2003). *Establishing a Select Committee on POW and MIA Affairs*. 108th Congress, 1st session, H. Res. 103. *Congressional Record*. 149, daily ed. (February 25, 2003): H1334.

U.S. Congress. Senate. Select Committee on POW/MIA Affairs. (1993). *Report of the Select Committee on POW/MIA Affairs, United States Senate*. Washington: GPO.

U.S. Department of Defense. (2001a). "Navy Changes Status of Cmdr. Michael Scott Speicher." January 11: http://www.dtic.mil/dpmo/newsre/2001/010111_osd_pr016_speicher.htm.

———. (2001b). "Statement of Secretary Rumsfeld on Accident in Vietnam." April 7: http://www.dtic.mil/dpmo/newsre/2001/010407_osd_pr148_secdef_helo.htm.

———. (2001c). "Remarks by Deputy Secretary of Defense Paul Wolfowitz, Fort Myer Memorial Chapel, Fort Myere [sic], VA, Wednesday, April 25, 2001." April 25: http://www.dtic.mil/dpmo/newsre/2001/010425_osd_depsecdef_speech_helo.htm.

U.S. Department of State. (1977). "Presidential Commission Visits Vietnam and Laos to Seek Information on Missing Americans" (Woodcock Commission Final Report). *Department of State Bulletin*. Washington, April 18: 363–74.

———. (1992). "Progress on POW/MIA Issues: Kenneth M. Quinn, Deputy Assistant Secretary for East Asian and Pacific Affairs." *US Department of State Dispatch*. Washington, December 7: 869–72.

———. (1993a). "U.S. Policy Toward Vietnam: President Clinton." *US Department of State Dispatch*. Washington, July 12: 499.

———. (1993b). "Presidential Delegation to Hanoi." *US Department of State Dispatch*, Washington, July 26: 534.

———. (1993c). "Progress on POW/MIA Issues: Winston Lord, Assistant Secretary For East Asian and Pacific Affairs." *US Department of State Dispatch*, Washington, August 2: 557–58.

U.S. Department of State. (1994a). "U.S.-Vietnam POW/MIA Progress:

Lifting the Embargo." *US Department of State Dispatch*. Washington, February 28: 105.

———. (1994b). "U.S. Commitment to Our POW/MIAS: Secretary Christopher." *US Department of State Dispatch*, Washington, March 28: 177-78.

U.S. President. (1983). *Public Papers of the Presidents of the United States: Ronald Reagan 1983*. Washington: USGPO, 131.

———. (1993). *Public Papers of the Presidents of the United States: George Bush, 1992-1993*. Washington: USGPO, 1933-34.

———. (1995). "Remarks at the Unveiling Ceremony for the POW/MIA Postage Stamp." *Federal Register* 31, no. 22 (5 June): 917.

Van Voorst, Bruce. (1992). "The Truth at Last." *Time*, November 2: 59.

Veith, George J. (1998). *Code-Name Bright Light: The Untold Story of U.S. POW Rescue Efforts During the Vietnam War*. New York: Dell.

Verdery, Katherine. (1999). *The Political Lives of Dead Bodies: Reburial and Postsocialist Change*. New York: Columbia University Press.

"Veterans Find Jobs Faster." (1968). *New York Times*, May 3, 35:7.

"Vietnam War Tomb of the Unknowns: Fact Sheet." (nd). Information from the website of the National League of Families of American Prisoners and Missing in Southeast Asia: http://www.pow-miafamilies.org/tomb.html.

"Vietnam's Ability to Account for Missing Americans, April 9, 2004." (2004). Statement by the National League of Families of American Prisoners and Missing in Southeast Asia, August 1: http://www.pow-miafamilies.org/vability.html.

"Vietnam's Collection and Repatriation of American Remains." (1999). Study compiled by the Defense Prisoner of War/Missing Personnel Office (DPMO), June: http://www.dtic.mil/dpmo/special/vietnam_collection_study.htm.

Vistica, Gregory L. (2001). "One Awful Night in Thanh Phong." *New York Times Magazine*, April 29: 50.

Warner, Daniel. (1999). "Searching for Responsibility/Community in International Relations." In *Moral Spaces: Rethinking Ethics and World Politics*, ed. David Campbell and Michael J. Shapiro, 1-28. Minneapolis: University of Minnesota Press.

Westmoreland, William. (1976). *A Soldier Reports*. Garden City: Doubleday.

White, Geoffrey M. (1997). "Museum/Memorial/Shrine: National Narrative in National Spaces." *Museum Anthropology* 21, 1: 8-27.

———. (1999). "Battleship Memories: 'Remember Pearl Harbor!' 'Remember the Maine!'" Presented at the East-West Center, Honolulu, Hawai'i: September 29.

White, Hayden. (1978). *Tropics of Discourse: Essays in Cultural Criticism*. Baltimore: Johns Hopkins University Press.

Williams, Rudi. (1996). "Some Missing May Never be Accounted-For."

Armed Forces Information Service, February 21: http://www.dtic.mil/dpmo/newsre/1996/960221_afis_sea.htm.

———. (1999a). "United States Helping Vietnam Find its MIAs." *Armed Forces Information Service*, September: http://www.dtic.mil/dpmo/6newsre/1999/990908_afis_sea.htm.

———. (1999b). "Dual POW/MIA Ceremony Slated Sept. 17 at Tomb of Unknowns." *American Forces Information Service*: September 10: http://www.dtic.mil/dpmo/newsre/1999/990910_afis_us_unknown_tomb.htm.

World Bank. (2000). *World Development Report 2000/2001*. Washington: World Bank.

Yarsinske, Amy Waters. (2003). *No One Left Behind: The Lt. Cmdr. Michael Scott Speicher Story*. New York: New American Library.

Young, James E. (1993). *The Texture of Memory: Holocaust Memorials and Meaning*. New Haven: Yale University Press.

Zasloff, Joseph J., and MacAlister Brown. (1978). *Communist Indochina and U.S. Foreign Policy: Postwar Realities*. Boulder, Colo.: Westview Press.

index

Abjection: gender and, 121–22; impaired masculinity and, 147–52; Vietnam veteran and, 27–29, 116–23, 132, 139–42, 156–57

Absent without leave (AWOL), 43

Accounting for the missing: aircraft crash sites and, 95; circumstantial evidence and, 3, 24, 79, 85–87, 100, 113–14, 243, 249–50; identifiable remains and, 3–4, 24–25, 42, 64, 82–86, 238; lists of the missing and, 59, 80–82; scavenging of sites and, 99. *See also* Identification of remains

Agnew, Spiro, 28, 125

Archival research, 24, 81, 84–85, 90–93, 104–5. *See also* Identification of remains

Arizona Memorial, 199–201

Arlington Memorial Bridge, 176, 190

Arlington National Cemetery, 1, 159, 189–93

Armed Forces DNA Laboratory (AFDIL), 104, 246

Armed Forces Identification Review Board (AFIRB), 105, 109

Armed Services Graves Registration Office (ASGRO), 109–10

Blassie, Michael J., 2, 33, 192

Body count: ethical relation and, 239; healing the body politic and, 198; knowledge of the soldier's body and, 14–15, 21–25

Body politic: *ancien régime* and, 31, 161–62; democracy and, 31, 162–63, 188–89; emasculation and, 148; gender and, 32, 164, 170–74, 206–7; healing and, 30–33, 36, 115, 139, 157–59, 161–56, 175–86, 193–202, 205–7, 209; names and, 31–33, 162–63, 168–69, 176–78; unaccounted-for bodies and, 51, 54, 159–61, 174, 178–80, 184–86, 194–95, 200–201, 205; war memorials and, 159–61, 169. *See also* Vietnam Veterans Memorial

Butler, Judith, 9, 117, 253 n.1

Calley, William, 134

Cambodia: accounting for the missing in, 89, 91–93; Americans missing in, 56–57, 88

Campbell, David, 230–31, 236

Captivity narratives: American victimization and, 15–18, 26, 220; perception of unaccounted-for soldiers and, 16–17, 67

Carter, Jimmy, 74, 191

Central Identification Laboratory (CIL), 26, 37, 85–88, 101–13, 246, 255 n.3

278 Index

Certainty: continuation of Vietnam War hostilities and, 26, 67, 82, 86–87, 106–14, 235–36, 243, 249; identified body and, 3, 23–25, 80; restoring the nation and, 18, 33, 196–98, 212; Vietnam veteran's body and, 26, 115–16, 123, 152
Charney, Michael, 109
CIL/CILHI. *See* Central Identification Laboratory (CIL)
Clarke, Douglas L., 46–48, 52–54, 259 n.2
Classification of missing soldiers during Vietnam War, 43–49, 53, 205. *See also* Status changes
Clinton, Bill, 78–79, 247
Connolly, William, 34, 235–36, 259 n.1

Defense Prisoner of War/Missing Personnel Office (DPMO), 88, 90–92
Dewey Canyon III, 120, 138
Discrepancy cases, 60–66, 76–77, 92, 260 n.7
Dodge, Ronald, 62

Engelhardt, Tom, 13–18
Ethical relation, 34–36, 211–41 passim
Excavation of remains, 24, 81, 85, 93–101

Family organizations, 3, 36–37, 49–54, 73, 89–90, 163, 199, 212. *See also* National Alliance of Families for the Return of America's Missing Servicemen; National League of Families of Prisoners and Missing in Southeast Asia
Ford, Gerald, 257 n.6
Fragmentation: of American body politic, 30, 139, 162, 213; of bodies during Vietnam War, 14; of recovered remains, 24–26, 42; remains identification and, 82–83, 86, 100–101, 105, 110
Franklin, H. Bruce, 11, 63, 258 n.8
"Fullest possible accounting, the," 24, 33, 83–84, 123, 215
Furue, Tadao, 106–10, 192

Garwood, Robert, 11, 19
Genealogy, 5–12, 40, 71, 79
Geneva Conventions, 44, 53, 56
Goodacre sculpture, 32, 172–74, 180–82, 197, 206
Go Public campaign: American victimization and, 15, 124; Honor America Week and, 125, 136; perception of missing servicemen and, 28, 49–52, 60; perception of Vietnam veteran and, 123–25, 130–31, 136, 217–19
Griswold, Charles, 176–77
Gritz, James "Bo", 68, 254 nn.3–4

Hart, Anne, 108–12
Hart, Lt. Col. Thomas, 108–13
Hart sculpture: masculinity and, 32, 170–74, 206; politics of, 179–82. *See also* Goodacre sculpture; Vietnam Veterans Memorial
Hart v. United States, 107, 110–13
Healing: normalization of relations and, 79; political implications of, 32, 163–66. *See also* Body politic; Vietnam Veterans Memorial
Herman, Ellen, 139–40, 143–44
Holocaust memorials, 165–66, 175, 180–84
Honor America Week. *See* Go Public campaign
House Select Committee on Missing Persons in Southeast Asia, 11, 17, 74–75, 95, 112, 256 n.8

Hrdlicka, Alfred, 181–83
Hrdlicka, David, 62
Humanitarianism, 35–36, 112, 211–13, 216–17, 230–37, 243

Identifiable remains. *See* Accounting for the missing
Identification of remains: certainty and, 24–25, 85–87; controversies over (Pakse, Laos case), 105–14; DNA and, 1, 85, 101–4; fragmentation and, 81–84; teeth and, 101–4; skeletal features and, 101–2. *See also* Accounting for the missing
Investigative Element (IE). *See* Joint POW/MIA Accounting Command (JPAC)

Jeffords, Susan, 117, 121, 150–51
Joint Casualty Resolution Center (JCRC), 56, 69, 72
Joint field activity (JFA), 89, 93–96, 100, 242
Joint POW/MIA Accounting Command (JPAC): archival research and, 90–93, 255 n.3; fieldwork and site excavation, 93–101; Investigative Element (IE) and, 93–96, 242; organization of, 88–90; Recovery Element (RE) and, 93, 96–100, 255 n.4; Research and Investigation Team (RIT) and, 92–93; Stony Beach group and, 92–93; Trilateral Witness Program and, 91
Joint Task Force–Full Accounting (JTF-FA), 65, 81, 89, 242, 255 n.3

Kantorowicz, Ernst, 162
Kerley, Ellis, 109
Kerrey, Bob, 118, 154–55
Killed in action/body not recovered (KIA/BNR): criteria to be classified as, 44–45, 80; definition of, 13; number of, at end of Vietnam War, 45. *See also* Classification of missing soldiers during Vietnam War
Kissinger, Henry, 58, 61, 73

Laos: accounting for the missing in, 89, 91–93, 97; Americans missing in, 56–63, 72, 76
Last known alive cases. *See* Discrepancy cases
Lefort, Claude, 161–63
Levinas, Emmanuel, 35, 213–14, 231, 237
Levine, Lowell, 109
Lin, Maya, 169–71, 178. *See also* Vietnam Veterans Memorial
Lincoln Memorial, 176–77, 258 n.6
Live-sighting reports, 60–67, 73, 76–78, 92, 245–49

Manhood. *See* Masculinity
Manila American Memorial and Cemetery, 200
Maples, William, 109
Masculinity: body politic and, 171–74; loss of Vietnam War and, 32, 117, 147–48, 206; psychological trauma and, 121, 141–42, 148–49; rejection of the feminine and, 28–29, 121–22, 149–53. *See also* Remasculinization
Materiality: certainty and, 80, 106, 152, 196, 212; as dissimulated effect of power, 9–10; normalization of relations and, 77; truth and, 19, 23–25, 36–37, 71, 214, 248–49; Vietnam veteran's body and, 116, 127, 152, 156–57, 159. *See also* Certainty
Mayaguez incident, 257 n.6

280 Index

McCain, John, 79, 118
"Mindset to debunk" 65, 71, 209, 250
Missing in action (MIA): criteria of classification of, 45; definition of, 13, 45, 205; estimated number of, in Laos, 58; expectation and odds of survival of, 48-49, 53-54; number of, at end of Vietnam War, 47; as rationale for continuing the war, 52, 130. *See also* Classification of missing soldiers during Vietnam War
Missing Persons Act, 47, 60, 79, 218, 254 n.1
Monument Against War and Fascism, 181-85, 205
Mosse, George, 30, 166-67, 171, 175, 186-87
My Lai massacre: image of Vietnam veteran and, 120, 126, 134-35, 147; memorial in Vietnam, 182-84, 259 n.8
"Myth of the War Experience," 167-71, 187

National Alliance of Families for the Return of America's Missing Servicemen, 37, 89, 247
National League of Families of Prisoners and Missing in Southeast Asia: founding of, 52-53; influence of, on U.S. government policy, 219, 260 n.4; POW/MIA Flag and, 31, 202-7; status changes and, 218-19, 259 n.2; on Vietnam's responsibility to account for American missing, 18, 219-24; Vietnam War unknown soldier exhumation and, 193-94
National Memorial Cemetery of the Pacific, 200-201
Nixon, Richard: cultivation of good vet/bad vet opposition and, 27-28, 120, 123-26, 128-30; promise of reconstruction aid to Vietnam and, 72; return of POWs and, 59-60, 124, 135. *See also* Go Public campaign
Normalization of relations (United States and Vietnam), 71-79, 226, 232-33; as aid to accounting process, 17, 93; discrepancy cases and live-sighting reports and, 66; economic embargo and, 93, 224; National League of Families and, 219-20

Operation Grand Eagle, 68
Operation Homecoming, 13, 55, 58-63; knowledge of absent Vietnam War body and, 48
Operation Lazarus, 68-69
Operation Rapid American Withdrawal (RAW), 120, 136-38
Oral History program, 91

Pakse, Laos case: *See* Identification of remains
Paris Peace Accords, 12; Americans KIA/BNR at time of, 45; Article 8(b) of, 45, 48-49, 55-56, 72, 75, 225; Article 21 of, 55, 72-73, 75; normalization of relations and, 224-26
Pathet Lao, 57-60
Persian Gulf War, 37, 244-52
Personnel recovery apparatus. *See* Joint POW/MIA Accounting Command (JPAC)
Post traumatic stress disorder (PTSD), 128, 149
POW/MIA activism: fraudulent photographs and, 69-71, 78; private POW rescue missions and, 67-69
POW/MIA bracelets, 51

POW/MIA Flag, 30–33, 158–59, 165, 199–210, 227
Presumptive finding of death. *See* Status changes
Prisoner of war (POW): criteria of classification of, 44, 205; lists of during the war, 56–61; Nixon and return of, 59–60, 124, 135, 154; number returned during Operation Homecoming, 13; opposition between Vietnam veteran and, 118, 129–31, 135, 151; public perception of, 51–54, 67; as rationale for continuing the war, 40, 50–52, 125, 130; significance to the accounting effort, 41–43, 81–82, 224–25; as symbols of American victimization, 15–17, 124; as symbols of American victory, 118, 146. *See also* Go Public campaign
Psychiatry and psychology, 27, 121, 139–53. *See also* Vietnam veteran; World War II veteran

Rambo, Johnny (*Rambo: First Blood, Part II*), 151–52, 254 n.4
Reagan, Ronald, 76
Recovery Element (RE). *See* Joint POW/MIA Accounting Command (JPAC)
Remains identification. *See* Identification of remains
Remasculinization, 28–29, 148–53
Research and Investigation Team (RIT). *See* Joint POW/MIA Accounting Command (JPAC)
Responsibility: discourse of, 33–36, 40, 51; ethical relation and, 212–40 passim; POW/MIA Flag and, 206–10

Sappol, Michael, 21–22
Senate Select Committee on POW/MIA Affairs, 11, 57, 70, 73, 78–80, 105, 254 n.3
Shell shock, 142
Silverman, Kaja, 148–50
Sparks, Donald, 63
Speicher, Michael Scott, 37–38, 244–52
Status changes, 47–49, 60, 108, 218–19, 259 n.2; presumptive finding of death and, 47–48, 62, 79, 108
Stony Beach group. *See* Joint POW/MIA Accounting Command (JPAC)
Sturken, Marita, 159, 258 n.3

Tomb of the Unknown Soldier: selection of World War I unknown, 188; as symbolic of the national body, 2, 30, 164, 187–90, 195; Vietnam War unknown, 1–3, 33, 158–59, 186–99, 207, 251
Trilateral Witness program. *See* Joint POW/MIA Accounting Command (JPAC)

Unaccounted-for: definition of, 3, 62, 79; total of servicemen from Korean War, 4; total of servicemen from Vietnam War, 2; total of servicemen from World War II, 4
U.S.-Russia Joint Commission on POW/MIA Affairs, 88, 254 n.2
U.S.S. Arizona Memorial. *See Arizona* Memorial

Vietnam Office for Seeking Missing Persons, 89, 233
Vietnam veteran, 26–30, 115–57 passim; antiwar activism and 120, 131–32, 136–39; first-person narratives of, 120, 131–34, 144; "good vet/bad vet" opposition and, 27–

Vietnam veteran (*continued*) 28, 120-21, 124-29, 131-32, 135-38, 143, 148, 152; Hollywood representations of, 28, 120, 123, 127-29; impaired masculinity and, 121-23, 141-42, 147-52, 172; opposition between unaccounted for body and, 27-29, 116-20, 122-32, 134-39, 147-53, 156-57, 159; postwar readjustment and, 27, 118-19, 131-32, 141, 145-47, 152-54, 156; psychiatric effects of the war on, 27, 118, 120-21, 127-29, 141-45; as responsible for atrocities in Vietnam, 126-27, 131, 134-38; as responsible for defeat in Vietnam, 116, 119-21, 129, 135-36, 147, 156-57

Vietnam Veterans Against the War (VVAW), 120, 125, 136-37

Vietnam Veterans Memorial, 30-32, 159, 166-86, 258 n.6; gender and, 32, 164, 170-75, 206; healing metaphor and, 159-68, 175-86, 193, 201-2, 207; masculinity and, 171-75; naming and, 31-33, 162-63, 168-69, 176-79; political work performed by, 32, 163-66, 174-75, 179-81, 184-85; tension between remembering and forgetting at, 31, 159-60, 164-65, 179-80, 184-86, 207-8; unaccounted-for bodies and, 30-32, 159-61, 178-80, 184-86, 194-96. *See also* Goodacre sculpture; Hart sculpture; Holocaust memorials

Vietnam Women's Memorial. *See* Goodacre sculpture

Warner, Daniel, 228-29, 235
War neurosis, 141-45
Washington Monument, 170, 176, 258 n.6
Westmoreland, William, 235, 254 n.4
Winter Soldier Investigation, 120, 137-38
Woodcock Commission, 11, 17, 74-75
World War II veteran: postwar readjustment and, 121, 144-47; psychiatric effects of the war upon, 121, 143-44; psychology and, 140-44

Yarsinske, Amy Waters, 251
Young, James, 180, 183-84

Thomas M. Hawley is assistant professor of government at Eastern Washington University.

Hawley, Thomas M., 1970–
The remains of war : bodies, politics, and the search for American soldiers unaccounted for in Southeast Asia / Thomas M. Hawley.
p. cm. — (Politics, history, and culture)
Includes bibliographical references and index.
ISBN 0-8223-3526-3 (cloth   ) —
ISBN 0-8223-3538-7 (pbk.   )
1. Vietnamese Conflict, 1961–1975—Missing in action—United States.
2. Vietnamese Conflict, 1961–1975—Casualties—United States. I. Title. II. Series.
DS559.8.M5H28 2005
959.704'38—dc22   2005002539

www.ingramcontent.com/pod-product-compliance
Lightning Source LLC
Chambersburg PA
CBHW070755230426
43665CB00017B/2362